This is not a diary

This is not a diary

Zygmunt Bauman

polity

First published in 2012 by Polity Press

Polity Press
65 Bridge Street
Cambridge CB2 1UR, UK

Polity Press
350 Main Street
Malden, MA 02148, USA

ISBN-13: 978-0-7456-5569-7
ISBN-13: 978-0-7456-5570-3(pb)

A catalogue record for this book is available from the British Library.

Typeset in 11 on 13 pt Sabon
by Toppan Best-set Premedia Limited
Printed and bound in Great Britain by MPG Books Group Limited, Bodmin, Cornwall

For further information on Polity, visit our website: www.politybooks.com

Contents

September 2010

3 September 2010

On the sense and senselessness of diary-keeping

I confess: as I am starting to write (it is 5 a.m.), I haven't the slightest idea what, if anything, will follow, how long it will go on and how long I'll need, feel the urge and wish to keep it going. And the intention, let alone a purpose, is anything but clear. The question 'what for' can hardly be answered. At the moment when I sat down at the computer, there was no new burning issue waiting to be chewed over and digested, no new book to be written or old stuff to be revised, recycled or updated, no new interviewer's curiosity to be satiated, no new lecture to be sketched out in writing before being spoken – no request, commission or deadline...In short, there was neither a frame nailed together waiting to be filled, nor a plateful of podgy stuff in search of a mould and a form.

I guess the question 'because of what' is more in order in this case than the question 'what for'. Causes to write are abundant, a crowd of volunteers line up to be noted, picked and chosen. The decision to start writing is, so to speak, 'overdetermined'.

To begin with, I've failed to learn any other form of life except writing. A day without scribbling feels like a day wasted or criminally aborted, a duty neglected, a calling betrayed.

To go on, the game of words is for me the most heavenly of pleasures. I enjoy that game enormously – and the enjoyment reaches its peak when, after another reshuffle of the cards, the hand I get happens to be poor and I need to strain my brains and struggle hard to make up for the blanks and bypass the traps. Forget the destination; it is being on the move, and jumping over or kicking away the hurdles, that gives life its flavour.

Another cause: I seem unable to think without writing...I suppose I am a reader first and writer second – scraps, snippets, bits and pieces of thoughts struggling to be born, their ghostly/ghastly spectres whirling, piling up, condensing and dissipating again, need to be caught by the eyes first, before they can be stopped, held in place and given contours. They must first be written down in a row for the tolerably rounded thought to be born; or, failing that, to be aborted or buried as stillborn.

In addition, while adoring solitude, I abhor loneliness. After Janina's departure I've reached the darkest bottom of loneliness (if there is a bottom to loneliness), where its bitter and most pungent sediments and its most toxic effluvia gather. Since Janina's face is the first image I see when switching on my desktop, the rest that follows the opening of Microsoft Word is nothing if not a dialogue. And dialogue makes an impossibility of loneliness.

Last, though not least, I suspect I am a natural or nurtured graphomaniac...an addict, needing another daily dose, or risking agonies of withdrawal. *Ich kann nicht anders.* And this, probably, is the underlying reason, one that makes the search for reasons as desperate and inconclusive as it is inescapable.

As to yet other reasons and causes, they can't be really counted, and for all I know their number will keep growing daily. Among those that figure most prominently at the moment is the gathering feeling that I am overstaying my welcome, that I have done already what my immoderately moderate capacities entitled or obliged me to, and that the time has therefore arrived to apply to myself Wittgenstein's recommendation to keep silent about things I can't speak of or about (I would add, things I can't speak of or about *responsibly*, that is with a bona fide conviction of having some-thing useful to offer). And things I can't speak about are increas-ingly those things that are nowadays the most worth speaking about. My curiosity refuses to retire, but my capacity to satisfy it or at least placate and alleviate it cannot be either cajoled or persuaded to stay. Things flow too fast to allow room for the hope of catching them in flight. This is why a new topic for scrutiny, a new theme for a full-length study hoping to do justice to its object, is no longer on my cards. And not for a dearth of knowledge available for consumption – but because of its excess, defying all attempts at absorbing and digesting it.

Perhaps this unfeasibility of absorption is an outcome of ageing and of fading strength – a fully or mostly physical and biological matter, rooted ultimately in the changing condition of my own body and psyche (a plausible guess, made still more credible by the impression that the resources needed to obtain and process new information, supplied in my younger years in the form, so to speak, of a limited number of banknotes of large denominations, are now on offer in huge heaps of copper coins, tremendously high in bulk and heaviness, yet abominably low in purchasing power – which makes them, to borrow Günther Anders's expression, 'overliminal' for an aged body and easily tiring psyche). Our time excels in pulverizing everything, but nothing as thoroughly as the world image: that image has become as pointillist as the image of the time that presides over its fraying and grinding.

I gather that at long last the fragmented world has caught up with the painters of its likenesses. An old Indian fable comes to mind, in which half a dozen people, having bumped into an elephant on their way, try to assess the nature of the strange object they have encountered. Five of them are blind, none of them able to reach far enough to touch and feel the elephant all over and tie together their scattered impressions into a vision of its totality; the only one who has his eyes wide open to see is, however, dumb...Or Einstein's warning that although a theory can, in principle, be proved by experiments, there is no path leading from experiments to the birth of a theory. That much Einstein must have known. What he did not and could not surmise was the advent of a world, and a way of living-in-the-world, composed only of experiments, with no theory to design them, no reliable advice on how to start them off, pursue them and evaluate their results...

What, after all, is the difference between living and reporting life? We can do worse than take a hint from José Saramago, my lately discovered fount of inspiration. On his own quasi-diary he reflects: 'I believe that all the words we speak, all the movements and gestures we make...can each and every one of them be understood as stray pieces of unintended autobiography, which, however involuntary, perhaps precisely because it is involuntary, is no less sincere or truthful than the most detailed account of life put into writing and onto paper.'

Exactly.

4 September 2010

On the usefulness of fighting windmills

At the threshold of the third millennium, France, like most of the planet, was in the throes of uncertainty. The entry into the new era was appropriately preceded by what might have been (we would never know for sure) one of the most successful hoaxes in history: the 'millennium bug' affair, which cast thousands of serious, down-to-earth business corporations and governmental offices, as well as millions of their clients and subjects, into a state of alert aroused by the horrifying, well-nigh apocalyptic vision of the routines of Planet Earth stopping dead, of life on the planet grinding to a halt, at the moment of encounter between New Year's Eve and New Year's Day. That end of the world having failed to arrive, the computer-service companies counted their blessings and summed up their profits, and the disaster that never struck was promptly forgotten, elbowed out of the endemically excitable and chronically agitated attention of the public by disasters that *did* strike, or were expected to hit at any moment; whereas the crumbling of public trust and the condensation of public uncertainties – the kinds of troubles the story of the 'millennium bug' symbolized – stood fast and refused to budge, let alone to bid farewell.

Perhaps the end of computerized civilization 'as we knew it' was not after all nigh, as was proclaimed on the outer edge of the preceding millennium, but the end of the happy-go-lucky years presaged by that proclamation may well have been. One by one, the habitual foundations of security trembled, cracked and fell apart, the prospects of steady jobs and incomes dimmed, once solid bonds and partnerships grew sickly and frail, many a lighthouse of allegedly unshakeable reliability collapsed or shook under the burden of its own corruptions or imploded together with the confidence of beguiled and straying sailors. As for the governments expected to make the insecure secure again and put the disorderly in order, they responded with a staunch and blunt 'there is no alternative' answer to the complaints and protests of their increasingly confused and frightened subjects; that is, if they stooped to responding, instead of returning the 'help me' and 'do something' petitions with 'wrong address' or 'addressee unknown' rubber stamps...

Against the background of all such noises and silences, the words (and the televised shows that shortly followed them) of Nicolas Sarkozy, newly appointed as Minister of the Interior – French Home Secretary (in 2002) – sounded like a message overflowing with just the right meaning – the first such message for years. The appointment, coming so quickly after the beginning of what seemed to many to be a millennium, or a century at least, of uncertainty, appeared to open the door to a new governmental role and strategy, and to usher in the time of a 'listening government', a government following the example set by the banks that were tempting their prospective clients by assuring them that they 'loved to say "yes" '. Sarkozy's appointment promised the advent of times that would render powers-that-be trustworthy once again, and their subjects confident once more that they would not find themselves abandoned to their atrociously scarce resources in their desperate struggle to find firm ground under their feet.

Sarkozy's message was threefold. First, the hothouse of the insecurity known to torment ordinary folks like you and me, that den of vice and gushing source of daytime horrors and nightmares, has been found, pinpointed and located: as a matter of fact, in the *banlieues*, the French wholesale name for rough districts and mean streets, populated by people of strange (read, not like ours) look and demeanour, and so probably strange (read, suspect) habits and intentions. Second, as the deepest roots of the adversities and inequities of Frenchmen's fate have finally been mapped, we the people-in-power, powerful guys, can and will at long last 'strike at the roots' of evil – something we are indeed beginning already to do (as seen on TV). Third, what you've just seen on TV (the forces of law and order flexing their muscles and raiding the fortresses of crime at dawn in order to round up and incarcerate past, present and prospective criminals, those ultimate culprits of your harrowing days and sleepless nights) is just one example, but a vivid one, of the government in action, determined from the start to end in victory. (Lest such optimism bewilders present readers, let me recall that it was the year 2002, a timing fortunate for the author of the message because, two or three years later, he could have added, to his subsequently yet greater shame, that the governmental actions were 'bound to end in triumph just like the wars in Afghanistan and Iraq are bound to'.) In short, what is said by the government is done by the government... or at least is already beginning to be done.

It is 2010 now. In the course of the passing years, that Home Secretary ran on his 'death to insecurity' ticket and was elected President of France (in 2007), moving from somewhat humbler premises on Place Beauvau to the dazzling splendours of the Élysée Palace. And now, eight years after the message first summoned Frenchmen and Frenchwomen to listen and take note, that identical triple message is being sent again, with the President's passionate endorsement and blessing, by Brice Hortefeux, his successor at Place Beauvau. According to Denis Muzet, writing in today's *Le Monde*, the replacement and heir of Nicolas Sarkozy followed point by point the 2002 feat of his boss and mentor, extending his own workday to twenty hours and using the impressively expanded time to show up and be seen 'where the action is'. He personally supervised the dismantling of Roma camps, rounding up the evicted and sending them back to 'where they came from' (that is, back to their previous misery), calling in local prefects for reporting and briefing, or catching them unawares 'in the field' in order to admonish them and spur them into more action: into one more try, one more effort, one more Summer (Autumn, Winter, whatever) Offensive against the perpetrators and culprits of the misfortune of decent folks known by the name of 'insecurity'; one more final drive to finish another war promised to end all wars. You are haunted by monsters? Let's start by getting rid of windmills. This doesn't stand to reason? Perhaps, but at least you know now that we don't sit idly by. We do something – don't we? As seen on TV!

The French warriors against insecurity-by-proxy are not alone in promising to burn insecurity out in the form of Roma and Sinti effigies. Their close ally is Il Cavaliere – The Cavalier – ruling neighbouring Italy. It so happens that today there is also a report by Elisabetta Povoledo, in the *New York Times*, from Italy, where Silvio Berlusconi's government, with an eye on the Roma, passed a decree in 2007 allowing it to expel citizens of the European Union after three months' stay in the country if they could be shown to lack the means to support themselves; following it in 2008 with another decree, granting the state authorities new powers to expel European Union citizens for reasons of public safety – if you are a threat to public safety, you may, should, and will be picked up and escorted to the nearest airport.

To profit from such brand-new wonder weapons in the war declared on insecurity, one needs first to make sure that the hated Gypsies do become, and above all are seen as, a paramount threat to public safety; just to make sure that the word of the powers-that-be becomes flesh indeed, and the forces of law and order do not flex their muscles in vain. Or, yet more to the point, to make one's prediction into a self-fulfilling prophecy: having foretold on *Good Morning TV* a forest fire, proceed right away to sprinkle trees with petrol and to strike matches, so that by the end of the day one's reliability and trustworthiness can be documented on *Newsnight*. 'When municipally authorized camps are built,' Povoledo reports, it is often on the outskirts of a city, segregated from the rest of the population, with living conditions well below standard. That allows governments 'to bypass the question of integration, a process that would include giving Roma permanent residences and access to schools'. Governments incite suspicion towards Roma on the ground of their nomadic inclinations, and then the same governments force Roma to stay nomadic despite their wish to settle, and try hard to force back into a nomadic life those who have already settled, willingly and quite a time ago – so that the original summary dismissal of the whole ethnic group as 'travellers' can after all be convincingly corroborated by statistics, those least debatable 'facts of the matter'. The Roma are resented as obtrusive beggars? Well, make sure they have no chance of 'decently' earning a living. And as to our forest-burning allegory,

> temporary camps are a hazard. Last week in Rome, a three-year-old Roma boy was burned to death when a fire broke out in the hut he was living in with his family in an illegal camp near Fiumicino Airport. Afterward, the mayor of Rome, Gianni Alemanno [another politician elected on a 'war on insecurity' ticket], said the city would begin dismantling 200 illegal camps this month.

In a flash of prevision, shortly before being crowned Queen of the United Kingdom, young, simple-hearted and plain-speaking Victoria noted in her diary under the date of 28 December 1836: 'whenever any poor Gypsies are encamped anywhere and crimes and robberies &c. occur, it is invariably laid to their account, which is shocking; and if they are always looked upon as vagabonds, how *can* they become good people?'

Marx said that history tends to happen twice: the first time as drama, the second time as farce. That rule came into action once more in the case of the two successive wars against insecurity declared by Sarkozy in the course of one decade. On the second of the two wars, Alain Touraine caustically observed that, in sharp distinction from the crowds who applauded the declaration of the first war, 'no one believes that the Roma or Gypsies are responsible for our misfortunes'. Few indeed do, even though some still swallow the bait and delay spitting it out. But it was not in order to debate the causes of evil, or make the nation believe the official version, that this particular campaign of fear was launched. Touraine hits the bull's eye when he observes that all that front-page headlines, hullabaloo and public excitement takes place 'in a setting remote from the great catastrophes we live through'. The effects of politics Sarkozy-style are not to be measured by the number of minds converted to, or continuing to cling to blaming the Roma, but by the number of eyes diverted (even if only temporarily) away from what is truly relevant to people's lives and their prospects – as well as away from assessing how far, if at all, the government of the country is acquitting itself in the duties which, as it claims, legitimize its prerogatives, its pretensions, and its very presence. If measured in this – proper – fashion, Sarkozy-style politics cannot be easily dismissed as a straightforward failure. Nor is it bankrupt – as vividly testified by the growing number of governments hurrying to concoct local imitations and put them into operation.

The eyes of the nation, you may comment, are unlikely to stay averted forever, so won't the respite gained by rulers be short-lived? But what these days, forgive me asking, is long-lived? And how many suckers still believe in long terms and ultimate solutions? It will be quite enough, thank you, if the respite lasts long enough to allow the rulers to find another attraction equally likely to draw eyes to itself before they have a chance to turn to what really *does* matter, to those things about which the rulers neither can nor want to do anything that matters.

There is also another collateral casualty of Sarkozy-style governance. Surprisingly, though not so very surprisingly, the additional casualty is the self-same value which such governance promised and continues to promise to promote and serve: the sentiments of safety and security, of being protected and insured against adverse fate. Frenchmen may now be more sceptical or even downright cynical about the effectiveness of the government's promises, and about the value of the videotaped and televised governmental undertakings, than they were at the beginning of the first of Sarkozy's wars; but it is sure that they are now more *frightened* than ever before. They have lost much of their past faith in the possibility of making their situation any better. They are beginning to believe that insecurity is here to stay, and that it is likely to turn into a normal human condition; and most certainly that state governments are not the sort of instrument which can be used to try to tinker with that particular verdict of nature, of history, or of human fate. Whether by design or by default, Sarkozy's warlike actions ploughed and fertilized the soil for lush fundamentalist and tribal crops... The soil so prepared is a temptation to adventurous conquistadores which few if any aspiring politicians will find easy to resist.

This kind of governance also needs *appointed* victims. In the events reported by Denis Muzet and Elisabetta Povoledo, such victims are, of course, the Roma and Sinti populations. But in the kind of politics increasingly à la mode, victims, whether appointed or 'collateral', are not just pawns in other people's games; in the games currently being staged they are also anonymous and expendable extras, easy to replace – supernumeraries whose demise or departure no players, and only a few spectators, are likely to notice and remember, let alone bewail and mourn.

5 September 2010

On virtual eternity

A bus from Tokyo disgorged a large group of youngsters on a beach at Atami, a little sea resort and a favourite weekend haunt for the capital's seekers after erotic adventure; this is what we learn from today's edition of Yahoo! News. Buses arrive from Tokyo several times a day, so how come that one of them earned space in the widely read online news bulletin? This particular bus brought to Atami the first batch of the new Nintendo Love+ game players; this bus was a swallow announcing a long and profitable spring for Atami restaurateurs and hoteliers.

The youngsters who alighted from the bus, unlike other passengers, paid no attention to the scantily clad 'girls frolicking on the sand'. Clutching their smartphone cameras, armed with AR ('augmented reality') software, they hurried instead straight to the genuine objects of their desire, the *real thing*: the *virtual girl-friends*, enchanted in a little barcode glued to the plinth of a love couple's sculpture. The software fed into the boys' smartphones allowed them to 'disenchant' from the barcode the one and only girl of their virtual dreams, take her for a walk, entertain her, ingratiate themselves in her eyes and win her favours just by following the clear-cut, unambiguous rules spelled out in the interactive onscreen instructions – results guaranteed or your money back. They can even spend a hotel night together: kissing is allowed and encouraged, though sex alas is for the time being barred; there are still some limits which even the cutting edge technology is unable to cross. One can bet, however, that the technowizards will be able to break this limit, as with so many other limits in the past, by the time Love++ or Love2 is launched.

A serious technological website, dbtechno.com, convinced that technology exists in order to serve human needs and satisfy humans' demands, is impressed: 'Love+ is a new game devoted to the man who cannot handle having a real woman in their life and in the country of Japan it has taken off big time,' it says. As to the services rendered, it is hopeful: 'For the men out there who do not want to put up with a woman in their life, the virtual girlfriend may be the answer.'

Another 'need niche' yearning to be filled is spotted by cream-global.com: 'A generation who grew up with Tamagotchi' (alas, no longer in fashion and so out of the market) has developed a 'caring habit', indeed, a sort of addiction (to virtual) caring for (virtual) beings (virtually) alive – a habit which they are no longer able to satisfy because they don't possess the appropriate tech-nogadgets to unload it. They need a new gizmo with which to practise the contrived habit, and possibly in a manner yet more exciting and pleasurable (for a time). Thanks to Love+, however, the worry is over: 'To keep the girlfriend, the player must tap a stylus on the DS touch-screen where they can then walk hand-in-hand to school, exchange flirtations, text messages and even meet in the school courtyard for a little afternoon kiss. Through a built-in microphone, the player can even carry on sweet, albeit mundane, conversations.' Note: inserting 'albeit' does not necessarily signal regret; remember that Tamagotchi did not manage to make conversing, let alone non-mundane conversing, into a habit.

On ChicagoNow.com, Jenina Nunez wonders: 'In the era of dating and virtual reality, have we become so lonely (and given up on real, human love) that we're willing to court the image of the perfect companion?' And she hypothesizes in response to that question: 'I'm starting to think that Love+, which seems to eliminate a human companion from the equation entirely, is a clear example of how far people would go to avoid feeling lonely...' The surmise underpinning that answer – a guess which Jenina Nunez unfortunately neglected to make explicit and failed to develop – is right on target. Yes, the revolution that the latest Nintendo game portends, and the secret of its instant marketing success, is the elimination of a human companion *entirely* from the human relations game. While being rather in the style of non-alcoholic beer, fat-free butter or calorie-free food, it is something hitherto attempted only cravenly, surreptitiously, or in inept, primitive, cottage-industry style and manner in its application to what for techno-boffins and techno-traders is the supreme challenge and the nearest equivalent to a can of worms or a lion's den: the sphere of human partnerships, bonds, friendship, love...

This is an ambitious new game, this Love+. In supplying virtual (read, sanitized, stripped of 'strings attached', of side-effects, of 'unanticipated consequences' and fears of pre-empting future liberty) substitutes, it aims at the very peak: at the *future itself*. It offers eternity for instant, on-the-spot consumption. It offers a way to keep eternity at bay and under control, and the ability to stop it the moment it ceases to be enjoyable and desired. It offers 'eternal love' to be imbibed and relished in full on a short coach trip to Atami – with no need to carry it back home. As Naoyuki Sakazaki, a man in his forties, put it: 'Love Plus is fun because the relationship continues *forever*' (italics added). He should know:

the Love+ campaign in Atami started on 10 July and had finished by the end of August...

For this kind of accomplishment, there has been, to my knowledge, only one known precedent, albeit apocryphal and unprovable. The Mogul emperor Shah Jahan was so deeply in love with his third wife, Mumtaz Mahal, that when she died he summoned, hired and paid the greatest architects of his time, and spent twenty-one years supervising the construction of a fitting monument to her charm and beauty: the Taj ('crown of buildings') of Mahal. When the last frieze was engraved and the last ornamentation polished, Shah Jahan allegedly inspected the masterpiece and found his love longings finally gratified and nostalgia for his lost love satiated.

What spoiled his delight, however, so obviously distorting the harmony and elegance of the supreme composition, was a strange, coffin-like box at the centre. It was the removal of that box that needs to be seen as the fully and truly last, ultimate and crowning finishing touch of the Jahan–Mumtaz romance...

11 September 2010

On farming words

About giving interviews, as about many other forcefully promoted customs of our times, José Saramago had his doubts. He noted on 16 November 2008, having turned eighty-six, a year older than I am now: 'I'm told that the interviews were worth doing. I, as usual, tend to doubt this, perhaps because I'm tired of listening to myself.' So am I...More than once, pressed by interviewers to reveal what they thought they did not know but their readers yearned to learn, I have felt humiliated by being forced to repeat what 'has with the passing of time turned into a reheated soup for me': discoveries once exciting and impatient to be shared now felt soporific in their banality...'Worse still,' as Saramago hastens to add, 'the handful of sensible things I've said in my life have turned out after all to be of absolutely no consequence. And why should they be of consequence?' Again, I know the pain: when urged by interviewers and reciting my own, incomparably tinier handful of once iconoclastic thoughts, all too often I have seen and could think only of icons that were meant and hoped to crumble long ago out of shame and belated remorse, but which instead hit back at me, even more unsightly than I remembered them and just as self-confident as they were in their tender years, if not more so – now staring me arrogantly in the face, sneering, jeering, jibing…

'Do we talk for the same reason we perspire? Just because we do?' Saramago asks. Sweat, as we know, promptly evaporates or is keenly washed away, and 'sooner or later ends up in the clouds'. Perhaps this is the fate for which, in their own manner, words are destined.

And then Saramago recalls his grandfather Jeronimo, who 'in his final hours went to bid farewell to the trees he had planted, embracing them and weeping because he knew he wouldn't see them again. It's a lesson worth learning. So I embrace the words I have written, I wish them long life, and resume my writing where I left off.'

'There can be', he adds, 'no other response'. So be it.

12 September 2010

On superpower, superbroke

Two days ago America celebrated/mourned/regurgitated another 9/11 anniversary.

'American pacifists need not worry any more about "wars of choice",' Thomas L. Friedman suggested a few days earlier. 'We are not doing that again. We can't afford to invade Grenada today.' The superpower is now superbroke, he opines, and bound to turn – for many years to come – superfrugal. 'America is about to learn a very hard lesson: You can borrow your way to prosperity over the short run but not to geopolitical power over the long run.'

Not that Friedman's opinion is universally shared. Hillary Clinton, for instance, is on record trying just four days ago to convince the members of the Council on Foreign Relations that the 'United States can, and shall lead, and in fact does lead' the world in the beginning century. Well, what else could the chief of diplomacy say? Another member of the federal government,

Robert Gates, in charge of the military, strikes a different chord. He recommends that quite a large dose of modesty and realism be inserted into American international initiatives. He does not elaborate, counting on the readers of *Foreign Affairs* to decipher his meaning without crib or prompting.

Nations are reluctant to learn, and if they do learn, it is mostly from their previous mistakes and misdeeds, from the funerals of their past fantasies. 'As the Pentagon rebrands Operation Iraqi Freedom as Operation New Dawn,' says Frank Rich, quoting Boston professor Andrew Bacevich, 'a name suggesting a skin cream or dishwashing liquid', 60 per cent of Americans believe – now – that the war in Iraq was a mistake, and 10 per cent more condemn it as unworthy of American lives, whereas only one in four Americans supposes that war to have made them safer from terrorism. The war's official costs to Americans is now (at the moment President Obama asks Americans 'to turn the page on Iraq') estimated to have been $750 billion. For that money, about 4,500 Americans and more than 100,000 Iraqis were killed, and at least 2 million Iraqis were forced into exile, while Iran was enabled to rev up its nuclear programme 'and Osama bin Laden and his fanatics' have been set free 'to regroup in Afghanistan and Pakistan'.

One mistake brings another in its wake. 'The biggest legacy of the Iraq war at home', observes Rich, 'was to codify the illusion that Americans can have it all at no cost.' Well, what the Americans are learning now, still reluctantly, is that even repulsive and abhorrent things they hadn't in the least bargained for cannot be bought without huge spending, and one of the most repulsive aspects of those repulsive things is running short of the money with which something else – good or bad, desired or feared, delighting or disgusting – can be purchased. 'The cultural synergy between the heedless irresponsibility we practiced in Iraq and our economic collapse at home could not be more naked,' Rich concludes. The fight-now-pay-later war, and almost universal blindness to its human costs, were aided and abetted by the same disregard of realities as in the flood of subprime mortgages, the housing bubble and other Wall Street games of hazard. The true reckoning of all those happy-go-lucky years is only beginning to be counted and weighed, but the interest to be paid on the federal debt is expected to rise to $516 billion by 2014, that is more than the US domestic budget – and half has to be paid to foreign investors. Fears are voiced time and again about the Armageddon that may follow if foreign creditors decide to sell the American debt. Those fears are mitigated, if not entirely quashed, by a gamble on the foreigners' prudence: a massive selling of that debt would provoke stock exchanges all over the world into a radical devaluation of stocks, and so it stands to reason, doesn't it, for the creditors to settle for a steady income from 'debt servicing' – at least as long as the US Treasury manages to repay the interest...

The other collateral casualties of the reckless adventure in Iraq are the trustworthiness and credibility of both halves of the American party establishment, of the American news media, and of the pundits, boffins and reputable experts, who all – with only a few noble exceptions (out-shouted as a rule and hunted down by a pugnacious and vociferous majority) – played up to the war-mongering spokesmen of unreason.

But there is another kind of collateral damage that just may (who can be sure it won't) haunt America, with its as yet unsung accomplices, willing, reluctant or inadvertent, for who knows how long a future. 'Instead of bringing American-style democracy and freedom to Iraq,' Rich muses, 'the costly war we fought there has, if anything, brought the bitter taste of Iraq's dysfunction to America.' Is the story of the 'hellenization effect', of Roman conquerors culturally absorbed, swallowed, converted, assimilated and recycled by the defeated and the conquered, about to repeat itself, if only as its gruesome caricature?

13 September 2010

On averages

'Americans are not being honest with themselves about the structural changes in the economy that have bestowed fabulous wealth on a tiny sliver at the top, while undermining the living standards of the middle class and absolutely crushing the poor. Neither the Democrats nor the Republicans have a viable strategy for reversing this dreadful state of affairs' – so writes Bob Herbert in today's *New York Times*:

There was plenty of growth, but the economic benefits went over-whelmingly – and unfairly – to those already at the top. [Robert] Reich (in his new book *Aftershock*) cites the work of analysts who have tracked the increasing share of national income that has gone to the top 1 percent of earners since the 1970s, when their share was 8 percent to 9 percent. In the 1980s, it rose from 10 percent to 14 percent. In the late-'90s, it was 15 percent to 19 percent. In 2005, it passed 21 percent. By 2007, the last year for which com-plete data are available, the richest 1 percent were taking more than 23 percent of all income. The richest *one-tenth of 1 percent*, rep-resenting just 13,000 households, took in more than 11 percent of total income in 2007.

Learning from the past, even from its mistakes and misdeeds, does not come easy. Particularly to those who made those mistakes and committed those misdeeds. Exactly one year ago, Alex Berenson noted in the *New York Times* 'little change on Wall St'. Today, he could surely reprint his conclusion unaltered, only with a much swollen store of data and much heavier factual backing. He could repeat, if anything with yet more self-assurance, that 'the biggest banks have restructured only around the edges', and that the pay of the bankers – responsible for the catastrophe of two years ago and still unpunished for their misdemeanours – is back to, if not above, its pre-crash levels, with 30,000 employees of Goldman Sachs (the company bailed out by the federal debt from the threat of bankruptcy) earning an average of $700,000 a year. According to Kian Abouhossein, a J. P. Morgan analyst, eight major American and European banks pay on average $543,000 to their 141,000 employees. The 'system', whatever that word may mean in that thoroughly deregulated setting, has grown riskier still. 'Investors will lend money to the financial industry on easy terms. In turn, financial institutions will use that cheap money to make risky loans and trades. The banks will keep the profits when their bets pay off, while taxpayers will swallow the losses when the bets go bad and threaten the system.' Bankers even have a special term for that tactic, IBG: by the time the bets are lost, 'I'll Be Gone' (with a handsome bonus, of course, and a platinum handshake). This is the other face of the labour market's deregula-tion that has already cast millions of workers, with more following them daily, into prospectless poverty; or, to borrow Peter S. Goodman's phrase, into 'the deserts of joblessness'.

It is a desert – for the 15 million people declared redundant, about 3 million of whom have already seen their unemployment assistance expire, with many more watching in despair as the same predicament relentlessly approaches. In their lives, unlike on Wall Street, everything has changed, and beyond recognition. People promised a middle-class income (fraudulently, as they find out now) and lured into middle-class spending, have now (most of them for the first time in their lives) no other choice except to hope for a lifeline from public assistance. But even that hope, their last, is growing more tenuous, more filigree and gaseous, by the day. Forty-four US states have cut off welfare payments from households with a total income less than one-quarter below the official poverty line. As Randy Abelda of the University of Massachusetts calculates, entitlements to public assistance stop when a family of three reaches $1,383 a month (that is, about $1.5 per person a day; though by the time of my writing that might have dropped again...).

Yours is a class society, Madame, yours is a class society, Sir – and don't you forget it, lest you wish to have your amnesia ended with shock therapy. It is also a capitalist, market-operated society – and it is an attribute of such a society to stutter from one depression/recession to another. Being a class society, it distributes the costs of the recession and the benefits of the recovery unevenly, using every occasion to give further firmness to its backbone: class hierarchy. The depth of the fall and the duration of the stay at the prospectless bottom are also differentiated by class. It all depends which rung of the ladder you fall off: if it was a high one, your chances of a climb-back are high. But if you fell from the lower rungs of the ladder, a return of sunshine to the boardrooms will not be enough to raise your hopes. After every successive bout of economic depression, fewer workers find themselves in employment than were registered before the economy contracted. In 2000, at the beginning of the previous recession, 34 million were employed; but the number never rose again, despite the 'economy growing again', above 30 million. And no wonder. Institutional investors are thirsty for a 'killing' – a quick profit on investment – and nothing slakes their thirst more promptly and thoroughly than a solid cut in the payroll. Disarming and disabling the trade unions made it possible to shift stable jobs to casual labourers. Automation is believed to be responsible for the disappearance of about 5.6 million industrial jobs in the last decade. Last but not least, a lot of blue-collar as well as white-collar jobs have recently 'emigrated' to the low-pay and no-union countries of Asia and Latin America, and are still doing so. At the moment, the average duration of unemployment among redundant American workers is growing by two weeks every month. Experts anticipate this trend will continue.

Crises are reputed to strike at random, but their consequences, and above all their long-term consequences, are class-managed. The severity of the crises may result from the intensity of deregulation, but the harshness and pungency of their human effects stay stubbornly – and tightly – class-controlled.

I have focused thus far on the US experience. But quite similar trends mark the rest of our deregulated globe. As Margaret Bounting notes in a trenchant warning addressed to an impending session of the United Nations, 'at the current progress more than a billion of the world's population will still be living in extreme poverty in 2015; half of all children in India are malnourished; in sub-Saharan Africa, one child in seven dies before their fifth birthday... [T]he goals are bypassing the poorest in the world... [T]hree quarters of the world's poorest now live in middle-income countries such as India or Nigeria.' While the 'UN prefers to talk of global inequality rather than the inequality within developing countries – India, for all its feted economic growth, has barely touched the proportion of those going hungry in the last twenty years.' Most UN members and managers wouldn't touch the idea of 'equity', let alone of 'equality', with a barge pole.

We go on routinely, duly and diligently computing statistical averages. Some of the averages are encouraging, a few are downright delightful and even justify some degree of self-congratulation. Others are considerably less heart-warming, while a few signal abominable failure and inspire questions to which no good answers have been found (or for that matter sought in earnest). But unlike the averages, the statistics of the collateral victims of the markets' free-for-all and catch-as-catch-can – the poor and hungry left out of the enrich-yourself thrust of the rest and badly hit by its results – are routinely, invariably, stubbornly and monotonously dismal and dreary, and with each successive fit of economic depression become ever more so. As Margaret Bounting implies, this is not a question of a different way of manipulating

the chronically insufficient aid funds. It is instead a question of
politics, a thoroughly political challenge and task.

14 September 2010

On multi-tasking

From the dawn of the consumerist era the main worry of marketing experts was the brevity of the time that prospective clients
could devote to consumption; time had its natural limits and could
not be stretched beyond twenty-four hours a day, seven days a
week. Time's inflexibility seemed in turn to set natural limits to
the expansion of the consumer market.

As stretching the size of the day or the week was out of the
question, the obvious way to deal with that worry was to try to
pack more consumption into each time unit – by training people
to consume more than one commodity at a time. Eating and drink-
ing was the most evident candidate to be piled on top of other
consumer activities: you can swallow fast food while driving a car,
queuing for a theatre ticket, or watching a film or a football
match. That was easily done: different parts of the bodily organs
and different pleasure-arousing senses were engaged in consuming
different goods, none of them demanding full and undivided
mental concentration, and they could be deployed simultaneously,
only minimally detracting from the intensity of the pleasure (the
total sensual relish was perhaps a little smaller than the sum of
the delights which each of the goods consumed could offer in its
own, separate time – but then there was not enough time to allow
them to be so consumed). But what if the goods on offer engaged
the same senses and called for the same aspect of our attention?
You can have music to dine by or to jog by, to fall asleep by or
to wake up by – but can you have music to listen to music by?

Well, it seems that at long last the consumer markets have found
their philosopher's stone. Time can finally be stretched beyond its
'natural' limits. Though, at least thus far, only one of the many
markets can cash in on that discovery/invention: that of electronic
gizmos and gadgets. As recent research conducted by Ofcom
revealed, media 'multi-tasking' now occupies 20 per cent of total
media-using time. That means that an average Briton manages to

squeeze 8 hours 48 minutes of media time into just over 7 hours of media consumption.

To be sure, considerable differences hide behind that average. Simultaneous media consumption is routine for a third of 16–24 year olds, but only for one in eight people beyond that age bracket. The younger generation is much more skilful than its elders at cramming in media consumption activities: they know how to thrust 9.5 hours of media consumption into a little more than 6.5 hours of 'real time' – and they practise this feat routinely, day in day out. As the data collected by Ofcom suggest, these 'multi-tasking' habits really took off in earnest with the introduction of smartphones. The impact of later novelties has not yet been measured, but it is widely anticipated they will intensify the multi-tasking trend. The data suggest that this acceleration is currently growing faster in the older groups of the population: for the first time, more than half of people over 55 years old have installed a broadband connection, whose main bonus is precisely its multi-tasking facility. Watching TV while using a laptop or a smartphone (and presumably also an iPad) is now a habit shared by all age cohorts.

This is how Krishnan Guru-Murthy, Channel 4 newscaster and self-confessed media addict, describes his own daily routine: 'On a working day I spend most waking hours in the company of one media device or another and I can easily see how people get more "media hours" out of the day than actual hours.' From 6:30, Guru-Murthy prepares for his working day in the company of breakfast TV, Radio 4, and news websites on his computer, while 'fiddling with an iPhone or Blackberry to get my Twitter'. He takes his headphones to the gym, and on the treadmill he watches 'a bit of TV'. On his office desk he keeps two computers permanently open: one as a workspace, the other to follow the TV news and for twittering. On the way home Guru-Murthy checks his iPhone for the latest Twitter responses to his programmes. It is only at 8:45 in the evening that he gets (not necessarily every day) 'a media-free hour or so'. But 'if my five-year-old hasn't swiped the iPad, I will use it to check what the newspapers have got on their front pages before my head hits the pillow'.

In my youth I kept being warned: 'quickly learned, soon forgotten'. But it was a different wisdom speaking: the wisdom of a time that held the 'long term' in the highest esteem, and when people at the top marked their high position by surrounding themselves with durables, leaving what was transient to those lower down the ladder; that was a time when the capacity of inheriting, keeping, guarding, preserving, bequeathing and altogether caring for things counted for much more than (regrettable, shaming and bewailed) facility of disposal.

This was not, though, the kind of wisdom many of us would approve of today. What was once merit has nowadays turned into vice. The art of surfing has taken over from the art of fathoming the best in the hierarchy of useful and desirable skills. If soon forgetting is the consequence of quick learning, long live quick (short, momentary) learning! After all, if it is tomorrow's commentary on tomorrow's events that you need to compose, the memory of the events of the day before yesterday will be of little help. And since memory's capacity, unlike the capacity of servers, can't be stretched, that memory may, if anything, constrain your ability to absorb and speed up the fresh assimilation. Multi-tasking is therefore doubly welcome: it doesn't just accelerate learning, but makes it redundant. When a number of unconnected bits of information rub at your diverse sense organs simultaneously, the odds are that none of them will rub in too deep to be quickly eradicated – and most certainly none of them will outstay their usefulness.

Multi-tasking is yet more welcome when you are not exposing yourself to those appliances piping information in order to search for knowledge, however brief the use you may need it for, but in order to give the stuff currently being piped a chance to please and amuse you. The prospect of instantly forgetting is then *neither* resented *nor* welcome. Purely and simply, it is *irrelevant*. The old caution 'quickly learned, soon forgotten' would be neither taken seriously nor derided. In all probability, it would be met with incomprehension.

19 September 2010

On the blind leading the impotent

Houellebecq...the author of *The Possibility of an Island*, the first great, and thus far unrivalled dystopia for the liquid, deregulated, consumption-obsessed, individualized era...

The authors of the greatest dystopias of yore, like Zamyatin, Orwell, or Aldous Huxley, penned their visions of horrors haunting the denizens of the solid modern world: the world of closely regimented and order-obsessed producers and soldiers. They hoped that their visions would shock their fellow travellers-into-the-unknown out of the torpor of sheep meekly marching to the slaughterhouse: this is what your lot will be like, they said – unless you rebel. Zamyatin, Orwell, Huxley, just like Houellebecq, were children of their times. This is why, *unlike* Houellebecq, they were bespoke tailors by intention: they believed in commissioning a future to order, dismissing as a gross incongruity the idea of a self-made future. They were frightened of wrong measurements, unshapely designs and/or sloppy, drunk or corrupt tailors; they had no fear, though, that tailors' shops would fall apart, be decommissioned and phased out – and they did not anticipate the advent of a tailor-free world.

Houellebecq, however, writes from the innards of just such a tailor-free world. The future, in such a world, is *self*-made: a DIY future which no DIY addict controls, wishes to control, or could control. Once each is set on his or her own orbit, never crisscrossing with any other, the contemporaries of Houellebecq have no more need for dispatchers or conductors than the planets and stars need road planners and traffic monitors. They are perfectly capable of finding the road to the slaughterhouse completely on their own. And they do – as the two principal protagonists of the story did, hoping (in vain, alas, in vain...) to meet each other on that road. The slaughterhouse in Houellebecq's dystopia is also, as it were, DIY.

In an interview conducted by Susannah Hunnewell, Houellebecq does not beat about the bush – and just as his predecessors did and as we do and our ancestors did, he reshapes into a programme of his choice conditions not of his choice: 'What I think, fundamentally, is that you can't do anything about major societal changes.' Following the same line of thought, he points out a few sentences later that even if he regrets what is currently happening in the world, he doesn't 'have any interest in turning back the clock *because* I don't believe it can be done' (emphasis added). If Houellebecq's predecessors were concerned with what the agents at the command post of 'major societal changes' might be able to do to stifle the irritating randomness of individual behaviour,

Houellebecq's concern is with where that randomness of individual behaviour will lead in the absence of command posts and agents willing to man them with a 'major societal change' in mind. It is not the *excess* of control, and of coercion, its loyal and inseparable companion, that worries Houellebecq; it is their *dearth* that renders all worry toothless and superfluous. Houellebecq reports from an aircraft with no pilot in the cockpit.

'I don't believe much in the influence of politics on history…I also don't believe that individual psychology has any effect on social movements,' Houellebecq concludes. In other words, the question 'what is to be done?' is invalidated and pre-empted by an emphatic answer 'no one' to the question of 'who is going to do it?' The sole agents in sight are 'technological factors and sometimes, not often, religious'. But technology is notorious for its blindness; it reverses the human sequence of actions following purpose (the very sequence that sets the agent apart from all the other moving bodies) – it moves because it can move (or because it can't stand still), not because it wishes to arrive; while God, in addition to an inscrutability that dazzles and blinds his watchers, stands for humans' insufficiency and their inadequacy to the task (that is, for humans' inability to face up to the odds and act effectively on their intentions). The impotent are guided by the blind; being impotent, they have no other choice. Not, at any rate, if they are abandoned to their own, jarringly and abominably inadequate resources; not without a pilot whose eyes are wide open – a pilot looking *and* seeing. 'Technological' and 'religious' factors behave uncannily like Nature: one cannot really be sure where they are going to land, until they do land somewhere; but that only means, as Houellebecq would put it, until it is no longer possible to turn the clock back.

Houellebecq, to be praised for both his self-awareness and frankness, puts on record the vanity of hopes, in case anyone is sufficiently stubborn and naive to go on entertaining them. Describing things, he insists, no longer leads to changing them – while forecasting what is going to happen no longer leads to preventing it from happening. A point of no return finally reached? Fukuyama's verdict of the end of history vindicated, even if its grounds are refuted and ridiculed?

I am questioning Houellebecq's verdict while being in almost full agreement with Houellebecq's inventory of its grounds. Almost

– because that inventory contains truth, only truth, but not the whole truth. Something tremendously important has been left out of Houellebecq's account: it is because the weaknesses of politicians and individual psychology are *not the only* things to blame for the bleakness of the prospects as they are (correctly!) painted that the point we have been brought to thus far *is not* a point of no return.

Houellebecq's despondency and defeatism derive from a two-tier crisis of agency. On the upper tier, at the level of the nation-state, the agency has been brought perilously close to impotence, and that is because power, once locked in a tight embrace with state politics, is now evaporating into the global, extraterritorial 'space of flows', far beyond the reach of the persistently territorial politics of the state. State institutions are now burdened with the task of inventing and providing local solutions to globally produced problems; because of a shortage of power, this is a load the state cannot carry and a task it cannot perform using its remaining resources and within the shrinking realm of its feasible options. The desperate yet widespread response to that antinomy is a tendency to shed one by one the numerous functions the modern state was expected to perform and did perform, even if with only a mixed success – while resting its legitimation on the promise of their continued performance. The functions successively abandoned or forfeited are shed to the lower tier, that of the sphere of 'life politics', the area in which individuals are nominated to the dubious office of their own legislative, executive and judicial authorities rolled into one. It is now 'individuals by decree' who are expected to devise and pursue, with their individually possessed skills and resources, their individual solutions to societally generated problems (this is, in a nutshell, the meaning of present-day 'individualization' – a process in which the deepening of dependency is disguised and redubbed the progress of autonomy). As at the upper tier, so at the lower one the tasks are grossly mismatched with the available and attainable means to perform them. Hence the feelings of haplessness, of impotence: the plankton-type experience of having been a priori, irreparably and irreversibly condemned to defeat in a blatantly unequal confrontation with overwhelmingly vehement tides.

The yawning gap between the grandiosity of the pressures and the meagreness of the defences is bound to go on feeding and beefing up sentiments of impotence as long as it persists. That gap, however, is *not* bound to persist: the gaps looks unbridgeable only when the future is extrapolated as 'more of the same' as present trends – and the belief that the point of no return has already been reached adds credibility to such an extrapolation without necessarily rendering it correct. It happens time and again that dystopias turn into self-refuting prophecies, as the fate of Zamyatin's and Orwell's visions at least suggests...

21 September 2010

On Gypsies and democracy

Maria Serena Natale of *Corriere della Sera* suggested to me that one possible interpretation of the expulsions of Roma people is to read them as another case of the old habit of societies of expelling elements that resist assimilation and classification. I agreed with her supposition. The resolve of the Italian authorities to expel Roma, I pointed out, is one of innumerable cases of what Norbert Elias half a century ago described as 'Established versus Outsiders' – a perpetually simmering and almost universal conflict. The 'established': people settled in an area of the city who suddenly see a growing number of unfamiliar faces on the street, of people strangely dressed, behaving peculiarly, talking incomprehensibly – in short, of 'outsiders' who 'do not belong here'. The 'outsiders': strangers – neither friends nor enemies, and so unpredictable, arousing anxiety and fear...

Strangers are dangers, because – unlike friends or enemies, with whom one knows what to expect and how to respond to their gambits – it is impossible to say of strangers what they are going to do, how they are likely to respond to one's actions, or how one ought to behave in their presence to avoid trouble. Because there is no knowing how to decode their conduct and intentions, one feels lost – *ignorant*; and because one can't be sure what to do in order to stave off possible danger (one can't even know what the danger is, and so one is inclined to imagine the worst...), one also feels *impotent*. And feeling ignorant and impotent is an undignified, *humiliating* condition! It's as if the very presence of strangers offended and denied one's dignity. No wonder one might wish them to go, just to restore tranquillity and balance of mind...

And the politicians are eager to indulge such cravings. They are all too keen to capitalize on the uneasiness, discomfort and anxiety of the 'established' in the presence of 'outsiders' by showing that the authorities *do* care about the security of their subjects and are ready to protect them from the peril. Roma are particularly vulnerable to such treatment. They are the most common 'usual suspects' – the very incarnation of 'strangeness'…Roma are nomads wandering among the sedentary. Untied to any place, they are free to move, they come and go, they resent settled life and so, unlike other diasporas, they seldom spend enough time in one place to 'grow into' a local population, to adjust to the local routine, to become, so to speak, on 'indispensable part of the familiar landscape', and to dissolve into the surroundings having negotiated a mutually acceptable 'modus vivendi'. They are 'perpetual strangers' everywhere; they serve in fact as symbols of disorder, they become 'emblematic strangers', 'strangers incarnate', the fullest embodiment of the menace which 'strangers' portend. As they visit many local communities on their perpetual travels, they carry with them the badges of stigma and the stories of their genuine or putative misdemeanours wherever they go. The list of charges against them grows over time, without ever being subjected to cool-minded testing and scrutiny. They are guilty until they prove their innocence, but are given no opportunity to prove it.

And another factor in their disfavour: unlike most other migrating or diasporic minorities, Roma are blatantly and obtrusively visible in every place they stop for however brief a moment, but simultaneously invisible (indeed, absent) in places where opinions are created, exchanged, debated and given the 'commonsensical' shape. Very seldom are Roma represented in national or local governments, and they have no learned, writing, opinion-forming elite to articulate and promote their point of view. They are visible, yet unseen. Audible, but not heard…

Maria Natale asked me whether there are nevertheless any differences between West and East European countries in the ways Roma (Tziganes, Gypsies) are treated. To which I responded that the feeling of being discriminated against is obviously more painful in poorer countries than it is in richer; the loaf to be sliced is smaller there, and so the chances of decent living are more meagre. Being or trying to be as rational as all the rest of us, migrants setting out on travels in search of bread and butter (and there are huge numbers of them around the globe, of all skin shades, religious beliefs, languages, customs, preferred forms of life) would naturally prefer to go to the better-off countries rather than to the worse-off ones. In this respect, there is nothing peculiar about the preferences manifested by the 'Gypsies' – to 'move West'. In lands with a higher standard of living, prospects for a satisfactory life are greater and opportunities more numerous; even the local poor are richer! Being impoverished in a wealthy country may seem like near paradise when compared with being sunk in prospectless poverty in a poor one.

Having replaced its previous programmatic interference through the so-called 'welfare state', with the existential uncertainty and insecurity produced by the market, and having on the contrary proclaimed the removal of all and any constraints on profit-oriented activities to be the prime task of a political power that truly cares for the well-being of its subjects, contemporary states must, however, seek other *non-economic* varieties of human vulnerability and uncertainty on which to rest their legitimacy. Alternative legitimation of this sort has now been located in the issue of *personal safety*: in the extant or still portending, overt or hidden, genuine or putative fears of *threats to human bodies, possessions and habitats*, whether they arise from pandemics and unhealthy diets or lifestyle regimes, or from criminal activities, anti-social conduct by the 'underclass', alien immigrants, or, most recently, global terrorism.

Unlike the existential insecurity emanating from the vagaries of markets, an insecurity all too real, profuse, and obvious for comfort, that *alternative* insecurity which is now being relied on to restore the state's lost monopoly on the role of people's guardian must be artificially beefed up, or at least highly dramatized to inspire a sufficient volume of fears, as well as to outweigh, overshadow and relegate to a secondary position *economically generated* insecurity – the kind of insecurity the state administration can do next to nothing about, and about which nothing is what it is particularly willing to do. Unlike in the case of market-generated threats to livelihood and welfare, the gravity and extent of dangers to personal safety must be presented in the darkest of colours, so that the *non*-materialization of the advertised threats (indeed, any disaster less awesome than predicted) can be applauded as a great victory of governmental reason over hostile fate: and as the result of the laudable vigilance, care and good will of the state organs.

'Blaming the immigrants' – the strangers, the newcomers, and particularly the newcomers among the strangers – for all aspects of social malaise (and first of all for the nauseating, disempowering feeling of *Unsicherheit, incertezza, précarité*, insecurity) is, under such conditions, a tempting alternative source of a government's legitimation – and so it is fast becoming a global habit. A permanent state of alert: dangers proclaimed to be lurking behind every corner, oozing and leaking from terrorists' camps masquerading as Islamic religious schools and congregations, from the *banlieues* populated by immigrants, from mean streets infested by the underclass, 'rough districts' endemically breeding violence, the no-go areas of big cities, paedophiles and other sex offenders on the loose, obtrusive beggars, bloodthirsty juvenile gangs, loiterers and stalkers...Reasons to be afraid are many, their genuine number and intensity being impossible to calculate from the perspective of a narrow personal experience; and yet another, perhaps the most powerful reason to be frightened is added – one does not know where and when the words of warning will become flesh...

My conversationalist was worried about the prospects of democracy in all these circumstances. I recalled in this connection Roger Cohen's article in the issue of the *New York Times* for 20 September 2010. He wrote of the 'decline of democracy', and explained: 'It's not that nations with democratic systems have dwindled in number, but that democracy has lost its lustre. It's an idea without a glow.' And there are many reasons for that: the bloody mayhem caused by the wars waged in Iraq and Afghanistan in the name of democracy hurt democracy's reputation. Particularly when you juxtapose it with the stable, eminently peaceful and anti-militaristic but dictatorial regime in China, presiding over 10 per cent annual economic growth...Cohen went so far as to suggest that the 'dichotomy between freedom and tyranny suddenly seems oh-so 20th century'. To the countries liberated from communist tyranny, Western-style democracy promised prosperity, growth and peace; in all these areas it delivered much less than it promised. Among old democracies, Belgium is blocked in a conflict which it is clearly unable to resolve; in Israel politics is saturated with corruption; in Italy democracy is turning into its own parody. The US Congress has been immobilized by an interparty stalemate and the only action it is capable of endorsing or promoting is inaction.

I could easily add more reasons for democracy fast losing its once uncontested allure. For instance, that being a leading star of worldwide democracy did not prevent the United States from also becoming a leader or an accomplice in the similarly worldwide disregard for human rights, and in particular the twenty-first century's resurrection of torture. Or that democracies everywhere failed to discourage their peoples from retreating into private shelters and turning their backs on the public space and on their citizens' duty to care for the common and shared good. Or that democracies blatantly failed to protect their own minorities, and their right to respect and to a dignified life. Or that they also failed in their obligation to enhance their subjects' willingness to engage in uninterrupted dialogue, mutual understanding, cooperation and solidarity – those *sine qua non*, defining attributes of democratic life. Democracy cannot rest on the promise of individual enrichment. Its greatest and unique distinction is the service rendered to the freedom of all.

All this is truly worrying. Particularly at a time like ours, a time of global interdependence, confronting us with an unprecedented challenge: the necessity to raise the sacrosanct principles of democratic coexistence from the level of nation-states, to which our ancestors lifted them and on which they left them, to the level of planetary humanity.

22 September 2010

On fading trust and blooming arrogance

For some time now, trust and the hard times on which it appears to have fallen have been the focus of attention of social and political pharmacists, worried by the obstinacy of the multiple ailments besetting their patients, and despairing of their staunch resistance to treatment and so also of the glaring ineffectiveness of the medicines kept on the pharmacy shelves. Trust, most of those pharmacists have come to believe, is the missing ingredient whose absence bears a major, perhaps even the main responsibility for the futility of the once efficacious therapeutic regimes – still customarily recommended and widely considered foolproof, in spite of fast accumulating evidence to the contrary. It is in the resurrection of trust that social and political healers now invest their hopes; and it is the infuriatingly short supply of trust that they now commonly blame for the continuous failure of traditional social medicines.

That it is by trust that the economic, political and social orders stand, and that it is by its absence that they fall has now become the doxa of political science – the foundation of current political science discourse already laid down, set, hardened and seldom revisited. When she addressed the participants of the Rencontres de Pétrarque held in Montpellier on 19 July 2010, Dominique Schnapper accepted it as an axiom, and presented it as an indisputable fact of the matter requiring neither theoretical nor empirical proof, that the practices of economic life as much as the legitimacy of politics ('and thus, so to speak, the social order') 'can't be maintained without a minimum of trust between people, and without people's trust in the institutions'. Having said that, the diagnosis of the semiology of the present troubles suffered by economic, political and social life was for Schnapper a foregone conclusion: in the 'society of generalized defiance' in which we currently live, 'the arguments from tradition or legality are no longer considered valid'. We don't trust such arguments, Schnapper went on – at least not as our ancestors presumably did. And if we don't, then no wonder that our economic, political and social arrangements grate, squeak, limp, get rickety, and threaten to fall apart. One question, though, failed to be asked: in that tangle of multifarious factors that brought that about, which are the carts and which are the horses?

In an interview given to *Le Monde* and published on 21 September, Pierre Rosanvallon picks up the substance of trust and confidence in agents as the 'ability to hypothesize their future behaviour'. He suggests that in the old-style politics (not so very old, to be sure – hardly a half of a century), organized around large political parties, each of them armed with rather firmly entrenched ideas and rather inflexible programmes, such an ability was relatively simple to practise and still easier to presume. We may therefore assume that in the politics of the present day, turning as it is into a game of personalities who come and go, and whose comings and goings are only loosely related, if at all, to extant ideas and programmes, any certainty as to the future behaviour of the powers-that-be is out of the question. Unlike the big, established and to a large extent impersonal parties of yore, blinking and flickering 'political personalities' cannot be trusted, since their future moves are as hazardous as the roles they play are wobbly, and since the cast of the next act of the political drama is just impossible to reliably predict.

Loïc Blondieu, on the other hand, suggests (in *Le nouvel esprit de la démocratie*, 2008) that the responsibility for the public's new scepticism towards the goings-on in the corridors of power rests on the ever more blatant illusoriness of citizens' participation in the political process, reduced as it increasingly is to periodical elections of 'representatives' whose 'representativeness' slips out of their hands they are moment they are elected and enter office. As Bastien François pointed out, however (in *Le Monde* of 22 July), there is little that can be done to repair that state of affairs so long as the idea of the accountability of elected rulers remains to be transferred from the area of political responsibility to that of criminality. Personalities now take the place of ideas on the defendants' benches. To all practical intents and purposes, unless incumbents of political office are caught *in flagrante* taking bribes, cheating in financial reports or engaging in illicit deals or scandalous sexual affairs, they are free to tear up their electoral manifestos with impunity.

More and more often such manifestos become superfluous anyway, ornaments which few if any people will study or indeed consider worthy of studying; catching sound-bites, like 'trust me' or 'we can', needing no elaborate manifestos, will do very well, thank you. The 'popular will', very much like the interests of the addicts of reality TV's *Big Brother*, is related to and fixed on the charms and glamour, sins and misdemeanours of the persons in the house, on their rise and, even more, their fall, on their entrances and even more their dishonourable discharges and brutal evictions – but hardly on the goings-on inside the house, and not on what is produced there, dismissed in advance as a waste rather than a useful product, as things or events eminently forgettable and of no consequence except for the stalwarts of TV quizzes. Something in line with the apocryphal opinion expressed by an Irish farmer: 'that pig does not weigh as much as I thought; but then I did not think it would.'

This is, let me observe, a transformation only to be expected, given the gradual but relentless dismantling and falling apart of societal and communal structures, and their equally gradual yet relentless replacement (or rather quasi-replacement) by frail, kaleidoscopic and eminently short-lived 'networks' – put together ad hoc, and ad hoc dismembered with little or no warning, stripped of all executive potential or not claiming executive powers in the first place. As Hervé de Tellier reports from inside one of those networks in today's edition of *Le Monde*: 'Fantastic, I have a mobile Facebook: hundreds of friends whom I don't know call me to tell me about the tricks with which I have nothing to do, which they apply in their lives of which I know nothing.' Alain Minc (in *Une histoire politique des intellectuels*, just published) has baptised network-politics as @gora...

The strength of certainty acquired reflects the degree of credibility and trustworthiness possessed by or imputed to the authority from which it has been obtained. The first cannot be greater than the second. When we are offered information to be believed, we ask well-nigh automatically: 'who told you that?' or 'where did you read (or hear) it?' Seldom, though, can we count on the answers coming anywhere near those we would consider satisfactory. A trustworthy authority is needed today perhaps more than at any other time – but in sharp opposition to that need, ours are not good times for it to arrive, and yet worse for it to settle and stay.

With the right to make choices, and the obligation to bear the responsibility for their consequences, both saddled firmly on our own shoulders, we may be self-governing as never before, but we also need as never before people-in-the-know who can be believed in and trusted to sincerely wish to assist and reinforce our entitlement and our ability to self-govern. After all, as Alexis de Tocqueville already predicted with uncanny prophetic intuition, even the greatest among philosophers is now bound to believe in millions of things just on the grounds of trust in people proclaimed or proclaiming themselves to be *the experts*; and even the greatest among philosophers are unable to check first-hand the truth of most of the information they need and have to resort to whenever they think or act. More than a hundred years have passed since Georg Simmel concluded that the products of the human spirit's vitality and creativity had already passed the point at which the spirit that conjured them up and brought them into being was still able to reabsorb and digest them. Since Tocqueville penned down his observation, the volume of information 'available' for consumption has been growing exponentially. Never before have so many free agents been tied by, and held onto, so many strings. Never before have so many of the moves of self-propelled agents resulted from so many outside pulls and pushes they could neither control nor resist...

Telling the right moves from the wrong ones has become a gamble. It can hardly be otherwise when the sheer volume of information deemed to be necessary to make a truly rational move (that is, a move based on *full* knowledge of the situation) precludes its ingestion. As most knowledge is available for processing only in a second- or third-hand condition, even that part of knowledge amenable to ingestion and fit for assimilation is of much less than indubitable quality. The spectre of a lie hovers over every truth circulated online or offline; over every reliable recommendation, a spectre of deception. And slowly yet steadily we are growing resigned and habituated to insincerity and double-crossing, high, low and in the middle.

Lies and deceit no longer feel scandalous and outrageous; liars and conmen are no longer banished from public life by common consent, just on the strength of breaking our trust; being 'economical with truth' and 'selective with facts', spinning and 'massaging' the news or making false reports are the bread and butter of today's politics. Few if any brows will be raised nowadays by news that another 'statesman' has been caught lying. We may deride spin-doctors and laugh at them, but politics without them has become as unimaginable for us as a circus without clowns was for our forebears. The lying, lie-denying and lie-debunking routines only add to politicians' entertainment value; not a minor virtue in a world obsessed with and addicted to infotainment.

My beloved Saramago, under the date of 18 September 2008, gave in his blog his opinion of George W. Bush as a cowboy who has inherited the world and mistaken it for a herd of cattle. 'He knows he's lying, he knows we know he's lying, but being a compulsive liar, he will keep on lying...' And he is not alone! 'Human society today is contaminated by lies, the worst sort of moral contamination... The lie circulates everywhere with impunity, and has already turned into a kind of *other truth*.' Let me recall that

George Orwell warned of its coming more than half a century earlier, baptising it 'newspeak'...

As things stand at the moment, the politicians' calls for more trust sound as suspicious and treacherous as sirens' songs. Why should we trust the sirens? Wouldn't it be more reasonable, and ultimately more honest, to follow Odysseus's example (more and more people do already, plugging their ears against the voices coming from on high)? Or better still, considering that sirens can no more alter their tunes than leopards can change their spots, try in earnest to redesign the public stage so that it stays off-limits to sirens?

I admit: easier said than done. But I believe it to be worth trying. And *needing* to be tried. Urgently. Just for the sake of recovering our trust in the possibility of truth...

29 September 2010

On the right to be angry

'Anger is sweeping America,' Paul Krugman noted in the *New York Times* of 19 September. Wouldn't one expect it to sweep? After all, as he reminds us, 'poverty, especially acute poverty, has soared in the economic slump; millions of people have lost their homes. Young people can't find jobs; laid-off 50-somethings fear that they'll never work again.' After a few decades of dreaming the American dream day and night on the pavements and road-ways of the land of the 'end of history' and on the piazzas of the Disneyland of the future 'as seen on TV' – a sudden, brutal awak-ening. The morning after an orgy. For enough people, enough reasons to be angry. After the sweet dream of the certainty of 'We can!', a bitter concoction of confusion and impotence. 'Uncertainty is pervasive,' as Roger Cohen notes in the *New York Times* of 27 September. 'The government's rescue of Wall Street combined with the acute difficulties of a middle class struggling to get by on stagnant or falling incomes has sharpened resentments.' Who was surprised when Velma Hart, until recently a whole-hearted and militant Obama supporter, shouted 'I'm exhausted of defending you!' As Cohen notes, Hart's cry of desperation 'struck a national chord because so many people feel the same thing'.

Contrary to what you might expect, however, this is not what Krugman has in mind when he observes that 'anger is sweeping America', or Cohen when he suggests that the deep unease of America has 'descended into tribalism' – political, economic and social. Millions of the new homeless, as well as the youngsters and the middle-aged with no job prospects, are so far keeping silent, and the wide echo of Velma Hart's cry of desperation seems to be due more to the vast and dumb wilderness in which it reverberated than to a crescendo of supporting voices. Krugman lays open his concerns in the title of his opinion piece: 'The angry rich'. It was the billionaire fund manager Stephen Schwarzman who compared Barack Obama to Hitler invading Poland when he deprived fund managers like him of a tax loophole. And it was *Forbes* magazine, the trumpet of the richest of the rich, that proclaimed Obama's taxing policy to be of Kenyan 'anticolonialist' provenance and announced that from now on the United States was threatened with rule 'according to the dreams of a Luo tribesman of the 1950s'. It was Dorothy Rabinowitz of the editorial board of the *Wall Street Journal* who on 9 June charged Obama with deriving his ideas from the salons of the foreign left – in an article under a title that said it all: 'The alien in the White House'. On 21 September another financial baron, Mort Zuckerman, denounced federal efforts to slow down the steep rise of home repossessions, invoking the orthodox act of faith of the superrich – that 'the markets ought to be allowed to seek their own equilibrium'; while four days later the stentorian and majestic voice of the Cato Institute, in another frontal assault against the alien (un-American?) White House taxation policy, restated the long-lived and long-discredited myth that in the long run tax cuts at the top benefit those at the bottom. All that against a background of a deafening chorale, sung daily from one coast of the country to the other, to tell of the tragic lot of people making between $400,000 and $500,000 a year, who are now faced with a return to the level of taxation before the Bush cuts (so losing a round sum of $700 billion to an emaciated national treasury in debt over its ears) and who will surely go bankrupt (and bereave the less fortunate rest) if they try to pay property taxes on their exclusive homes and the fees of the elite private schools in which their kind spend their gilded youth.

'The spectacle of high-income Americans, the world's luckiest people, wallowing in self-pity and self-righteousness', so Krugman concludes, 'would be funny, except for one thing: they may well get their way.' They may, and the odds are that they will, because they are 'different from you and me: they have more influence'. Influence is the difference that makes the difference. It is thanks to their influence that when they call on the nation 'to be willing to make sacrifices', they can mean, with impunity and fearing no backlash of popular outrage, that 'sacrifice is for the little people'. They have the *right* to be angry; they are allowed to pump their anger through loudspeakers installed on public squares in front of the offices of supreme powers – without any fear of being charged with selfishness, breaking solidarity, anarchy, anti-Americanism, or the mentality of a Luo tribesman.

October 2010

7 October 2010

On the right to get richer

Credit in the United States has hardly ever been so cheap. The Federal Reserve lends money to banks for peanuts, at an interest close to zero. But what proves to be an incentive to the rich to borrow in order to get richer also proves to be a hurdle for the poor and the not so rich who dearly wish to borrow in order not to fall deeper into poverty. Once more, Operation 'salvaging the country's economy' turns out to mean allowing the rich to get richer. As to the poor, who cares?

As Graham Bowley informs us in the *New York Times* of 3 October, it is the biggest American companies – the Microsoft, Johnson & Johnson, PepsiCo or IBM kind – that have started borrowing lavishly. They would hardly miss such an opportunity to amass cash at almost no cost of storing it until the time when the economy 'gets back to normal', that is, when investments start to bring in right and proper profits once more. As an analyst at Microsoft, Richard J. Lane, observes, for a company 'borrowing new money on the debt market is now cheaper than bringing its own money back from overseas'. And so the big money-users who can afford it borrow money to store it; if they put it back into circulation, it is with a mind to repurchase their own stocks or to finance new (mostly hostile) mergers and acquisitions. Prudently, they do not hurry to build new factories or hire more labour. Thus far, the big corporations have accumulated a mind-boggling treasure trove of $1.6 trillion to sit on. And as Michael Gapen, an economist at Barclay Capital, muses, they most probably intend to, and will, use that cheap money to obtain labour-replacing technology and to cut jobs.

To cut a long story short, the much advertised 'trickle-down effect' has once more failed to materialize. So far, it is the opposite effect that appears all too real. As Bowley points out, low-interest lending and borrowing 'have in fact hurt many Americans, especially retirees whose incomes from savings have fallen substantially' – like the rates of interest, well-nigh to zero. But pensioners forced to bite deeply into their life savings are just one category to suffer the darkest and most painful consequences of the credit collapse, as well as of the current fashion of reviving credit. Most if not all of the almost 15 million unemployed in the US, and the uncounted number of adults and children they were presumed to provide for, fall into another category. Yet another category is made up of small businesses, as the cheap credit blatantly refuses to 'trickle down' even to their level. For those categories, borrowing remains a daunting task, requiring an uphill struggle with little if any chance of success. Many face the prospect of bankruptcy, most can't dream of expansion and job creation – which rubs more salt into the wounds of the already un- or under-employed. Like a magic wand, all measures undertaken in the name of 'salvaging the economy' turn out to be measures to enrich the rich and impoverish the poor.

While I am writing these words, the administration initiative most hotly resisted and fought against by the US Congress is the termination of George W. Bush's tax cuts for the super-rich (the contentious sum is around $700 billion). One of the most successful investors in the world, often called the 'legendary investor Warren Buffett', consistently ranked among the world's wealthiest people (according to his Wikipedia biography, the world's second wealthiest person in 2009, and currently the third wealthiest person in the world), is said to have announced: 'there's class warfare, all right. But it's my class, the rich class, that's making war, and we're winning.'

How right that legendary investor is proving to be…

13 October 2010

On many cultures, and one cover-up

Cultural difference is what sets you apart from those behaving differently; or at least this definition or explanation (mostly tacit, and axiomatically embraced) is one of the least shakeable pillars of both the current social-scientific doxa and abominably unscientific, because common, sense. Those people out there conduct themselves differently from these down here? Those people are more likely, statistically, to suffer a different lot from these? In both cases, culture is the cause – and so, obviously, the explanation. And the reason.

'Cultural', by definition, applies to patterns of behaviour, or habits, or attitudes that could be different if the people practising them made different choices. They are 'soft' attributes of the *homo eligens*, the 'choosing agent'. They may be adopted or renounced at will (even though, admittedly, powerful odds may conspire against it). And so, ultimately, it is the agent who adopts or renounces them who bears the responsibility for their presence and absence.

When teaching at the Memorial University of Newfoundland a quarter of a century ago, I read in the *Globe and Mail*, the leading opinion-shaping daily of Canada, that according to the latest research the mortality among people diagnosed with cancer was closely correlated with their income: among the rich, cancer led to death significantly less often than among the poor – and if the cancer discovered among the richer Canadians did ultimately end in death, it took on average more time than in the case of their less well-off compatriots. The editors, with the help of learned experts, explained those statistics by pointing out that the poor smoke more than the rich (i.e., than the more educated and so more prudent and rational); there was, however, no mention of factors less easy to get rid of than the smoking habit – such as, for instance, chronic undernourishment and inferior life conditions, or just the absence of the money a thorough therapy would most certainly require. In other words, it was the 'culture of the poor', that is the cultural precepts *chosen* by the poor, that were guilty of killing them more often and more promptly in the event they fell victim to cancer. That explanation, as far as I can judge, was one of the first signs of the impending era of 'culturalism': times in which the different fates suffered by different categories of humans tend to be explained, as a rule and all but automatically, by differences in the choices (preferences, priorities) which those different categories are likely to make – whereas the possibility that the 'dice might be loaded' (that the sets of options confronting different categories, and among which they are realistically able to choose, might have been varied well before the question of individual choices arose) was seldom, if ever, invoked and still less often seriously pondered.

A week ago Didier and Eric Fassin remembered in *Le Monde* (in 'Misère du culturalisme') the cases of lead poisoning discovered among French, American and British children a few years ago. French epidemiologists hastened to announce that cases of that serious, in many cases terminal, illness were particularly widespread among families from sub-Saharan Africa – and proceeded right away to add two and two together: in Sahel culture, children often pick and suck bits of coating flaking off walls. At the same time, though, the infant victims of lead poisoning in the United States proved to be found mostly in Afro-American families not originating in the Sahel, and in any case settled in their new homeland for many generations. In Britain, by comparison, children most affected by lead poisoning came from families which had arrived from India and Pakistan. Clearly, similarities in the incidence of the illness could hardly be traced to imported similarities in cultural training. The factors common to all three groups were obviously social, not cultural: all three categories of recent or early immigrants lived in impoverished urban districts and inhabited dilapidated, time-worn, god-forsaken slums, where they were bound to inhale the dust of lead-based wall-paints daily or drink water from lead pipes well beyond their use-by dates.

If anything, the tendency to put a 'culturalist' gloss on worrying social problems at the centre of public attention has gathered force since the cases of lead poisoning vanished from newspaper front pages and headlines. Today, the most salient instance – since it is the most common and has the most 'commonsensical' status – is the 'culturalist' interpretation of the statistical correlation between high incidences of juvenile delinquency, anti-social behaviour and inferior school performance, on the one hand, and urban locations with dense immigrant populations, on the other. Obviously forgetful of the time-honoured warning from Hume (*post hoc non est propter hoc* – preceding does not mean causing), Hugues Lagrange (author of *Le déni des cultures*, 2010) or Michèle Tribalat (in *Le Monde* of 14 September) take a time sequence for a causal connection. Lagrange charges the blacks who arrived from the Sahel of 'carrying into our [urban] universe large swathes of distant customs, often rural and very retrograde'. Whereas Tribalat castigates (selected) fellow social scientists for 'harnessing themselves to the service of anti-racism' by apparently preferring to stay ignorant of cultural differences, and by being inclined to blame social structures for misdeeds determined culturally; in other words, for a deliberate cover-up of the unpleasant fact of a prospectless incompatibility of 'our' and 'their' cultures.

In this version at least, 'multiculturalism', and more generally 'culturalism', in straining to supply a scholarly underpinning (more to the point, a PR gloss) for multiculturalist practice, is itself a cover-up exercise. What it tries to cover up and elbow out of public debate are the brute realities of social discrimination and deprivation.

14 October 2010

On don't say you haven't been warned

This needs to be recorded before tomorrow's headlines and the headlines of the day after tomorrow do what their main (even though latent rather than manifest) function requires them to do: before they efface the message from human memory... What I am saying demands to be recorded and saved from extinction is today's *New York Times* editorial under the tell-all title: 'The Next Bubble'.

It informs us that buying out the stocks of the 'emerging economies' is the latest fashion and passion on Wall Street. This year alone, Wall Street will spend $825 billion on buying them (a 42 per cent increase on last year), while spending on buying out the debt of the emerging economies will triple and reach $272 billion: all that money having been saved thanks to the new reluctance of Wall Street to invest in the no-longer-solvent American debtors. In other words, as one would expect from capital – to following its familiar strategy of a parasite desperately searching for a new host organism after killing the old – a new virgin land has been discovered by the intrepid scouts of Wall Street: one apparently unexploited or underexploited, untapped, promising fast and high profits, garnered quickly before the grossly underpaid labourers become hard-nosed and demand to join the consumerist orgy in which their American or European counterparts are accustomed to wallow, and in which they intend to go on wallowing for as long as they can manage it...

The writer of the editorial observes that the initial benefits to the natives notwithstanding, massive foreign investments 'push up the value of their currency, boosting imports and slowing exports, and they promote fast credit expansion – which can cause inflation, inflate asset bubbles and usually leave a pile of bad loans. This money turns tail at the first sign of trouble, tipping countries into crisis.' And then the author reminds readers of the patterns likely to be repeated again, as they are bound to be monotonously repeated in the life of all parasites: the 1994 tequila crisis in Mexico, the 1997 Asian crisis, the 1998 Russian catastrophe, the 1999 Brazilian debacle or the 2002 Argentine collapse. One would add more recently Greece's, Ireland's and Latvia's bitter awakening...

The author wouldn't go as far as questioning the 'economic wisdom' of the current Wall Street frenzy: 'Still, it is not time to panic. Developing countries are in relatively good economic shape, while interest rates in the wealthy countries are likely to stay low for years.' In other words, profits are likely to flow uninterruptedly into stockholders' pockets and bank accounts for some time yet. What worries the author, and should worry the readers, is the possibility that another shock – replicating the recent defaults in Ireland or Greece, for instance – may unmask the organs designed, expected and hoped to stop capitalism before it drains dry, exhausts and wastes away the pastures that feed and sustain it as unable to do their job, and especially their inability or reluctance to start doing that job in earnest before it is too late. Are not the assurances that 'it is not time to panic' among the major causes of that inability cum reluctance, routinely discovered after the fact – only to be, similarly routinely, promptly forgotten? How many virgin lands need to be forced into catastrophe for that routine to be broken? Or does capitalism, and the polities servicing it, mean the very impossibility of learning?

17 October 2010

On the quandaries of believing

The detractors of religion, doubting the desirability of its human uses and the value of its impact on human life, aim to strip religious beliefs of their authority by pointing out that – unlike the secular knowledge supplied by 'experts' – they are accepted on *faith*, not on *evidence*. The explicit assumption invoked by this argument is that knowledge based on evidence is more reliable than knowledge ('merely') taken on trust in the authority of its purveyors; but the tacit yet nonetheless decisive assumption is that the reliability and truthfulness of a proposition depends on what can pass for evidence and ultimately for 'how things truly are', which in turn translates into the question of who is a legitimate spokesman for the truth and who is only a false pretender. The Gospels, after all, or for that matter the Old Testament, are brimming with 'empirical proofs' of their messages. Jesus, much like Moses, convinced witnesses that he had access to true knowledge and so that he was in-the-right and deserving-of-trust by demonstrating his exquisite ability to do things that transcended the capacity of his adversaries and traducers: as Tertullian was to observe a little later, the story of Jesus' miraculous accomplishments had to be believed precisely for that reason – for 'being absurd' (uncanny and unbelievable...). We can safely assume that people to whom the story of such demonstrations was reported by people who vouched they had witnessed them were fully prepared, indeed eager, to believe what they heard and trust the messengers. Just as we, born and brought up in the age of science and technology, are prepared to believe what we hear from the scientists and trust them, the messengers of Science.

It was Ludwik Fleck, the formidable philosopher of science and cognition, who pointed out that theory precedes seeing; an uninitiated (untrained, unindoctrinated) person who was asked to look through a microscope would look but not see. What would present itself to his eyes would be a disorderly, meaningless accumulation of colourful spots which would fall into shape and acquire meaning only if they were allocated to the preconceived sites of a theoretical matrix. Such a matrix needs to be already in place and so must already have acquired the status of axioms no longer questioned and, indeed, no longer noticed. And this may happen solely as a product of 'thought collectives', distinguished by their own 'thought style' (defined by Fleck as 'directed perception, with corresponding mental and objective assimilation of what has been so perceived'), sustained and continuously reproduced in ongoing mutual communication: 'a community of persons mutually exchanging ideas or maintaining intellectual interaction'. As Wojciech Sady, the author of a 2001 article 'Ludwik Fleck: thought collectives and thought styles', commented, such communities are formed by 'relatively small esoteric circles of experts and much bigger exoteric circles of school teachers':

> The training introducing one into a thought style is of a dogmatic character. Students attain competence in applying some principles, but their critical attitude to those principles is out of question. If they do not accept the set of beliefs common to all members of a given thought collective and if they do not master the same set of skills, then they will not be admitted to the community.

And he adds:

> It is to be understood not as a set of *constraints* that society imposes on our cognitive practices, but as something that makes cognitive acts *possible* at all. The word 'knowledge' is meaningful only in relation to a thought collective. And if for any reason someone formulates ideas that are beyond the limits of what is socially acceptable at a given time, they will remain unnoticed or misunderstood.

What follows is that the people who speak for modern science and advocate its methodological superiority over religious beliefs gloss over the fact that ultimately the knowledge conveyed by scientists is also accepted on faith and trust, since those who accept its conclusions rarely have the opportunity, or indeed the will, to subject their beliefs to the testing procedure which science claims to be its distinctive mark and the grounds for its superiority. What is presented as 'episteme' – systematically tested knowledge – is in the last account accepted and deployed in the same fashion as the 'doxa' so derided and held in such contempt – the knowledge *with* which lay people (that is, those outside the 'esoteric circles of experts' and 'exoteric circles of school teachers') think but which they don't think *about*; whereas properly trained and drilled and so certified experts and teachers accept the propriety of their cognitive procedure in a way not qualitatively distinct from doxa. The 'obvious' and 'self-evident' character of *scientific* findings is arrived at through a long string of collectively reiterated and collectively reaffirmed acts of *faith*. Bringing Galileo to court, the church prosecutors were not in fact out of order when they questioned his insistence that the smudges he saw when he pressed his eye to a telescope indeed stood for stains on the sun...They merely followed – well before its discovery by Ludwik Fleck in the working of modern science, and Fleck's recording of it in his 'Genesis and development of a scientific fact' – the well-nigh universal pattern of 'the tenacity of systems of opinion and the harmony of illusions'. In Fleck's rendition, that pattern consists in making whatever contradicts the system unthinkable, while concealing from the eyes whatever does not fit into the system; or – in the event that 'abnormalities' force their way into the field of vision – explaining them away in a fashion that does not clash with the system's integrity.

The true substance of the modern campaign of 'secularization' was a power struggle; and the object of that struggle, its stake and its yearned-for prize, was the right to select from the array of competing legitimating formulae one procedure entitled to claim truth-value for its results, by the same token disqualifying the claims of all other competitors. The conflicts between episteme and doxa or between empirical and revealed knowledge, or indeed between knowledge and faith, glossed over the power conflict between the established church and the academy. Another way to put it is to say that the process of 'secularization' was effected by the redistribution of the rare resource of public trust, seen from *both* sides of the main frontline as the object of a zero-sum game.

Thus far, we've watched the two contenders deploying their different weapons in a war conducted with identical objectives in mind; they are vying for the same trophy, the right to speak with authority – ultimately, or at least preferably, with an exclusive, indivisible and unshared authority. The game played by both contenders has acquired the name, on the religious side of the frontline, of monotheism (on science's side, a name – a distinguishing device, needed to set certain objects apart from a plethora of others – has not been coined; thus far science has been not so much dismissive as neglectful of and oblivious to the possibility of an alternative to itself). Science's a priori intolerance for all and any alternative entitlement to be the one speaking-with-authority is a secular extension of monotheism; a monotheism without God. Both inspired and moved by the spirit of Jerusalem, the two contenders agree on the indisputable need to tame, curb, check, and suppress the cheerful and carefree wantonness of Athens that left truth to the vagaries of the agora.

20 October 2010

On Cervantes, father of humanities...

Below is the text of the acceptance speech I delivered in Oviedo at the ceremony for the Prince of Asturias prizes:

'Your Royal Highness, Mr President of the Prince of Asturias Foundation, Ladies and Gentlemen!

There are many reasons to be immensely grateful for the distinction bestowed upon me, but perhaps the most important among those reasons is that you have classified my work as part of humanities, and as an effort relevant to human communication. All my life I have tried to do sociology in the way in which my two Warsaw teachers, Stanisław Ossowski and Julian Hochfeld, taught me sixty years ago, and what they taught me was to treat sociology as a discipline of *humanities*, whose sole, noble and magnificent purpose is to enable and facilitate human understanding and interhuman ongoing *dialogue*.

Which brings me to another crucial reason for my joy and gratitude: the distinction you have bestowed on my work comes from Spain, the land of Miguel de Cervantes Saavedra, the author of the greatest novel ever written, but through that novel also the founding father of humanities. Cervantes was the first to accomplish what we all working in humanities try, with only mixed success and within our limited abilities, to do. As another novelist, Milan Kundera, put it: Cervantes sent Don Quixote to tear up the curtains patched together of myths, masks, stereotypes, prejudgments and pre-interpretations, curtains that cover up tightly the world we inhabit and which we struggle to understand – but are bound to struggle in vain as long as the curtain is not raised or torn up. Don Quixote was not a conqueror – he was conquered. But in his defeat, as Cervantes showed us, he demonstrated that "all we can do in the face of that ineluctable defeat called life is to try to understand it". This was Miguel de Cervantes' great, epochal discovery; once made, it can't be ever forgotten. We all, in humanities, follow the trail which that discovery laid open. It is thanks to Cervantes that we are here.

To tear up the curtain, to understand life...What does this mean? We, humans, would prefer to inhabit an orderly, clean and transparent world in which good and evil, beauty and ugliness, truth and lie are neatly separated from each other and never mix, so that we can be sure how things are, where to go and how to proceed; we dream of a world in which judgements and decisions can be made without the arduous labour of understanding. It is of this dream of ours that *ideologies* are born – those dense curtains that stop looking short of seeing. It is to this incapacitating inclination of ours that Étienne de la Boétie gave the name of "voluntary servitude". And it was the trail out and away from that servitude that Cervantes blazed for us to follow – by presenting the world in all its naked, uncomfortable yet liberating, reality: reality of the *multitude of meanings* and irreparable *shortage of absolute truths*. It is in such a world, in a world in which the sole certainty is the *certainty of uncertainty*, that we are bound to attempt, ever again and each time inconclusively, to understand ourselves and each other, to communicate, and so live *with* each other and *for* each other.

This is the task in which humanities try to assist fellow humans; at least what they ought to be trying, if they wish to remain faithful to Miguel de Cervantes Saavedra's legacy. And this is why I am so immensely grateful, Your Highness and Mr President, for qualifying my work as a contribution to humanities and human communication.'

30 October 2010

On one more war of attrition, CE 2010–?

Today's papers bring another serving of mind-boggling, blood-curdling and nerve-shattering news. Two unnamed Yemeni women put in the mail two brand-new varieties of 'highly sophisticated' weapons, this time so skilfully hidden in a computer printer and a printing cartridge that none of the sophisticated X-ray devices installed in all the large and not-so-large airports of the world could have spotted them. (How on earth they were nonetheless discovered and defused, the people who issued the press release did not say; it is left to us, on the receiving end of the channel of communication, to assume that foiling the shrewd plot can only be ascribed to the superhuman perceptiveness and unsleeping vigilance of security agents, in the same way as the discovery of Saddam Hussein's weapons of mass destruction, as well as the 'dirty bombs', 'liquid bombs' and the other exquisitely murderous contraptions added to the terrorists' arsenal.)

The first commentaries are concentrating on the possible impact of this dramatic announcement on the coming mid-term elections in the United States. How will Obama react to the news? Will he play it up or down? I don't know the answers, and frankly I am not particularly interested in finding or guessing them. Of one thing, though, I am sure. As today's *New York Times* chose to express it, 'The foiling of the package plot was a sobering reminder to officials around the world that quick response to timely intelligence rules the day' (as if the officials needed to be reminded, or for that matter wished to be sobered...). A spate of brand new security measures will be designed and promptly put into place, new spying techniques will be developed and supported by newly produced technical devices, and a 'new and improved' regime of airport checks and searches will be introduced. To pay for all and each of these measures, the new orders filling the order books of security companies, new holes will be burrowed in state budgets as well as in the funds earmarked to meet the urgent social, cultural and educational needs of nations. Two 'highly sophisticated' bombs have been intercepted. To seize the uncounted and uncountable numbers of their replicas still to be produced, millions of new and 'even more highly sophisticated' contraptions and thousands of people to operate them will be needed. As always since the discovery of the self-propelling escalation of security expenditures that is now proving to be the most seminal and lasting heritage of the Cold War, the stables will be overhauled at a cost dwarfing the price of the horse(s) that bolted.

It is not only generals who are prone always to fight the last victorious war, and the current 'war against terrorism' (I am sorry for adopting that oxymoron, for lack of another accepted, publicly recognizable name) is in some crucial and seminal respects a repetition of that Cold War. The combatants, the weapons and the modes of military actions have changed – but not the strategic doxa, the logic and above all the in-built mechanism of exponential self-escalation (I guess that precisely such an expectation was the hub of Bin Laden's war plan). It was the permanent feature of Cold War battles not to be fought in the field. New weapons were produced at a steadily rising pace, not in order to be used in action, but to render the weapons stocked by the enemy useless and force the enemy to replace them with new ones, thereby forcing one's own warehouses to be emptied and suppliers to refill them. The story is now repeating itself. At every step the probability grows that the ending will also be repeated. The Cold War, remember, ended with one of the players in the rearmament game becoming impoverished and going bankrupt. Imploding, not having been exploded...

November 2010

30 November 2010

On why Americans see no light at the end of the tunnel

Frank Rich writes in today's *New York Times*, in an article under telling-it-all title 'Still the best Congress money can Buy':

> The Great Depression ended the last comparable Gilded Age, of the 1920s, and brought about major reforms in American government and business. Not so the Great Recession. Last week, as the Fed's new growth projections downsized hope for significant decline in the unemployment rate, the Commerce Department reported that corporate profits hit a record high. Those profits aren't trickling down into new jobs or into higher salaries for those not in the executive suites. And the prospect of serious regulation of those at the top of the top – the financial sector – is even more of a fantasy in the new Congress than it was in its predecessor.

He wrote these words, presumably, to explain why – after the recent elections punishing the Obama administration, held by univocal, media-incited opinion to be the main reason for the widespread feeling that something had gone wrong in America – the proportion of respondents to a *Wall Street Journal* poll who judged that America was on the right track rose from 31 per cent to...32 per cent. 'Regardless of party or politics,' Rich concludes, 'there's a sense of a broken country that can't be fixed.'

As Peter Drucker prophesied quite a few years ago, few if any nowadays expect salvation to descend from on high. In Rich's view, unloading popular spleen on the Democrats' Congressional majority was wide of the mark; as should have been expected, nothing has changed – the mood is no less melancholy today than it was before, and it is still vainly looking for culprits. That majority went as swiftly as it came, but reasons to rejoice failed to appear. Evidently, that 'something' that has 'gone wrong' in America needs to be sought and (hopefully, hopefully...) may be found elsewhere. And equally obviously, that 'something' has not moved an inch and stays firmly in place.

And where is that 'elsewhere' to be found, and that 'something' to be dug out? The answer is in an industry that grasps, swallows and digests a quarter of America's business profits (having almost doubled its share in just a quarter of a century), in stark opposition to the rest of America's industries (in the words of John Cassidy, another *New York Times* columnist, it 'doesn't design, build or sell a tangible thing'); an industry whose speciality is the massive purchase and conspicuous consumption of... politicians. The insurance lobby alone, joining together to fight Obama's health care reform, contributed $86 million to a 'purchase fund' of undisclosed, yet commonly agreed to be unprecedented, size. According to an independent news agency, Pro Publica, about sixty-nine members of Congress, together with hundreds of big business lobbyists, currently belong to a highly secretive 'New Democrat Coalition', described by the agency as 'one of the most successful political money machines' – 'most' in American history? In human memory?

In the view of David Axelrod, also writing in the *New York Times*, that particular genie can't be put back into the bottle. He thinks, I presume, what most of us think – because, following the convulsions of an incurably stalemated Capitol Hill, he, like the rest of us, can't see a power potent and resolute enough to force that genie back under control. What is left is to update Peter Drucker's prophecy: salvation can no longer be expected from that particular 'high up' where the powers ruling America currently reside.

December 2010

2 December 2010

On the war to end wars

In one of the full-length sequels of the *Star Trek* series on TV, we, the viewers, are invited to visit a planet (called, by the way, 'Nimbus', a halo, or aureole, believed to emanate from the heads of saints, heroes, and powerful rulers) on which the use of weapons is strictly prohibited. As the plot briskly develops, we come to realize (even though – who knows? – that might not have been the film-makers' intention) just how many weapons, supreme weapons, state-of-the-art weapons, cutting-edge weapons and damned costly weapons he who prohibits the use of weapons needs, and must use, in order to make sure that the prohibition of the use of weapons is obeyed.

Deliberately or not, knowingly or not, the film-makers made a point: the very point from which all other antinomies endemic to the human, only human, all-too-human mode of being spring – and on which they feed. The specifically and uniquely human mode of being is marked by a refusal to take things for granted and by an effort to make them different than they are. The most common names for the combination of those two attributes are 'ordering', 'order-making' or 'bringing order into things': to put it in a nutshell, humans are 'order-making beings'. When they are engaged in bringing order into things (that is, throughout their lives), humans are busy in manipulating the probability of eventualities: making the occurrence of some events more probable than it would be in the absence of their efforts, while reducing and hopefully altogether eliminating the probability of others. If they are successful, they are 'in control (or "in command") of things': no longer are they taken by surprise, caught unawares, forced to improvise defences against turns of events not to their liking and not of their making. Being 'in command' in its turn requires being the sole 'free agents', capable of making choices and changing their minds, while reducing all other potential actors to reciting set lines and reiterating set moves – in essence, to the status of the *objects* (targets, sufferers) but not the *subjects* (originators and designers) of action.

To put this all together and to draw (inescapable) conclusions: order-making means forcing some people – whose exclusion from the company of (appointed, invited, permitted or inadvertent) actors is what distinguishes an orderly setting intended-to-be-made from a setting intended-to-be-ordered – to accept a status they resent and engage in actions they have neither the taste nor the stomach for. Whenever an order is built (and that means twenty-four hours a day, seven days a week), force is applied to compel some people to surrender their ambitions and desist from acting on their preferences, and to impose upon them the condition of (to deploy Étienne de la Boétie's term once more) 'voluntary servitude'. The big question, therefore, is whether the elimination of the use of violence to compel, coerce, disable and incapacitate is at all conceivable as a realistic objective of order-making. In other words, whether – given the nature of the human mode of being – such a result is a viable and feasible task…or whether, on the contrary, every and any endeavour to 'eliminate compulsion and enforcement' is that compulsion's and enforcement's most profuse and inexhaustible source.

Joanna Tokarska-Bakir recently recalled Arthur Koestler's observation that a common feature of altruistic utopias is cruelty perpetrated in the name of love, condemning or licensing people to do what repels and revolts them. Such utopias call for murder for the sake of putting an end to murders, for whipping people in order to teach them to refuse to be whipped, for scruples to be cast aside in the name of fulfilling the highest of moral commandments, and for an awakening, beefing up and bringing to the boil human hatred, in the name of the love of humankind. Koestler was not the only one to expose such toxic concoctions. Far from it: the need for them (indeed, their unavoidability) had been firmly established in popular wisdom, and in the practice of that wisdom's most devoted, eager and most business-like spokesmen, since antiquity: *si vis pacem, para bellum.* You want peace? Be ready to wage war. Those who are ready are winners. Those who emerge defeated were not, obviously, ready. QED. Who would dare to object? Who would wish to object? Certainly not those responsible for ushering the nations over which they presided into the world of modernity – that brave (and pugnacious) new world vociferous about the winners, dumb about the defeated. The world promising to use violence (sorry, legitimate coercion...) solely in order to put, once and for all, an end to violence (coercion illegitimized...). To be done by drawing a clear and unchallengeable line separating violence (from now on a name for illegitimate coercion) from legitimate coercion; and making sure that the line stays impassable and is observed: courtesy of legitimate coercion, of course – a resource available solely to those resourceful enough to draw that line and keep it intact.

Koestler himself, in the first volume of his monumental autobiography, notes that on 5 September 1905, the day of his birth, the London *Times* waxed lyrical and eulogized Japan's victory over Russia, lavishing praise on Japan's supreme readiness for the war effort. Whoever wrote the *Times* editorial must have been impressed and wished his readers to share his enthusiasm: the examples of Japan, in his view, 'indicate one or two directions in which it may perhaps tend to mould thought and character in the world'. And he does his best to spell out what that welcome thought and character will, shall and ought be like:

> The great end of all this training has been the subordination of the individual to the family, the tribe, and the State...It teaches that [man's first duty] is his collective duty to the different social groups into which he is born. From his boyhood he is hourly and carefully trained to the fulfilment of this duty. He is taught not merely to school his actions and his features, but his very thoughts and feelings and impulses in obedience to it...

'That was the lesson', Koestler comments acridly, 'which, in his [the editorial author's] opinion, the West, with its excessive individualism, had to learn from the "monastic discipline" of the first modern totalitarian state.' What for? Presumably, to flex its own muscles in order to fulfil the noble purpose history had placed on its shoulders: the white man's mission to extirpate all residues of barbarism and blaze a trail to the ultimate triumph of civilization over savagery, progress over backwardness, power over impotence...

The most awesome, most gory and blood-curdling atrocities in history have been committed in the name of the most elevated, noble and for that reason most commendable and alluring aims. It was in the name of salvaging their souls that heretics and witches were burnt at the stake, and in the name of establishing the Kingdom of God on Earth that heathens were put to the sword and their homes set on fire. It was in order to make the state and its repressive organs redundant that Stalin proclaimed the necessity of unleashing, building up and perpetually sharpening state repression. It was to bring about and secure the worldwide rule of the German race that Hitler sent German males to their deaths, old and young alike, while causing their family homes to be gutted and their families to be decimated. It is in the name of peaceful coexistence with their Israeli neighbours that Israeli troops are ordered to bulldoze and raze to the ground the homes of Palestinians, uproot their olive groves and destroy their livelihoods. It was to promote the cause of democracy that the ad hoc alliance of democratic powers sent its expeditionary forces to bomb and destroy the lands where the enemies of democracy were hiding, deemed to be hiding or suspected to be seeking hideouts.

The saddest point of all is that we all find it just about impossible to conceive of any other way of proceeding. We can hardly imagine creation free from destruction. And we tend to consider destruction an acceptable price to be paid for creation. We scratch our heads in disbelief when someone suggests that it can be otherwise. We shed a tear or two when we hear of 'innocent victims', the 'collateral casualties' of the drive to a better life, the march of progress, or the holy war against warmongers; all in all, of the drive to a world that no longer needs and allows violence. But then we can always console ourselves by remembering that omelettes can't be made without breaking some eggs. And that, for the time being, it is not our turn to be those eggs.

Michelangelo is reputed to have been asked how he managed to recycle his visions into the exquisitely beautiful, indeed perfect sculptures that made him famous. He is also reputed to have answered that his method was simplicity itself: he just took a block of marble and cut out and threw away all the unnecessary parts. We are all trying to do what Michelangelo did, following his method whatever the material in which we are carving our designs. Sometimes it is marble. Sometimes it is human flesh. We haven't found another method. And, as a matter of fact, we haven't looked for one particularly keenly. By now, we seem to have stopped looking altogether.

4 December 2010

On hurting flies and killing people

Slavenka Drakulić, indefatigable Croatian journalist and essayist, has documented the lives and deeds of the criminals brought to the international Tribunal in The Hague in the aftermath of the civil war that tore apart the country known for seventy years under the name of Yugoslavia – and its population. She collected the results of her unique first-hand, face-to-face investigation in a book called *They Would Never Hurt a Fly* (2004).

One of her reports contains the reflections of a witness to one of the tribunal's first trials, conducted against Dragoljub Kunarac, Radomir Kovač and Zoran Vuković, a driver, a waiter and a shop assistant, three Bosnian Serbs from the little town of Foča. Having witnessed the trial proceedings, Drakulić reports her feelings: if she had met any one of them before the war, it wouldn't have occurred to her that they were particularly brutal. Just three ordinary guys of the kind she meets daily. But there was a war, and it is now known that all three were guilty of torture, kidnap, rape and cold-blooded murder. Is this possible?! One seeks in vain for some evident sign of perversion allowing murderous potential to be spotted. In vain, in vain! And there must be a great multitude of such cases, since during that war 60,000 women were raped and 200,000 people were murdered. Hundreds of thousands of people must have believed that while they did all that they were in the right...

Another defendant facing the tribunal, Goran Jelisić, sentenced to forty years in prison for murdering thirteen men and women arrested at the police precinct he commanded, 'looks like a person you can trust'. A man like that 'usually helps old people across the street, stands up in a tram to offer his seat to an invalid, lets others move forward in the supermarket queue. He would return a found wallet to its rightful owner...Best friend, trustworthy neighbour, ideal son-in-law...' Seriously, you wouldn't find the slightest hint of pathology in his prewar life. He was a quiet, in fact a rather timid boy, self-effacing but known to be eager to help others...

Well, beginning on 7 May 1992, the day he shot his first victim, and for eighteen consecutive days, Goran Jelisić, twenty-three years old, was reincarnated as a sadistic beast. Survivors among his prisoners remember him walking and shouting as if drugged and in a trance. His gaze froze his victims before his gun murdered them. He picked his victims at random (though he was not choosy; he picked an old man for dropping a bottle on the floor and a young man for marrying a Serbian girl), ordered them to kneel and lower their heads over a sewage grill, and pressed his gun to their necks. Sometimes he invited Monica, his girlfriend, to watch and admire his efficiency. All that, day in, day out, for eighteen days...Why? What was the secret?!

Slavenka Drakulić's son-in-law, also a Croat, was in many ways just a nice young man like Jelisić, addicted like Jelisić to fishing. But unlike Jelisić, who volunteered to join the newly formed Croat police, he went to Canada before the civil war started. 'Could it all happen the other way round?' Drakulić asks, desperately trying to crack the mystery. 'Could my son-in-law volunteer for the Croat police?' 'It was the first time in his life that Goran Jelisić had power...He was given a gun and told to use it freely,' she muses. And she adds: 'I still think that even if he indeed turned into an oppressor, in a deeper sense he was a victim. He and all his generation were deceived. They embraced the nationalist ideology and did nothing to stop the war that grew out of it. They were too opportunistic and too frightened to refuse to follow their commanders.'

Before 7 May 1992, anyone who set eyes on a friendly, handsome young man called Goran Jelisić would swear that this man wouldn't be able to hurt a fly.

16 December 2010

On Jerusalem v. Athens revisited

God is a prototypical 'social fact'. It exists the way all other social facts exist, if one believes Émile Durkheim: it cannot be removed (or, for that matter, inserted) by a sheer effort of mind, 'wished away' (or in), or 'argued away' (or in). God 'exists' through imposing itself and cropping up uninvited and unsummoned – winking from every blank spot, every 'non sequitur' in the chain of explanations and train of comprehension, and squeezing itself into every gap in the sequence of acts separating desire for fulfilment and expectation from things as they are, staunchly refusing to budge. God will exist as long as human existential uncertainty does, and that means forever. Which means God will die together with the human species and not a second earlier.

'God' is another name we tend to give to the experience of human *insufficiency*: of our ignorance (inability to understand and so to know how to go on) and impotence (inability to act with success) – as well as for the summary impact of both, our humiliation (the blow to our self-confidence and self-esteem). But it is not the only name: it has competitors, among whom blind, numb and dumb nature, fate, or a conspiracy of evil forces tend to loom larger than the rest. What unites all the names is the suggestion of the supra-humanity of the entities they designate: and by implication, human incapacity to grasp their logic (or rather the ability of those entities to ignore and violate 'logic' as humans know it), and man's inability to reach the goals he sets – suggested by the popular wisdom that man proposes, but it is God who disposes (to wit, the entities' ability to ignore, confound and thwart human intentions). In the face of such entities, begging favours or mercy is the sole expedient to which humans may resort; though it is not up to humans to decide whether their supplications or prayers are listened to or accepted. The entities are 'decisionist' in the sense of the status ascribed by Carl Schmitt to human sovereign rulers:

in the sense of owing their subjects no explanation, let alone an apology.

Schmitt himself had no doubt that assigning earthly rulers a decisionist status was tantamount to their deification – situating them among gods. The de-routinization of the ruler's decisions and their exemption from law-imposed rules aimed at regularity, monotony and repetitiousness are, in Schmitt's view, the political equivalents of God's miracles in religion. Gods are they who owe their subalterns nothing – and particularly no explanation of their own divine actions or inactions by reference to a rule of which they are the application. Gods are those whom one is obliged to listen to without having the right of being listened to. Being God means having an inalienable and indivisible entitlement to the *monologue*.

Politics and religion both operate in the same space: that of human uncertainty. They vie to conquer, colonize and annex the same ground, continuously vacillating from an alliance through competition to enmity. Allies or enemies, they vie for the same constituency: people groaning under the burden of an uncertainty transcending their singular or collective capacity for comprehension and remedial action. Allies or enemies, they tend to learn and borrow their expedients and stratagems from each other. And they both aspire to the right to monologue. Hence a permanent – latent, and sometimes manifest – temptation and inclination to the 'religionization of politics'. Politics is being 'religionized' whenever it oscillates towards the Schmittian pattern of focusing on the 'appointment and naming of an enemy' as the primary function of a political ruler, and when policies and their declared aims are couched in the phraseology of absolutism, as for instance in the language of George W. Bush: a language of an ultimate battle between good and evil, right and wrong – a 'middle' being a priori excluded as much as a dialogue with the enemy or building any sort of bridge over the abyss separating 'us' from 'them'.

The Schmittian model of sovereign political power has been made to the measure, and in the image, of the dictatorial, tyrannical or totalitarian state. Its sudden resurrection and rising popularity in political science has been triggered in all probability by the gradual yet steady accumulation of symptoms of the ever more evident ineptitude of democratic regimes (long viewed as an alternative to every and any variety of authoritarian state) in coping with the current transformations in the social setting in which it operates: in particular, the emergent status of 'difference' (or, more to the point, polymorphism combined with polycentrism) as a permanent and rather undetachable attribute of political as much as social life. Conversation and dialogue, to which democracy has been committed from the start as the ruling principles of the making of public decisions, used to be seen as an interim procedure leading to consensus; in Jürgen Habermas's memorable assault on 'distorted communication', an open and unlimited polylogue was assumed to work itself out of a job: a means rather than an aim. It was a procedure that set democracy apart from authoritarian regimes; a more humane, but also in the end more effective fashion in which a unity of the popular will, shared with other political systems, could be attained. That procedure was considered more humane and so preferable thanks to its deployment of freedom instead of servitude and conformity as the principal engine of its drive to consensus; and it was believed to be more effective because (it was tacitly assumed) it was based on undistorted communication (that is, unconstrained, open, free from coercion and any interference from the powers-that-be) – communication that must at some stage put an end to all controversy over value-laden preferences and choices. A suspicion that there might be controversies resistant to reconciliation, such as those that arise from something more than a one-sided or reciprocal miscomprehension (and therefore from an obstacle of the sort that cannot be removed by a dedicated, earnest and sincere thrashing out of their differences by discussants of good will) does not appear in the model of undistorted communication, as it also did not in the models of democracy of the now bygone era of the unholy trinity of TSN (territory, state and nation). The present situation, in which numerous divisive issues show signs of being permanent features of shared life, immune to argument and stubbornly non-negotiable, and when numerous controversies seem bound to continue for the duration rather than being defused and smothered in the course of a finite number of sittings around a negotiating table, this fully and truly novel situation has caught political theory and practice unawares and unprepared.

The new situation in question is a joint product of two relatively recent and certainly interrelated developments: a polycentric planet, and the increasingly diasporic character of the populations ensconced within the boundaries of most of its state or quasi-state units. Between them, the two developments have put paid to planet-wide and intrastate hierarchies – both spatial and temporal: in space terms, to a hierarchy of coexisting cultures; and in time terms, to the presumption of a unilinear evolution of culture. In a practical sense, the demise of those two mutually supportive hierarchies makes all but impossible the *imaginaire* construed with the help of such oppositions as cultural superiority versus inferiority and 'progressive' versus 'backward' or 'retrograde'. All such terms sound increasingly meaningless, while attempts at applying them are as a rule hotly contested. Under such circumstances, the current relations between cultures, faiths, or forms of life tend to be acknowledged as temporary, renegotiable and volatile settlements; most certainly, the direction of their future mutations looks anything but preordained and all in all unpredictable.

And so we seem to find ourselves once more facing the ancient Jerusalem–Athens alternative: that is, the choice between monotheistic and polytheistic designs of religious faiths and political formulae. With few exceptions, such as Japan, where people feel no incongruity between attending Shintu shrines on specific annual occasions, marrying according to Christian rites and being buried by a Buddhist monk, most populations of the planet have lived for many centuries in the shadow of three monotheistic cults, all three of Jerusalem's provenance. Our well-nigh universally shared conditioned reflex of putting an equation mark between religiosity and monotheism we probably owe to that historical coincidence; what we are now inclined to identify with 'religiosity as such' also derives from the legacy of Jerusalem. This reflex, however, fits ill with the new reality of the plurality of gods simultaneously outside and within the territorial boundaries of any state/national unit. Gods, just like their devotees, have spread over the globe in a web of criss-crossing and overlapping diasporas. They live, daily, in close mutual proximity – and however hard they try, they cannot ignore each other's presence and avoid various forms of interaction and interchange. Settings in which most of us act daily are, to most practical intents and purposes, routinely polytheistic, even if the three major players tend to cling devoutly to their monotheistic pretences. Our situation, after several centuries of the strenuous, coercive and from time to time gory rule of the *cuius regio, eius religio* principle (of the ruler setting the religion), is becoming ever more reminiscent of the state of affairs that preceded the replacement of the Roman Pantheon by the unified, indivisible, uncompromisingly monotheistic and intolerant of other gods, that of the Church of Christian Europe and its overseas outposts. Ulrich Beck, in his most recent trenchant and provocative study *Der eigene Gott* (translated into English under the title *A God of One's Own* and published by Polity Press in 2010), succinctly characterized the emerging reality as one of a 'worldwide involuntary confrontation with alien others' (p. 68).

Alongside the growing diasporization of the planet's population and its consequence, the plurality and ongoing multiplication of gods cohabiting inside the 'lifeworlds' of its steadily expanding section, another change, fateful for the plight of religion, politics and their relationship, is in the offing and fast gathering momentum. This change, signalled in the title of Beck's book, is an outcome of another aspect of the current 'modernization mark two' (or, in the terminology I prefer, the passage to the 'liquid' phase of the modern condition): a progressive, accelerating and increasingly intense process of individualization (shifting onto individual shoulders a steadily growing number of functions until recently performed, and jealously guarded, by power-assisted communities – including, notably, the task of identification, now transformed into a duty of self-identification, with the emphasis on 'self'). As essential principles of individualization, Beck names the 'dismantling of tradition, the necessity and possibility of individual decision-making, and, as the presupposition of that, a (more or less limited) horizon of options, as well as the custom of accounting for consequences'. With such principles in operation, 'the individualization of belief simply has to be accepted as a reality' (pp. 86–7).

A 'God of one's own' is a totally new kind of god: a DIY god. Not an institutionally composed and promoted god, but a 'grassroots' god (related to the previously prevailing variety in the same way as the liquid modern 'networks' are to earlier solid modern communities). Not a God *received*, but *contrived* – and contrived individually, even though it is done by arranging individually selected patches which have been cut out, again individually, from the available prefabricated offers into a totality composed and sewn together by the individual, following an individually sketched design, using individual instruments, resources and skills, and following the logic of individual preoccupations and priorities. A 'God of one's own' is, like all gods, an emanation, derivative or projection of insufficiency – but unlike institutional gods, it is a *personal*, individually suffered insufficiency that is projected; something to be expected in an era of 'life politics' (to borrow Anthony Giddens's term), marked by individual responsibility for the resolving of life problems and for the consequences of life choices.

'Insufficiency' in such an era confronts the individual in the shape of a *personal* inadequacy repeatedly revealed whenever it is juxtaposed with the grandiosity of the tasks to be confronted (assigned or assumed): the difficulty, and suspected impossibility, of coming to grips with, measuring up to and tackling (let alone properly responding to) the challenges posited by the conducting of life politics day in, day out. If the God of the congregational church reflected the insufficiency of the human species (or of one of its communal segments) when it was confronted with the awesome, uncontrollable and unpredictable powers of nature and fate, the 'God of one's own' reflects the insufficiency – the ignorance, impotence, and the humiliation they jointly produce – of the individual abandoned to his or her own sorely inadequate resources, while being commanded and nudged to cope on their own with the awesome powers of socially produced contingencies.

17 December 2010

On why students are restless again

Again, some Italian journalists have sent me questions... Again, they have been roused by the most recent 'extraordinary event' hitting the headlines, but this time, unlike the last time, they are not worried by the eviction and expulsion of the Roma, but by students' street protests. They asked: 'In these days, all around Europe, students are protesting. These youngsters are called Generation Zero: Zero opportunities, Zero future. How it is possible to rebuild the future of these youngsters? Which model of society can again give hope to people twenty-years old?' Some of my conversationalists were clearly worried about the degree of violence that accompanied the student demos: 'Some provoca-teurs started it, but the youngsters did not isolate them. Is there in students some kind of profound rage? How similar is it to the one we know from the past? What motives can trigger it?'

I tried, to the best of my ability, to risk some answers...I said: There is indeed quite a lot of sound and fury, signifying an explo-sive mixture of well-justified fear of the future and a desperate search for outlets to off-load the resulting anxiety and aggrava-tion. Successive explosions are rendered still more likely because day in, day out, the student population is crowded into and con-centrated on campuses (whereas comparable concentrations of industrial labourers are increasingly rare and far between): the intensity of rage, the degree of inflammability and the inclination to violence all tend to rise with the size and density of the crowd...Once condensed, the most gentle and peaceful individu-als may amalgamate and gel into a furious crowd.

But let's beware of jumping to conclusions and resist the temptation of facile extrapolations. It is too early for conclusions. What we should try hard to achieve, however, is *not to forget* that the spectacular lesson of the current student unrest needs to be thoroughly reflected upon, learned and absorbed. Alas, such for-getting may start right away, as soon as the street demonstrations are over and their 'news value' no longer inflates the TV ratings. The tendency to forget and the mind-boggling speed of forgetting are unfortunately seemingly indelible marks of contemporary liquid modern culture. Because of that affliction, we tend to stumble from one explosion of popular anger to another, ner-vously and perfunctorily reacting to each one separately as it comes, instead of trying seriously to come to grips with the issues they signal.

The present plight of students (future graduates who, on enter-ing universities a couple of years ago, were promised and expected plum jobs once they were armed with university diplomas and moved into the labour market) is another version of the pitiable fate of millions of equally frustrated home-buyers, promised and made to expect a perpetual rise in property values and thus a trouble-free and effortless repayment of mortgage loans, together with their accumulated interest. In both cases, prosperity based on allegedly unlimited availability (of employment opportunities in one case, of credit in another) was assumed, and believed to last indefinitely. More and more people bought houses with loans whose repayment they could not afford – and more and more people went to colleges dreaming of the kinds of jobs they could not reasonably hope for unless they obtained a university degree. As has now become clear, the assurances loudly voiced by banks, issuers of credit cards, marketers and neoliberal philosophers, as well as by neoliberalism's political practitioners, and flowing profusely from official (authoritative!) optimism into the public mood, were deceitful and in large part dishonest. Neither the volume of plum jobs in the City and advanced outposts of cutting-edge technology, nor the inflation of real estate prices and the supplies of consumer credit are (or indeed could be) infinite. The bubble was blown up beyond its capacity, and it had to burst, which it promptly did. Students are among the most frustrated and aggravated of the victims of its bursting. They are also the most active and resolute: they try to fight back against the damage perpetrated and its perpetrators. Pugnacity, the animus for collective action and the resolve to stand fast shoulder to shoulder come much easier, after all, to people trained to congregate daily in lecture theatres, as students do, than to the scattered and ultimately lonely victims of house repossessions, or to millions of newly redundant office and factory workers, who have got used to sulking and licking their wounds in solitude – each on their own.

For the first time in decades, the whole annual output of university graduates is facing labour markets inundated and glutted by job-seekers who cannot be accommodated, and therefore a perspective opens up of long-term unemployment or the necessity of accepting jobs well below their skills and ambitions: exceedingly frail jobs, casual and unreliable, without built-in career tracks. The kind of predicament in which this year's graduates found themselves and next year's graduates surely will was not confronted for long enough for us to learn its plausible consequences; but in the past the swelling ranks of unemployed and frustrated educated youngsters used to portend a parallel rise in aggressive political extremism. It also spelled grave troubles for democracy...

Next came a series of other questions, concerned with the need for university reform ('renewal', as one of the journalists phrased it) and the prospect of students' unrest in the event the need is not attended to. To which I answered:

Whatever 'renewal' universities might require will take much more time than composing ad hoc responses to the challenges presented by the current students' protest. The two tasks have completely different time scales. The student riots will be relatively short-lived, but their consequences (or rather the consequences of the condition of which the students' unrest is just a timely symptom) will be lasting; and it is those consequences that we should seriously worry about. And reflecting on the possible ways out of the predicament, not to mention implementing the results of our reflections, will take much more ingenuity and hard and protracted effort than is implied by off-the-cuff guesses offered on the spot.

One thought, though, leaps to mind right away: all consumer markets are known to be in the habit of overshooting their targets; markets are in the habit of counting on much larger demand than they are able to find or conjure up – but also of trying earnestly to tempt and seduce many more clients beyond those to whom the products on offer can be of any genuine use. Consumer markets are highly effective, but also exceedingly wasteful mechanisms of 'needs satisfaction': they are known to produce a lot of waste. In order to hit a target at all, they must shower it, inundate it with bullets! The 'education market' in our society of consumers has not been an exception to that general rule. Most countries have experienced an unprecedented growth in recent decades in the number of institutions of higher education and the volume of their students. That development was bound to result in a devaluation of college education and higher education diplomas. Besides, as Gresham and Copernicus found out several centuries ago, in a free market competition the inferior (and that includes fraudulent or forged) currency tends to crowd out and in the end marginalize or squeeze out of exchange the superior variety. None of these processes could leave universities unaffected. Engaged, for the sake of their own attraction to students, in a futile chase after increasingly volatile and elusive market-insinuated and market-propagated fashions, universities have lost from view the tasks that they, and only they, were born for and can perform; busy in trying to serve the fleeting, eminently short-lived needs or fads of a business-led 'economy', universities are in fact losing much of their past capacity to perform those tasks – even though they continue, on festive occasions, to pay them flowery tributes...

Finally, there were some questions about egalitarianism versus meritocracy. My answer was as follows:

I can't say whether there is more meritocracy in Italy than elsewhere. The sole thing I am qualified to say is that the idea of 'meritocracy' has been seen for some time now as one of the most essential planks in present-day political platforms where 'fairness' tends to replace the idea of 'justice', 'equity' replaces 'equality of living standards', and the principle, promise and criterion of allocating rewards according to merit elbows out the issue of the satisfaction of needs.

This much is seldom questioned, but the point is that the meanings of 'rewards' and 'merit' are two sorely underdefined and hotly contested elements of those political platforms. Currently, 'rewards' are reduced to monetary remuneration and the perks associated with allocated social standing, while 'merit' is measured by the relative market price attached to the kinds of services assumed to be rendered by people to whom that standing has been allocated. The resulting pleonasm (which, like all pleonasms, covertly presumes what it overtly pretends to prove) masks the relativism (indeed, questionability) of both definitions, as well as the tacit partisan assumptions that underlie them: what the practice of 'meritocracy' pretends to *create* and promote is in fact not much more than an ideological gloss over the already *existing* social reality – and that reality owes its genesis more to the random games of market forces than to any deliberate, ethically inspired policy. To cut a long story short, let's ponder which of these is likely to be the case: are the six-figure sums paid *in recognition* of merit, or is merit *assumed* on the strength of six-figure sums having been paid? And the second question: does all merit and all rewards have price-tags attached?

Youngsters, who have been fed quite a lot of promises without recording thus far any personal experience of putting them to the test, are the most vulnerable among the people hit. Those entering the labour market now have been caught unwarned and unprepared. Their first encounter with realities is for that reason particularly painful, unpromising and off-putting. Older people have some harsh memories but also some acquired knowledge and habits to fall back on, and so they can treat the current hardships as temporary hiccups, an abnormality which at some point will be cured, allowing things to 'return to normality'. Besides, many of them have some sort of 'second line of trenches' prepared for such an occasion. Not the youngsters, though: when they face the need for a long and risky leap from protected youth to adult independence they find their legs seeking the ground in vain – and they can easily assume that such a condition is the norm in the adult life they are entering. If this is the case, the thought is horrifying...

In the end, our subject switched to the frightening rise of unemployment, in Italy as in the rest of Europe. The question was put to me: 'Can there be a society post-work?' An *impromptu* answer did not come easily...

We, at least we in the 'developed' part of the planet, are in for a long and tortuous stretch of mass unemployment; and, to make it still worse, accompanied by a severe reduction in support from unemployment insurance and assistance – prompted by the enormous debts our governments have imposed on current and future generations in struggling to salvage the banks from insolvency and their stockholders from losses. We are still not fully aware of the volume of hardship and social dysfunction which rising and protracted unemployment is bound to visit on people directly affected by redundancies, as well as all the rest of us. The price for the short-lived orgy of 'enjoy now, pay later', charged in the currency of broken, wasted and lost lives, may yet prove enormous.

Speaking of 'post-work' does not, however, make sense. Even if the 'consumerist life pattern' becomes extinct and gets consigned to oblivion, humans will not stop being consumers, and what is to be consumed must first be produced. There will be no 'post-work' era, except after the extinction of the human species... What is fast changing instead is, so to speak, the 'geography of work'. Jobs are presently moving to countries where few if any laws and rules constrain the liberties of capitalists, whereas the workers are compelled to work for survival wages or less, while being deprived of communal assistance as well as of organizations of self-defence – and so also stripped of any significant bargaining power. No wonder the latest statistics show that while the distance between the 'developed' and the 'emergent' economies is shortening, the distance between the rich and the poor inside the 'developed' countries is stretching again, moving back ever closer to the abominable standards of inequality remembered from the early capitalist era...

18 December 2010

On respect and scorn

Respect belongs to the family of moral attitudes, and in the same way as the rest of morality its necessary or obligatory nature cannot be discursively 'proved'. Respect for the other is a value; and as in the case of other values, one can only compose a case in its favour, and then try to convince listeners of its merits, appealing to their moral conscience in order to persuade them to adopt and apply it in choosing their own attitude to other human beings.

In that job of persuasion one can neither count on, nor resort to, empirical arguments or authoritative credentials. If, for instance, one urged someone to respect other humans by pointing out that most people are inclined to approve of such an attitude, one wouldn't be appealling to the listener's moral conscience, but to her or his herd instinct. If one tried to convince them that showing respect to others would be repaid by the others being respectful to them, the appeal would be made to a selfish concern with their own gains: a kind of concern that would seldom, if ever, coincide or be reconciled with a moral impulse. If, on the other hand, one demands respect on the grounds that the showing of respect is a command that can be disobeyed solely at a high and unacceptable cost to the disobeying person (because of the power differential separating the command-giver from the commanded) – rather than arguing the case in terms of respect's intrinsic value – one would be appealing to the egotistic instinct of survival instead of invoking the concern with the well-being of others that is the attribute of every moral stance: and as Albert Camus correctly pointed out, there is hardly anything more contemptible than respect arising from fear.

Let me repeat, I can only approve of, praise and recommend respect for other humans as part and parcel of a moral attitude, without being able to 'prove' that taking that attitude is, for one reason of another, a 'must': a foregone conclusion or a necessary, inevitable or unavoidable decision. Necessity and inescapability belong to the vocabulary of reason – they are out of place in the discourse of morality. In speaking of a moral attitude whose hard core, according to Immanuel Kant, is precisely respect for an-other as a subject endowed with autonomy, reason and will, I need to surrender the use of instruments routinely deployed at academic seminars, such as cause and effect, inevitability and determination, correct and incorrect, norm and exception. When Emmanuel Levinas insists on ethics being *prior* to ontology, he by the same token denies ethics the right to the kind of self-promotion which science matter of factly adopts: ethics is not superior to ontology due to the unquestionability of its *truth* (its agreement with reality), but thanks to being *better* than reality ('better' being a house-term for ethics, but a foreign notion in ontology). But he adds right away: from the fact that I bear responsibility for you and you for me, it does not follow that I or you will inevitably and without fail take up our respective responsibilities. Calls to responsibility, including the calls to respect, may fall on deaf or plugged ears and remain hanging in mid-air. On this point, Levinas and Kant radically differ.

For Kant with his categorical imperative, for beings endowed with reason, paying respect to another human being is, as it were, a necessity – full stop. He supplies the biblical commandment 'love your neighbour as you love yourself' with the imprimatur of Reason: make your rule out of what you would desire to be a universal rule; in other words, don't do to others what you wouldn't wish to be done to you. If you prefer to be treated as a subject rather than as an object (as you most certainly do), treat others as subjects; if you don't want to be an instrument serving other people's objectives (as you certainly don't), don't treat others as your tools; if you wish to be loved (as you surely do), love those whose love you desire – and respect those whose respect you crave. The categorical imperative draws its power of persuasion from the principle of *reciprocity*: an anticipation that others will treat you as you treat them. To put it briefly, respect is a transaction of *exchange*. When offering respect, just as in any anticipated exchange, an equivalence between the goods exchanged is expected. The ideal of exchange is *symmetry*; the most telling symbols of fair exchange are perfectly balanced scales.

For Levinas, on the contrary, respect, just like morality, is a definitely *asymmetrical* relation. My responsibility is always one step ahead of yours. I am always already responsible for you, I am responsible before (and regardless of whether) I become aware of it, and most certainly before I start to ruminate over the mode of conduct I need or might choose in order to follow it. Questions along the lines of 'what is in it for me', 'how much effort and sacrifice on my part do they deserve', 'can I expect them to reciprocate my gambits in a similar manner', much as they are justified when calculating my actions according to Kant's suggestions in relation to the 'categorical imperative', have no place in thinking inspired by Levinasian 'unconditional responsibility'. My responsibility for you is not in the category of *amitia* or *philia*, one that presumes a symmetry of the relationship, but *agape*: it is the responsibility of the strong for the weak, of the agent richer in resources for someone poorer in resources, of someone with no restraint on choice for someone deprived of choice. Responsibility *for* an-other is not a responsibility *to* a superior, boss, command-giver, task-master or oppressor. That 'other' for whom I am responsible has no power over me, cannot command me to do anything, or force me to do it; nor can he punish me for desisting or neglecting my responsibilities. I am commanded, so to speak, by her or his weakness and through the unobtrusive silence of his or her presence...

As such, responsibility is unconditional and tolerates no exceptions, insists Levinas – it stops short of going into detail and remains silent about its precise demands. Once discovered and recognized as such (Levinas calls that moment of discovery 'awakening', 'sobering up', 'recovery of sight' – all names suggesting the spontaneity of the event and a rupture in continuity), it therefore confronts the discoverer with the need to fill it with content. The discovery of unconditional responsibility and its acceptance are not determinants but stimuli for the exploration that follows; they prompt a seeking, though that does not guarantee a finding – and above all they do not define the moment when the search can be taken to have reached its objective and so be brought to a stop. Once recognized and accepted, responsibility for an-other burdens the moral self with responsibility for the interpretation of its practical requirements. Nothing defines those requirements *a priori*; whereas the meaning ascribed to them *a posteriori* lacks grounds for perceiving them as a universally valid precept.

The discovery of responsibility (waking up, so to speak, to the fact of bearing it) is not a single, one-off act, triggering a chain of events and undertakings that will entrench unconditionality once and for all. Responsibility needs and tends to be discovered over and over again, in every encounter with an-other, or even at every successive stage of that encounter. It therefore casts the discoverer into a state of chronic, and perhaps incurable uncertainty that tends to grow rather than being reduced as the chain of actions lengthens. In the universe of Law, the absence of a paragraph equals the absence of crime; in the world of Morality, however, the absence of paragraphs means on the contrary the absence of innocence – or at least the impossibility of proving its presence. In the absence of authoritative and unambiguous prescriptions for acquitting oneself of responsibility, nothing a moral subject can do will offer the certainty that everything responsibility requires to be accomplished has been fully and satisfactorily performed. The natural habitat of morality is a state of chronic underdefinition and underdetermination. Morality acquires a voice when and where the imperatives of reason fall silent – or when and where they are denied a voice: when and where the decision to assume responsibility for the well-being, autonomy, integrity and subjectivity of an-other suspends the legitimacy and authority of the judgements of reason and deprives reason of its credentials as a Court of Appeal – of being an authority to which one can turn in order to question the actions prompted by a moral impulse.

But to return to the issue of respect, a concept notoriously open to a variegated range of extending and limiting interpretations: I suggest that attention and authority in the field of human relations be transferred precisely from the domain of reason (rationality, rules, prescriptions and proscriptions, the calculation of gains and losses and calculus of probability) to the domain of morality (that is, the priority of the human-in-need) for its essence.

The German term which Kant's translators convey as 'respect' is *Achtung* – meaning, in its primary and essential sense, 'attention'. What opposes respect to disrespect (or a snub) is the difference between paying attention and ignoring. 'Disrespect' means, first and foremost, indifference or equanimity. In the last account, the postulate of respect forbids snubbing: 'passing by' an-other without acknowledging their presence: without 'paying attention' – dismissing an-other beforehand as 'unworthy of attention'. It demands instead stopping, listening attentively to an-other's voice while suspending other interests for a time, stopping for long enough to grasp, digest and comprehend in full what sort of content their message may transmit. In other words, the postulate of respect requires according to an-other, whether explicitly or implicitly, the right to set the agenda – or at least accepting another's suggestion of an agenda as deserving full attention and thorough consideration. In a nutshell, respect for an-other consists in recognizing her or him as an *equal partner in dialogue*, as a subject having something significant to say; something that – just as defendants remain innocent so long as their guilt has not been proven – remains worthy of listening to attentively until and unless the triviality or futility of his or her locutions is convincingly demonstrated. The alternative to respect in the case of a person from whom paying respect is expected is indifference and a snub; in the case of a person to whom respect was expected to be paid, it is contempt and humiliation.

Entering into a dialogue (more precisely, giving the green light to polylogue, considering that open access is dialogue's indispensable attribute) equals in practice a suspension of self-assurance and a surrender instead to an uncertain and unpredictable course of events: accepting that the result of the exchange will be a derivative of an interplay of a number of initiatives, none able to plead the right to the last and decisive voice (or at least have such a right granted and assured in advance). *There is no bona fide dialogue unless the equality of participants is assumed and observed.* For the duration of the dialogue, hierarchies and assignments of 'superiority' and 'inferiority' are (in intention at least) suspended. What is more, also suspended are any presuppositions that the differences between conversationalists are too big for mutual communication and eventual consent to be plausible; the participants in a dialogue need to presume that what is common to all of them is more important than what sets them apart – and therefore capable of prevailing over and cancelling the antagonizing impact of discord. As St Paul put it in his letter to the Galatians: 'There is no such thing as Jew and Greek, slave or freeman, male and female; for you are all one person in Jesus Christ... Thus the law was a kind of tutor in charge of us until Christ should come, when we should be justified by faith; and now that faith has come, the tutor's charge is at an end' (Gal. 3: 28, 24–6). These words remain the prototype for all later approaches, including those of the present-day, to the essence of respect and respectfulness. As Robert Pawlik perceptively and clearly expressed it (in *Kronos* 2(2010), p. 44), 'Ecclesia is formed through messianic suspension of all extant dividing lines. A messianic event is a breakthrough and upturn so radical that it results in "de-activation" of legal orders heretofore in operation – religious as much as political...From this moment on (in the "messianic era"), human relationship is no longer regulated by law and by associated hierarchies and power relations, but by love of one's neighbour.'

One is tempted to ruminate that we now live in another 'messianic era' – though this time, at least thus far, with neither a 'messianic event' nor an expectation of its impending arrival. That ours is a 'messianic era' is suggested by the gathering signs that the 'de-activation of extant legal orders', the 'suspension of current lines of confrontation' and ceasing to be 'under the tutorship of old faith' are all long overdue. But we lack and miss a 'messianic event' comparable to the good tidings sent by St Paul to the Galatians in its potential to 'make us one'.

Because of the abysmal disproportion between the grandiosity of the challenge and the paltriness of our box of tools, we have found ourselves, as Antonio Gramsci observed almost a hundred years ago (one is tempted to add 'prophetically'), in a period of *interregnum*, that is a condition in which the old is fast losing its grip and its potency to act, while the new that could conceivably replace it either hasn't yet been born or remains too small and whimpers too softly to gain our attention. In times registered under the name of 'interregnum' anything can happen, though nothing can be undertaken with total self-assurance and no one can be fully sure of an action's result. The bane of our time is the incommensurability between intentions and the forces required to fulfil them. The most harrowing of quandaries is no longer 'what is to be done', but 'who is capable of doing it' in the event that we manage to agree on what is to be done.

That 'old' which is losing its grip and potential for action is the slicing of the planet into nominally sovereign local orders based on an increasingly fictitious overlap and coagulation of territory, state and nation. That 'new' which has failed to demonstrate its presence thus far is a global, genuinely 'ecumenical' order, based on the planet-wide human community – though, unlike in the past, not necessarily on its denominational, ethnic, cultural and political unity. To rub salt into an open wound, we will seek in vain for a historical precedent to assure us that this kind of a novelty is a plausible one. The idea that it is the birthright of every human being to participate in a humanity-wide community, and so the right to recognition, respect and dignity owed to all human beings just because they are human and regardless of all and any qualifiers setting them apart from other human beings, is striking in its jarring opposition to what thus far has been perceived as the unalterable nature of human cohabitation.

Carl Schmitt, widely thought to be the most acute and perceptive theorist of the politics of the era of nation-states and their absolute and indivisible territorial sovereignty, took the 'appointment of an enemy' as the defining feature of politics, and the opposition between 'friends' and 'enemies' (in practice, between 'us' and 'them') as its constitutive axis. Without an enemy, there is no state, politics, communal unity and state sovereignty, and cannot be. Association, the sovereign's main objective, can be attained solely through dissociation; inclusion (of 'friends') cannot and will not be performed without simultaneous exclusion (of 'enemies'). The realm of the rule of law is inconceivable without its borders being drawn and superimposed on the frontier separating friends from enemies. The political organization of post-Westphalian Europe, in whose practices Schmitt most certainly grounded his generalizations, would not be viable without the agglomeration of animosities and conflicts. It goes without saying that in the world emerging from the pages of Schmitt's *Political Theology* there is no room for the category of respect – while the idea of a universal right to be respected would smack of pure absurdity. That world after all was articulated and brought to life by the will of a territorial sovereign – a will that is expressed in his might to appoint enemies and exempt them from the rule of law.

Starting from different premises, René Girard arrived at practically identical conclusions. The birth act of a human community, in Girard's view, is an 'original crime', one that renders both contemporaries and their descendants accomplices, whether co-temporal or 'after the fact'. By the logic of that assignment, accomplices develop a vested interest in closing ranks in defence of that community and to assure its survival – as the sole shield protecting them from court and a verdict of guilty. Whole-hearted dedication to the cause of community requires from its members vigilance, distrust and enmity towards non-members, as well as unconditional approval of whatever is taken to be indispensable, or even only useful, for the strength of the community. Communities stay alive by way of regular rituals restaging the 'founding act' (or rather the etiological myth) in the course of which enemies conspire but have their iniquitous intentions spotted in time and their evil deeds thwarted, so that the plotters are disabled before they have a chance of putting their schemes into operation; though they are never completely disarmed, let alone annihilated – such a denouement of the story would be counter-productive, removing the reasons for continuing the uncritical discipline (the 'voluntary servitude') demanded by the community from its members in the name of its (and so, by proxy, their) continuing existence.

The stories told by Schmitt and Girard differ in their subject-matter and argumentation, but they are confluent in their ultimate message: respect is not promised much chance of promotion to the rank of a universal value. The realities of social life, its historically formed patterns and fashion of self-reproduction cannot be easily reconciled either with Kant's rational arguments or with the ethical postulates of Levinas. Conflict and consent, enmity and friendship are Siamese twins, unable to live separately and resistant to the efforts of the best of surgeons. Unity derives from division, respect from denial of human dignity…Ronald Reagan, a president not particularly famous for his academic abilities, yet a man endowed with a solid measure of folk wisdom, is reputed to have consoled Mikhail Gorbachev that even if US and Soviet interests couldn't be reconciled at that time, the Soviet and American armies would surely join forces to repel the common enemy once invaders from outer space assaulted the earth. He might well have been right, but the snag is that the aliens are not yet rushing to help us fulfil the longstanding dream of universal human dignity and an ecumenicity of mutual respect. In their absence, we, the native residents of the earth, have no alternative but to reach for armaments in holy intertribal wars waged in the name of recognition – that is, of the right to respect.

We, by the verdict of history, or rather by decrees issued and composed by humans, are presented with the right of choice while being burdened with the duty to choose, and so we have to struggle for social recognition of our form of being, always already pre-interpreted as a result of our own voluntary choices; recognition of the way we live individually or collectively, in the company of 'others like us' – whether by design, by default, or in response to other people's overwhelming pressures. What is commonly understood as 'social recognition' is the opinion of the 'people who count' on the merits and demerits of our way of life, and above all their judgement as to whether respect is due to a certain kind of creatures in view of their way of life, and needs to be accorded to them in the same measure as it has so far been given to others.

Politicians worthy of that name are quick to spot an untapped source of electoral support. Since few if any electors feel truly immune to the threat of a sudden reversal of fate portending a denial of their dignity, but all – high and low – equally strongly wish to be respected for what they presently are, have been forced to remain or are struggling to become, sooner than one might guess, the right to respect may be denied or withdrawn under the slogan of 'no respect for the enemies of respect' (meaning here by 'enemies of respect' those people who refuse to respect the verdicts of those in charge of its allocation and distribution), all in the name of its defence and promotion.

21 December 2010

On some (not all!) of my idiosyncrasies

On the occasion of my eighty-fifth birthday, I was pressed (in the most friendly of manners) by Simon Dawes on behalf of my friends at *Theory, Culture & Society* (*TCS*, one of the liveliest, most indefatigable, innovatory and courageous periodicals I know, a constant supplier of fresh air in the rather seedy and stolid intellectual atmosphere of the present-day humanities) to publicly confess to the perpetually off-the-main-track character of my kind of sociology. It was a pressure to which I promptly and gladly surrendered, all the more willingly because it came from circles owing their excellence precisely to this deficiency, considered by the vociferous majority as a sign of imperfection. I quote below some fragments of that confession:

Simon Dawes: To begin with, I'd like to ask you to what extent you think the liquidity of your own life experiences has influenced your interpretation of (liquid) modernity (as Martin Jay suggests in his *TCS* article)? Do you recognize yourself, for example, as an 'ambivalent outsider' who has 'learned to walk on quicksand'?

Zygmunt Bauman: I'd gladly (and, I presume, prudently) leave an answer to this question to psychoanalysts, who specialize in tracing these sorts of links, or just coincidences, and re-presenting them as causal connections. Having been a bird in the story rather than an ornithologist (and birds, as we all know, are not particularly prominent among ornithologists), I am perhaps the last person to be asked this question in the search for an authoritative answer. A rather mundane observation that the experience of the frailty of the settings in and through which I found myself moving in the course of my uncannily long life itinerary must have (mustn't it?) influenced what I saw and how I saw it is really as far as I feel entitled to go... And, to be sure, the art of walking on quicksand is still beyond me. What I have learned is only how difficult this art is to master and how hard people need to struggle to learn it.

As to being described as an outsider throughout, and an outsider through and through (I owe this discovery to Dennis Smith, in *TCS* in 1998), I have no reason to disagree. Indeed, I did not truly 'belong' to any school, monastic order, intellectual camaraderie, political caucus or interest clique; I did not apply for admission to any of them, let alone do much to deserve an invitation; nor would I be listed by any of them – at least in unqualified terms – as 'one of us'. I guess my claustrophobia is incurable – feeling, as I tend to, ill at ease in any closed room, always tempted to find out what is on the other side of the door. I guess I am doomed to remain an outsider to the end, lacking as I do the indispensable qualities of an academic insider: loyalty to a school, conformity to its procedure, and readiness to abide by the criteria of cohesion and consistency endorsed by the school. And, frankly, I don't mind...

SD: You rely on the dichotomous metaphor of solid/liquid in your accounts of modernity, but to what extent are these terms mutually exclusive? Could this relation be seen as a dialectic?

ZB: I did not and do not think of the solidity/liquidity conundrum as a dichotomy; I view those two conditions as a couple locked, inseparably, in a dialectical bond (something like what François Lyotard probably had in mind when he observed that one can't be modern without being postmodern first...). After all, it was the quest for the solidity of things and states that most often triggered, kept in motion and guided the liquefaction of those things and states; in turn, it was the formlessness of the oozing, leaking and flowing liquid that prompted the efforts of cooling, damping and moulding. If there is something that permits a distinction between the 'solid' and 'liquid' *phases* of modernity (that is, arranging them in an order of succession), it is the change in both the manifest and latent purpose behind the otherwise continuous and still ongoing effort.

Originally, solids were melted not because of a distaste for solidity, but out of dissatisfaction with the degree of solidity of the extant, inherited solids: purely and simply, the bequeathed solids were found to be *not solid enough* (insufficiently resistant and immunized to change) by the standards of the order-obsessed and compulsively order-building modern powers. Subsequently (in our part of the world, to this day) solids have been acknowledged to be transient condensations of liquid magma. They are temporary settlements, 'until further notice', rather than ultimate solutions – where *flexibility* replaces *solidity* as the ideal condition to be pursued. Even when they are desired, solids are tolerated only in as far as they promise to remain easily and obediently fusible on demand; before the effort of putting a structure together, firming it up and solidifying it is undertaken, an adequate technology for remelting it must be already in hand. A reliable assurance of the right and the ability to dismantle the constructed structure must be offered before the job of construction starts in earnest. Fully 'biodegradable' structures are nowadays the ideals and the standards which most, if not all structures, struggle to meet.

SD: Could you explain how the real freedom and genuine autonomy of the Enlightenment differs from the (false, liquid, consumerist) freedom of the market? And what do you make of John Milbank's claim that you lack a metaphysical basis for speaking of such freedom?

ZB: In a nutshell: where the freedom visualized by the Enlightenment and demanded and promised by Marx was made to the measure of the ideal *producer*, the freedom promoted by the market is designed with the ideal *consumer* in mind; neither of the two is 'more genuine' than the other.

This is, though, in my view, a *sociopolitical* problem, not a *metaphysical* issue. I was, and remain, and in all probability will stay until I die, interested in the *sociopolitical* mechanisms that generate 'enabling' and 'disabling' pressures in tandem, tying them together and intertwining them, all in all rendering them virtually inseparable, in the way Siamese twins share their pulmonary and digestive systems...

An ideal and flawless freedom, 'complete freedom', enabling without disabling, is, I believe, an oxymoron in metaphysics as much as it is an unattainable goal in social life.

SD: In her article in the special section, Julia Hell identifies a frequent emphasis on acts of looking in your writing. What is the link, for you, between looking and 'the other', or how significant for you is the gaze of/at 'the other'?

ZB: I guess Julia Hell is right, the visual does seem to me the most thoroughly grasped and recorded among my impressions; sight seems to be my principal sense organ, and 'seeing' supplies the key metaphors for reporting perception. It is the same with the constitution of the perception/imagination of Levinas, my ethics teacher: it is the *sight* of l'Autre that triggers the moral impulse and recasts me as a moral subject by exposing me and surrendering and subordinating me to the object of my responsibility (this happens even *before* l'Autre has a chance to open her or his mouth, and so before I can *hear* any demands or requests) – even though the tactile, the caress, is a better metaphor for Levinas's model of what follows that sight and awakens the moral self.

What seems to me unmentioned and missing, however, in Julia's awesomely insightful vivisection of the 'gaze' is another variety of gaze – tremendously important in the unpacking of the complex relation between eyes and ethics. The gaze she so perceptively and inspiringly focuses on, the Orphic gaze, is so to speak a 'killing through love' or 'murder by love' gaze (though also, potentially, saving and liberating). There is also, however, the 'Panwitz gaze' experienced, identified and vividly reconstructed by Primo Levi: a 'killing through unconcern' or, more adequately, 'murder by indifference' gaze, a gaze immune to the bacillus of the morality, inoculated against the responsibility-awakening impact of meeting-an-Other. I believe that tracing the societal ways and means of replacing Orpheus' gaze with Panwitz's, of stripping the gaze of its inborn ethical power (the process I dub 'adiaphorization'), is quite crucial in any serious attempt to map the convoluted and contorted itinerary of the moral self inside the liquid modern world.

SD: Moving on to other things: Could you tell us more about your forthcoming book, *Collateral Damage* (Polity Press, 2011)? What's it about, and how does it connect with your other writings?

ZB: To put it briefly: The foremost strategy of every and any power struggle consists in a 'structuring' of the counterpart's condition while 'unstructuring', that is deregulating, one's own – that used to be and remains a permanent feature of modern power strategies. However, in the society of producers, the solid modern settlement represented by the 'Fordist factory' cum 'social state' paradigm, both sides of the conflict had a vested interest in preventing inequality running out of control – whereas this is no longer the case.

As a result, the odds in favour of those 'close to the sources of uncertainty', and against the others, fixed and tied down at uncertainty's receiving end, have been radically multiplied. What has changed is that the efforts to narrow the hiatus and to mitigate the polarization of chances and the resulting discrimination have been made marginal and transient: these efforts are now spectacularly ineffective, indeed impotent, in stopping the runaway rise of fortune and misery at the two poles of the present-day power axis. They are afflicted by a chronic deficit of power to act and get things done, while power continues to be amassed and stocked on the side of forces pressing in the opposite direction. State governments vainly seek *local* remedies for *globally* manufactured deprivations and miseries – just as individuals-by-the-decree-of-fate (read, by the impact of deregulation) vainly seek individual solutions to their socially fabricated life problems.

'The inequality between the world's individuals is staggering,' says Branko Milanovic, the top economist in the research department of the World Bank. 'At the turn of the twenty-first century, the richest 5 percent of people receive one-third of total global income, as much as the poorest 80 percent.' While a few poor countries are catching up with the rich world, the differences between the richest and poorest individuals around the globe are huge and likely to be growing...

In 2008, Glenn Firebaugh pointed out that 'we have a reversal of a longstanding trend, from rising inequality across nations and constant or declining inequality within nations, to declining inequality across nations and rising inequality within them. That's the message of my 2003 book *The New Geography of Global Income Inequality*' – a message since confirmed.

SD: What do you make of the recent surge in interest in inequality and economic and environmental crises that proposes de-growth, sustainable economies, post-capitalism or the continuing salience of communism as solutions to these problems?

ZB: Poignantly and succinctly, the great José Saramago has already answered your question, pointing out that 'people do not choose a government that will bring the market within their control; instead, the market in every way conditions governments to bring the people within its control'. Several decades ago, in *Legitimation Crisis*, Jürgen Habermas spelled out the function of capitalist states as ensuring that a meeting *between capital and labour* takes place, and that both sides come to the meeting fit and willing for the transaction. As the society of producers run by capital has since turned into a society of consumers run by capital, I would say that the main, indeed 'meta' function of governments has now become to ensure that it is meetings *between commodities and consumers* and *credit issuers and borrowers* that regularly take place – as has been recently proved by governments, if proof was needed, as they fight tooth and nail over every penny needed by the 'underclass' (that is, 'flawed [useless] consumers') to keep their bodies alive, yet miraculously find hundreds of billions of pounds or dollars to 'recapitalize the banks'.

I have recently pointed out, following Keith Tester's hint, that we have found ourselves in a period of 'interregnum': 'the old' no longer works, 'the new' has not yet been born. But an awareness that unless it is born we are all marked for demise is already very alive, as is an awareness that the hard nut we must urgently crack is not the presence of 'too many poor', but 'too many rich'. Let me quote Saramago once more: 'I would ask the political economists, the moralists, if they have already calculated the number of individuals who must be condemned to wretchedness, to overwork, to demoralization, to infantilization, to despicable ignorance, to insurmountable misfortune, to utter penury, in order to produce one rich person?' I suppose that this and similar calls will gather in pitch in the coming years – and hopefully also in audience...

SD: Could you say a little about what you're reading at the moment, or what you've read recently that you've been impressed by?

ZB: For me, the last couple of years have discouraged voyages of discovery. Not many attempted, even fewer seen through.

But as you can gather from our chat thus far, Saramago was one (regrettably, late) discovery. I am sad that just a couple of his oeuvres, still unread, are waiting for me to savour – as he won't write any more of them...

Other discoveries were the first dystopias composed for the liquid modern world, codifying and extrapolating and bringing to their logical (that is, if our collective art of the illogical and the unexpected doesn't interfere in time) conclusion. In film, Michael Haneke. In literature, Michel Houellebecq: bound to do for the twenty-first century what Zamyatin, Orwell and Aldous Huxley did for the twentieth.

My latest discovery, not in the same class, yet great all the same: Sarah Bakewell's study of Montaigne under the enigmatic title *How to Live* (mind you, emphatically not 'How Should One Live'...).

I am fascinated by Keith Tester's studies in film art – both the already published and the forthcoming. They open quite new vistas where one would think everything that could be said has already been said. I am still trying to come to grips with their import.

SD: One final question: *TCS* is committed to the process of peer review, and many of our contributors (both rejected and accepted) are grateful for the feedback given by our editors and anonymous reviewers, and for the subsequent strengthening of their articles, but you are critical of peer review and no longer act as a referee for us. Could you tell us why?

ZB: There are, at the most conservative estimate, two grave and deeply regrettable collateral victims of the gruesome stratagem of peer review: one is daring of thought (wishy-washed to the lowest common denominator), and the other is the individuality, as well as the responsibility, of editors (those seeking shelter behind the anonymity of 'peers', but in fact dissolved in it, in many cases without a trace). Much other harm is also done, of course: like the deceptive safety suggested by the 'committee resolution', thereby dampening the reader's critical impulse, or suppressing the temperance and sometimes also the honesty of 'peers' provoked by assurances of anonymity into actions they would otherwise desist from. The overall result is a reinstating of the state of affairs bluntly described by Hannah Arendt as one of 'floating responsibility' or the 'responsibility of nobody'.

Last but not least, I would single out yet another instance of collateral damage: the multitude of the trails blazed and the heterogeneity of what inspires them. I suspect that the peer review system carries a good part of blame for the fact that something like 60 per cent or more of journal articles are never quoted (which means they leave no trace on our joint scholarly pursuits), and (in my perception at any rate) that 'learned journals' (with a few miraculous exceptions that entail, prominently, *TCS*) brandish stultifying repetitiousness and ooze monumental boredom. To find just one new enlightening and inspiring idea (as distinct from finding a recipe for getting safely through the peer-built barricade), browsing through thousands of journal pages is all too often called for. With my tongue in one cheek only, I'd suggest that were our stone-age ancestors to discover the peer-review dredger, we would still be sitting in caves...So perhaps the stratagem under discussion is in addition guilty of a massive waste of time and intellectual power. In short, not the sort of game in which I'd be inclined willingly to take part...

25 December 2010

On the new looks of inequality

Frank Rich, a leading op-ed columnist on the *New York Times*, observes in yesterday's issue, about the voice of the liberal America: 'economic equality seemed within reach in 1956, at least for the vast middle class. The sense that the American promise of social and economic mobility was attainable to anyone who sought it...' That was, he reminds his readers, not counting on their memories, the nation's mood fifty-five years ago. As to the American middle class of today, Rich needs only to ask a purely rhetorical question: 'How many middle-class Americans now believe that the sky is the limit if they work hard enough? How many trust capitalism to give them a fair shake?' – meaning how many Americans have managed to preserve and retain the old trust, so very alive a mere half-century ago, trust in the 'social equality of mobility', or 'equality on the move', 'equality coming nearer and nearer', 'equality within reach'...A rhetorical question indeed, since in this case Rich can rely on his readers to answer, unhesitatingly: not many. This is, roughly, what has happened to the middle-class dream 'that everyone can enter Frontierland if they try hard enough, and that no one will be denied a dream because a private party has rented out Tomorrowland'.

A day earlier, another *New York Times* op-ed columnist, Charles M. Blow, noted the latest statistical evidence:

> According to the National Center for Children in Poverty, 42 percent of American children live in low-income homes and about a fifth live in poverty. It gets worse. The number of children living in poverty has risen 33 percent since 2000. For perspective, the child population of the country overall increased by only about 3 percent over that time. And, according to a 2007 Unicef report on child poverty, the U.S. ranked last among 24 wealthy countries... [T]he reaction to this issue in some quarters is still tangled in class and race: no more welfare to black and brown people who've made poor choices and haven't got the gumption to work their way out of them.

There is no need to tell the parents of the 42 per cent of American children, struggling as they are day in, day out, trying to make ends meet, that the chances of equality are nowhere near for their children, while the parents of the 20 per cent of children living in poverty would hardly recognize the 'chances' whose vanishing the latest figures describe. Both categories of parents, however, would have little difficulty, if any, in decoding the message flowing loud and clear from the lips of those who set the laws of the land and translate them into the language of rights and duties for the citizens of that land. The message is simplicity itself: This is no longer a *land of opportunity*; this is a land for *people with gumption*. Socially manageable 'equality of mobility' foundered on the hard rock of the inequality of individual gumption. The 'gumption' of the parents is the only lifeboat on offer to those who wish to navigate their children out of poverty. The boat is small; you'd be lucky to procure a boat capacious enough to accommodate the whole family. More likely, only a few of the family's members, the most daring and tight-fisted among them and so the ones with the largest supply of gumption, will manage to squeeze into the dinghy and keep their place for as long as it takes to reach the coast. And the journey is no longer (if it ever was) a voyage to equality. It is, rather, a chase to leave others behind. The room at the top is pre-booked and only the chosen are admitted. As Frank Rich aptly puts it, 'a private party has rented out Tomorrowland'.

The land of opportunity promised more equality. The land of people with gumption has only more inequality to offer.

26 December 2010

On resocializing the social

Today's editorial in *Le Monde* ('Contre crise et pauvreté, la protection sociale') shares with its readers a remarkable discovery: little by little, gingerly taking one step at a time, but recently at a pace accelerated by the spectre of worldwide economic collapse, the realization has dawned on opinion-makers and doers-of-things alike that social protection endorsed and run by the state is a necessary condition of *both* a healthy economy *and* protection from the worst consequences of an unhealthy one. It is not just a question of generosity and charity, as the dominant ideology of

Reaganomics and Thatcheronomics would have us to believe. In other words, restoring old mechanisms of a collective insurance policy against individually suffered misfortune, or building new ones from scratch, is not only in the interest of the unfortunate, but a matter of *common interest* and indeed of *common survival*. A conflict of interest between taxpayers and recipients of welfare provisions is largely a figment of an ideologically fed and boosted imagination. It is not the largesse of a welfare state but its mean-ness that hits the taxpayer most painfully – since it hits at the source of his own welfare, the income from which taxes are paid.

There are growing numbers of material signs, though somewhat fewer declarations of faith, testifying that this truly watershed shift in high-level thinking is indeed taking place. The International Labour Organization's idea of including social security in the list of fundamental human rights is still widely decried as not much short of utopia; but in international political practice that idea is steering closer and closer to present-day – or at any rate foresee-able – reality. In July 2010, the United Nations, in an act almost unrecorded by the world's press and hardly reaching public aware-ness, took the bold step of appointing Michelle Bachelet, the former president of Chile, to promote the cause (indeed, the crusade) of spreading social welfare practices to parts of the world that have so far lacked them. This has been done with the whole-hearted support of the International Monetary Fund and the World Bank, two institutions on record as fighting tooth and nail for merciless cuts in states' expenditure and against state-guaran-teed social protection in developing countries. A formidable change of heart indeed, if it is true. The big question, though, is whether the new mood (steadily turning into the new mantra) will survive the reverberations of the current instability in credit and finance.

Even if it proves to be more lasting than the current tremors that triggered it, the new (still emergent) consensus has a long and tortuous way to go to reach its declared purpose. We learn from the editorial in *Le Monde* that while social protection consumes up to one-fifth of national wealth in the 'developed' (read, well-off) countries, poor countries can so far only afford (and let me add, are allowed) to set aside an average of just 4 per cent of their budget for social provision purposes; many of them, moreover, earmark only 1 per cent of national product or less for social assistance. Three-quarters of the world's families, and 90 per cent of African families, at the moment cannot count on any form of social security.

All the same, the signals are multiplying from every continent that governments are flexing their muscles to cut through the Gordian knot of economies pulled down by the burden of mass poverty and misery, both growing even more massive because of continuing economic weakness. Attempts to do so, albeit with varying degrees of determination, can be seen in places as scattered and different as South Africa and Nepal. On a grander scale, Brazil has managed to pull out of the depths of poverty, insecurity and prospectlessness as many as 13 million families, equal to an estimated 50 million adults and children, with the help of the state-administered programme Bolsa Familia, initiated by Lula. Mexico is trying to do the same, with the help of the Oportunidades programme; while in characteristically wholesale style, China has recently decided to shift its accumulated surpluses to build up, virtually from scratch yet within the next five years, a comprehensive web of social protection for hundreds of millions of its citizens hitherto deprived of any social provisions.

27 December 2010

On the friends you have and friends you think you have

Professor Robin Dunbar, an evolutionary anthropologist in Oxford, insists that 'our minds are not designed [by evolution] to allow us to have more than a very limited number of people in our social world'. Dunbar has actually calculated that number: he found that 'most of us can maintain only around 150 meaningful relationships'. Not unexpectedly, he's called that limit, imposed by (biological) evolution, the 'Dunbar number'. This hundred and a half is, we may comment, the number reached through biological evolution by our remote ancestors, and where it stopped, leaving the field to its much nimbler, more agile and dexterous, and above all more resourceful and less patient successor – called 'cultural evolution' (that is, triggered, shaped and driven by humans themselves, and deploying the teaching and learning process rather than changing the arrangement of genes).

Let's note that 150 was probably the topmost number of creatures that could come together, stay together and profitably cooperate while surviving just on hunting and gathering; the size of a proto-human herd couldn't go beyond that magic limit without summoning, or rather conjuring up, forces and (yes!) tools other than fangs and talons. Without those other forces and tools, called 'cultural', the continuous proximity of larger numbers would have been unsustainable, and so a capacity to 'hold in the mind' a larger number would have been superfluous. 'Imagining' a totality larger than that accessible to the senses was as uncalled for as it was, under the circumstances, inconceivable. Minds did not need to store what senses had no opportunity to grasp...The arrival of culture must have coincided, as it did, with trespassing beyond the 'Dunbar number'. Was crossing that number the first act of transgression of 'natural limits', and given that to transgress limits (whether 'natural' or self-set) is culture's defining trait and its mode of being, was that also the birth act of culture?[1]

Let's note as well that with the start of the cultural sequel of evolution, the field of recognizably 'meaningful' relationships split, for all practical intents and purposes, into two spaces according to two different, autonomous though interrelated, kinds of 'meaningfulness': sensual/emotional or specific, and mental or abstract. It is the first variety of 'meaningfulness' that can conceivably have 'set limits', in as far as it continues to depend on the (essentially unchanged) equipment with which evolution has supplied the human species; the second variety, however, is manifestly emancipated from constraints imposed by 'natural limits' – though eminently free at the same time to set (and revoke or transgress in practice) limits of its own. Much of culture's work has consisted thus far, and continues to consist, in drawing and redrawing the boundaries separating 'here' from 'there', 'in' and 'out', 'us' and 'them', and further subdividing and differentiating the terrains inside them; and given the plurality of cultures and of the interfaces of cultural interventions, it consists also in generating 'grey areas' of ambivalence between bordered-off territories, and so also bones of contention that in turn offer a further stimulus to the border-drawing urge. 'Dunbar's number' is itself a typical example of the cultural exercise of drawing borders (an activity going back, according to Lévi-Strauss's etiological myth, to the 'birth of culture', namely the prohibition of incest, that is, the division of women into permitted and forbidden sexual objects).

Electronically sustained 'networks of friendship' promised to break through the recalcitrant, intrepid limitations to sociability set by our genetically transmitted equipment. Well, says Dunbar, they didn't and will not: the promise can't but be broken. 'Yes,' says Dunbar in his opinion piece for the *New York Times* of 25 December, 'you can "friend" 500, 1,000, even 5,000 people with your Facebook page, but all save the core 150 are mere voyeurs looking into your daily life.' Among those thousands of Facebook friends, 'meaningful relationships', whether serviced electronically or lived off-line, are confined as before within the impassable limits of the 'Dunbar number'. The true service rendered by Facebook and the other 'social' websites of its ilk is the maintenance of a steady core of friends under the condition of a highly mobile, fast-moving and fast-changing world.

Our distant ancestors had it easy: they, much like their near and dear, tended on the whole to dwell in the same place from cradle to coffin, in close proximity to each other and within reach and sight of each other. This so to say 'topographic' foundation of long-term, even lifelong bonds is unlikely to reappear, and still less likely to be immune to the flow of time, vulnerable as it is to the vicissitudes of individual life histories. Fortunately, we now have ways of 'staying in touch' that are fully and truly 'extraterritorial' and so independent of the degree and frequency of physical proximity. 'Facebook and other social networking sites', and only they – so Dunbar suggests – 'allow us to keep up the friendships that would otherwise rapidly wither away.' This is not the end of the benefits they offer, though: 'They allow us to reintegrate our networks so that, rather than having several disconnected subsets of friends, we can rebuild, *albeit virtually*, the kind of old rural communities where everyone knew everyone else' (emphasis added). In the case of friendship, at any rate, so at least Dunbar implies, even if not in so many words, Marshall McLuhan's idea of the 'media being the message' has been refuted; though his other memorable suggestion, that of the arrival of a 'global village', by comparison, came true. 'Albeit virtually'...

But is not 'virtuality' a difference that makes a difference – a bigger one, and much more consequential for the fate of 'meaningful relationships' than Dunbar is willing or cares to admit? Living in 'the old rural communities' made it difficult to tie together bonds that were not tied together already, so to speak, 'by themselves', and more precisely by the circumstance of people rubbing shoulders inside the same 'rural community'; and it made it similarly difficult, if not more so, to untie the bonds that were already there, to render them null and void, short of the death of one or more of the bonded people. Living online, on the other hand, makes 'entering' a relationship childishly easy; but it also enormously facilitates opting out from a relationship, while making it treacherously easy in the meantime to overlook the loss of content in the 'relationship', as it becomes emaciated, fades and in the end dissolves for mere absence of attention.

There are reasons to suspect that it is precisely those facilities that have secured and assured the tremendous popularity of 'social networking' sites, making their self-proclaimed inventor and surely chief marketer, Mark Elliot Zuckerberg, an instant multibillionaire. Those facilities allowed the modern drive towards effortlessness, convenience and comfort to finally reach, conquer and colonize the hitherto stubbornly and passionately independent land of human bonds. They made that land risk-free, or almost; they made it impossible, or almost, for ex-desirables to overstay their welcome; they made cutting your losses cost-free, or almost. All in all, they accomplished the feat of squaring the circle, of eating your cake and having it. By cleansing the business of interrelating from all and any strings attached, they strained out and removed the ugly fly of unbreakability that used to blight the sweet ointment of human togetherness.

Dunbar is right that the electronic substitutes for face-to-face communication have brought the Stone Age inheritance up to date, adapting and adjusting the ways and means of human togetherness to the requirements of our *nouvel âge*. What he seems to neglect, however, is that in the course of that adaptation those ways and means have also been considerably altered, and that as a result 'meaningful relationships' have also changed their meaning. And so must the content of the 'Dunbar number' concept have done. Unless it is precisely the number, and only the number, that exhausts its content...

28 December 2010

On the front pages and other pages

The front-page headlines, true to the Christmas mood, are joyful and raise the spirits. They announce the imminent end of the

Depression: the United States is nearing that elusive light at the
end of the tunnel called a 'return to normality'. Namely: shoppers
have come back, in droves, to the shopping malls – as if to repent
their momentary loss of shopping verve and compensate for lost
time. Once again, and just as in the good not-so-old times, their
hands do not tremble when they pull credit cards out of wallets.
Jewellery and luxury goods are again in high demand, and the
optimism filling the boutiques cannot but spill over to high street
shops and market stalls. As a result, the revenues of sellers of gifts
promise to rise above pre-Depression levels this year. And this can
have only one meaning: our lord and angel guardian, the Economy,
is again on the move.

This is what you would have learned about the state of your
country if you had moved straight from the front pages to the TV
or the other entertainment pages. Though not if you happened to
be one of the many who failed to contribute to the revenues of
shopping malls and so have been omitted from their statistics; or
one of the 15 million Americans officially classified as jobless. 'In
the real world,' as Bob Herbert observes in his op-ed piece in the
New York Times of 27 December, 'where families have to feed
themselves and pay their bills, there are an awful lot of Americans
being left behind.'

At the John J. Heldrich Centre for Workforce Development at
Rutgers University, Professors Carl Van Horn and Cliff Zukin run
a research panel which has been recording the meandering where,
what and how about of the same sample of workers since summer
last year. Their last report, published at the same time as the san-
guine headlines summarized above, was given the gruesome and
alarming title: 'The Shattered American Dream: Unemployed
Workers Lose Ground, Hope, and Faith in Their Futures'. What
that report shows (and what others must have noted yet failed or
omitted to mention) is the ongoing social downgrading of people
thrown out of their jobs. Three-quarters of the sample remained
unemployed for the duration of the study; two-thirds have now
been without job-related income for a year or more, one-third for
two years or more. Their life savings are gone, they've sold any
sellable possessions and they live on money borrowed from relatives or friends. As to the older people among the jobless, they
make up a new class – of 'involuntarily retired'. Most of those
over fifty years of age do not believe they will ever again have a

full-time job. And as to the quarter of the sample lucky enough to be back in work, almost all of them were offered and accepted jobs for less pay and with fewer or no benefits. Of the 50,000 new jobs added to the employment statistics in November, the month leading to the 'return of the shoppers' celebrated in the front-page headlines, 80 per cent were temporary. One of the most prominent traits of the present mood dominant in the sample, according to Van Horn, is the loss of faith in the precept 'that if you are determined and work hard, you can get ahead'. Degraded and humiliated, these former workers no longer count on better times to come. And as Bob Herbert comments, 'jobless people don't buy a lot of flat-screen TV' – and so, to add insult to injury, their sorry lot is unlikely to find much compassion among that part of the nation returning to the shopping malls. They, the jobless, who have now turned into consumers who are not just flawed but disqualified as substandard, are unlikely to join the crowd heralding and promoting the 'robust recovery' spied out by the headline writers.

We can soon expect statistics to appear showing that the most lasting and corrosive consequence of the two-year-old credit collapse and the ways in which the powers-that-be reacted to it is a further deepening of the social inequality already eroding American society from the inside. As Tony Judt pointed out in *Ill Fares the Land* (Penguin, 2010, p. 175), his last warning of the many he addressed over the years to the American nation:

> Inequality...then, is not just unattractive in itself; it clearly corresponds to pathological social problems that we cannot hope to address unless we attend to their underlying cause. There is a reason why infant mortality, life expectancy, criminality, the prison population, mental illness, unemployment, obesity, malnutrition, teenage pregnancy, illegal drug use, economic insecurity, personal indebtedness and anxiety are so much more marked in the US and the UK than they are in continental Europe.... Inequality is corrosive. It rots societies from within. The impact of material differences takes a while to show up: but in due course competition for status and goods increases; people feel a growing sense of superiority (or inferiority) based on their possessions; prejudice towards those on the lower ranks of the social ladder hardens; crime spikes and the pathologies of social disadvantage become ever more marked. The legacy of unregulated wealth creation is bitter indeed.

When the statistics confirming Judt's dark premonitions are finally available, on which page of the newspaper are they likely to be printed?

29 December 2010

On (selected) quandaries

One year ago Janina left me.

On Eleanor Roosevelt, Adlai E. Stevenson opined: 'She would rather light candles than curse the darkness, and her glow has warmed the world.' In her turn, Eleanor Roosevelt opined about the human's power of setting limits to powerlessness: 'No one can make you feel inferior without your consent' – and she knew that power from finding it in herself. *Toutes proportions gardées* (Janina was never a president's wife, and she had just enough candles, but no more than that, to disperse the darkness in a room, and to warm those inside it), I felt as if I were reading words spoken about Janina, and by her; words spoken to describe the logic of her life and to convey the essence of her faith, her own way of being-in-the-world.

Arthur Koestler writes in his autobiography, *Arrow in the Blue*:

> one cannot act, or write, or even live guiltlessly. Train a dog to run after bicycles but not to run after motorcars, and then ride past him on a motorcycle; he will react with an experimental neurosis. Train a nation to believe that tolerance is good, persecution is bad, and ask them whether or not to persecute people who want to abolish tolerance; they will react in much the same way.

Struggling to find a way of living with that philosophical truth – the awareness that guilt may be shifted, but not removed, from acting, writing and living – he continued:

> If the pessimism of the philosopher is a valid attitude, the duty of the militant humanist to go on hoping against hope is no less valid...We have to accept the perpetual contradiction between the two. If we admit that defeatism and despair, even when logically justified, is morally wrong, and that active resistance to evil is a

moral necessity even when it seems logically absurd, we may find a new approach to a humanist dialectic...

Well, perhaps we may. Though we wouldn't know for sure unless we went on trying and refused to take a lack of certainty for a reason to stop.

31 December 2010

On whether 'democracy' still means anything, and in case it does, what is it?

The question is anything but new. In *Arrow in the Blue*, a book penned in 1952 but summarizing the bitter lessons delivered by the twenty years of frustrated hopes and lost chances recorded by historiographers under the name of the 'inter-war period', Arthur Koestler reminisces:

> We fought our battle of words and did not see that the familiar words had lost their bearing and pointed in the wrong directions. We said 'democracy' solemnly as in a prayer, and soon afterwards the greatest nation of Europe voted, by perfectly democratic methods, its assassins into power. We worshipped the will of The Masses, and their will turned out to be death and self-destruction...The social progress for which we fought became a progress towards the slave labour camp; our liberalism made us accomplices of tyrants and oppressors; our love for peace invited aggression and led to war.

Let's try to understand what sets that bizarre process in motion – uncannily reminiscent of the alleged habit of chickens to go on running for quite a few more yards after their heads have been chopped off. Signifiers may abandon, cut off and change their 'signifieds' (the 'referents' to which they are meant to 'refer') without losing their constituency. It is similar to such defining signifiers of our 'Western civilization' as 'democracy', 'freedom', 'progress', 'tolerance' and 'peace'. Propelled and given momentum by the enthusiastic support of their electorate for the causes and promises they originally stood for, the signifiers may be switched and tied to signifieds remote from, or even opposite to the original ones, without significant damage to the enthusiasm of their supporters. Once they are won, honed, cultivated and set in place – learned and absorbed – the loyalty, conformity and herd-style discipline attached to the words embroidered on the banners, and the habits that spring into action at the mere sound of those words being spoken, will withstand a potentially infinite multitude of reversals. Those words turn from the names of causes into the names of camps, and obedience can be (and is) demanded and obtained by recalling the ultimate confrontation between 'us' and 'them' – without the cause and the purpose of the ongoing war being mentioned ever again, let alone subjected to a test.

In an article displayed on the website of the internet journal *truthout* under the title 'Living in the age of imposed amnesia: the eclipse of democratic formative culture', Henry A. Giroux wonders how one can possibly explain 'the electoral sweep that just put the most egregious Republican Party candidates back in power?' After all, the victors are

> the people who gave us Katrina, made torture a state policy, promoted racial McCarthyism, celebrated immigrant bashing, pushed the country into two disastrous wars, built more prisons than schools [I would add that 758 persons in every 100,000 are currently in prison in the United States, constituting by far the highest number in the world, while if people on probation and on parole are added, 6 million Americans are under the surveillance of the state organs of coercion], bankrupted the public treasury, celebrated ignorance over scientific evidence ('half of new Congressmen do not believe in global warming') and promoted the merging of corporate and political power.

Indeed, how can one explain such a verdict of the electorate?! Giroux suggests two possible explanations. One is the successful making of 'punitive justice and a theater of cruelty' into a political formula accepted by (or at least acceptable to) the majority of Americans. The other is the accelerated pace of 'social amnesia': the most outrageous misdemeanours of rulers, not so long ago the subject of public outcry, are pushed aside or forgotten altogether in time for the mid-term elections...

But there is another possibility as well, perhaps too gruesome for the future of democracy to be willingly brought into the open

and seriously broached. It is the possibility, nay likelihood, that
the link between the public agenda and private worries, the very
hub of the democratic process, has been broken – each of the two
spheres now rotating in mutually isolated spaces and set in motion
by mutually unconnected and non-communicating (though certainly not independent!) factors and mechanisms. To put it simply,
these are situations in which people who have been hit don't know
what's hit them – and have little chance, if any, and hardly the
will any more to find out. What are on offer to the seekers and
dreamers of reconnection are 'short-circuits', known to emit a
dazzling light for a brief moment – but then they make the darkness that follows even deeper, more impenetrable and frightening
than it was before. Whatever remains of their desire to return from
an exile from the commonality of fate that sent them into a
prospectless loneliness and abandonment is dissolved, dissipated
and disappears in an apparently unending succession of frustrated
hopes. The overall effect of being immersed in this kind of situation has been succinctly summed up by Danilo Zolo: 'We are', he
has suggested, 'in the presence of a regime that I believe can be
called "post-democratic tele-oligarchy": a post-democracy in
which the vast majority of citizens do not "choose" and do not
"elect", but ignore, silently and obediently.'[2]

There is one other factor that enormously speeds up that descent
into the 'post-democratic' era of a 'don't care' *je m'en fous* kind
– of an 'ignoring, silent and obedient' electorate. To follow the
expression coined by Paul Krugman in his op-ed contribution to
today's *New York Times*, 'The new voodoo': 'Hypocrisy never
goes out of style, but, even so, 2010 was something special. For
it was the year of budget doubletalk – the year of arsonists posing
as firemen, of people railing against deficits while doing everything
they could to make those deficits bigger.' The overall message
exuded by information dripping from the upper regions of politics
was one of incongruence, if not downright inanity. One of the
fundamental syllogisms of elementary logic warns that 'if p and
non-p, then q'; meaning (in a simplified yet honest translation)
that if a proposition and its negation are simultaneously accepted,
then everything may follow (and therefore nothing has more basis
than anything else, and so nothing can be relied upon); in other
words, that everything can be asserted, but (or rather as) nothing
stands to reason. But headlines like 'McConnell blasts deficit

spending. Urges extension of tax cuts' have now become the common fare served by the American press to its readers. Confronted with these kinds of conflicting assertions offered in a single breath for their simultaneous approval, readers have little choice except to admit that things that decide their well-being and their life prospects are beyond their comprehension and bound to stay there; and where there is ignorance, impotence is sure to follow.

It has been averred since the beginning of the modern science of politics that, given that state authorities must deal with affairs much too involved to be understood by ordinary folk, democracy is bound to be the rule of highly educated experts, with the role of ordinary folk being reduced to the periodical approval or disapproval of the experts' actions. Contemporary political practice has gone far beyond the political scientists' expectations, however. The experts on high no longer need to repeat that things are too complicated to be properly judged by the layperson and so should be left to those in the know. They demonstrate day in, day out, and beyond reasonable doubt (if 'reasonableness' is still a recognizable quality, that is), that in applying their inborn inclination and their inherited or learned tools of setting the right apart from the wrong (the only tools at their disposal), laypersons are incapable of arriving at (as distinct from repeating or just echoing) a judgement. On its journey upwards to the murky regions where political judgements are reached and political decisions are taken, the logic guiding our ordinary folks' life pursuits stops (or, rather, is brutally stopped) well below the level it struggles to reach.

One shudders at such a surmise – but is not illogicality fast becoming the latest wonder weapon of state authorities, torn as they presently are between an acute deficit of power and the harsh demands of ruling which their powerless politics is much too weak to meet? It is a miracle weapon as cheap as it is easy to deploy (to borrow another of Krugman's phrases, 'all it takes is disgruntled voters who don't know what's at stake – and we have plenty of those'). Is it not the baffling and reason-defying incongruity that prompts the disheartened and dispirited 'ordinary folk' to turn their backs on and avert their eyes from Politics with a capital 'P', thereby allowing its practitioners to get away with their games of false pretences and promises to square circles and reconcile irreconcilabilities? The most effective prescription for grinding communication to a halt and preventing its resumption is, after all, to rob it of the presumption and expectation of meaningfulness and sense. No longer can one placate one's fears and premonitions by blaming rising anxieties about the future of democracy, and about its ability to fulfil the job in whose name it was called into being, either on the art of hypocrisy in which sectors of the political elite have become grandmasters, or on their ineptitude coupled with personal dishonesty and corruption. That wonder weapon may be, as the V2 was for Hitler, the last weapon left to the operators of a politics that has outlived its age; their last hope for a stay of execution...

January 2011

1 January 2011

On the Angel of History, reincarnated...

Angelus Novus shows an angel looking as though he is about to move away from something he is fixedly contemplating. His eyes are staring, his mouth is open, his wings are spread. This is how one pictures the angel of history. His face is turned towards the past. Where we perceive a chain of events, he sees one single catastrophe that keeps piling wreckage upon wreckage and hurls it in front of his feet. The angel would like to stay, awaken the dead, and make whole what has been smashed. But a storm is blowing from Paradise; it has got caught in his wings with such violence that the angel can no longer close them. The storm irresistibly propels him into the future to which his back is turned, while the pile of debris before him grows skyward. This storm is what we call progress.[3]

So wrote Walter Benjamin, looking at Paul Klee's drawing. Inspired by the suggestions oozing out of that drawing, Benjamin debunked the creed of worshippers, venerators, court poets, sycophants and fellow travellers of 'historical progress', their representation of history as a process set in motion and kept going by the forward pull of designs, visions and hopes of greater happiness; we are not pulled by a luminous future, Benjamin insisted, but repelled, pushed and forced to run by the dark horrors of the past. Benjamin's most seminal discovery was that 'progress' was all along, and continues to be, an *escape from*, rather than a *movement to...*

But let's note that the Benjamin/Klee Angel of History, much like the storm that blows him into the future, is *mute*. The Benjamin/Klee allegory does not stand for words but for happenings; not for what human beings, the involuntary agents and victims of history, say about their reasons to live on the run, but for what is *happening to them*. Benjamin was a self-proclaimed 'historical materialist'. In tune with the prevailing wisdom of his time, he believed in the laws of history (laws designed by and for moderns and hoped to fill the void left by divine design and providence); and he shared the similarly widespread belief in historical determination, a 'natural' as much as an indispensable concomitant of the ambitions to build and manage order of the up-and-coming modern state.

All those beliefs, however, including the idea of 'history' as a superhuman power that disposes what man proposes, have lost much of their credibility and appearance of being self-evident, together with the emaciation of history's 'material substratum': that up-and-coming state, self-confident and (at least in its intention) all-powerful, pushing, boundlessly ambitious, and jealous of current or potential competitors in the manner of the monotheistic God. States as we know them now, from our own, current experience, are bent on contracting out, hiving off, outsourcing and subsidiarizing everything the state – as it was recollected in Benjamin's obituary and as it was in the days when it was still alive behind the mask of the 'Angel of History' – aimed at monopolizing and taking under its exclusive management (the fading of the '*social* state' being just one of many undetachable facets of its departure).

Were we looking for a fitting allegory for what is going on nowadays, we would need to lay aside the one and only Angel of History and put in its stead a swarm of 'biography angels'. We would confess to being a crowd of loners, propelled into the future to which our backs are turned, while the pile of debris (of our dashed hopes, frustrated expectations and lost chances) before us grows skyward... We have been sentenced, each and every one of us, to what Anthony Giddens calls 'life politics'; told to struggle or pretend to be, simultaneously, our own legislative, executive and juridical powers. No more salvation by society, in Peter Drucker's timely reminder. It is up to us now, as Ulrich Beck caustically observed, to find individual solutions to the predicament we all share (or, closer to our theme, to conjure up in individual biography what in the past was presumed to reside in collective history). The point is no longer how to calm and pacify the turbulent waters, but (as for the shipwrecked sailor in Edgar Allan Poe's *A Descent into the Maelstrom*) where to find or how to nail together a nicely rounded barrel and, by leaping from one tide to another, manage somehow and perhaps escape drowning...

So whatever happened to Benjamin's Angel of History? Like so many other intentions, designs, functions and promises of state-administered collective action, disguised as 'progress', it has been *privatized*. At any rate it has been put on the market for private sale. The haute couture original adorned with the logo of 'God' or 'History' is now mass-produced, advertised and sold at discount prices in high street shops: a personal, do-it-yourself angel of biography, for everyone to assemble. Exactly what happened to God himself, as Ulrich Beck has pointed out in his latest book, *A God of One's Own*.

And so ultimately it all comes down not to the narratives we are taught to recite, but to the stubborn, recalcitrant, resistant social realities we try to narrate (while being forced to do so). In our pulverized, atomized society, spattered with the debris of broken interhuman bonds and their eminently frail and breakable substitutes, there is plenty for the diminutive angels of little biographies to be horrified by and compelled to run away from. Among the other revolting and offputting sights and odours, those of the rotting and malodorous zombies of 'society' and 'community' are perhaps the most salient...

2 January 2011

On finding consolation in unexpected places

The Spirit Level, the eye-opening study by Richard Wilkinson and Kate Pickett that demonstrated and explained why 'greater equality makes societies stronger', is at long last beginning to worm its way into American public opinion (thanks to Nicholas D. Kristof's comment in the New Year issue of the *New York Times*). The delay is all the more thought-provoking, because in the United States, the country firmly perched at the very top of the global premier league of inequality (according to the latest statistics, the wealthiest 1 per cent of Americans control more wealth than the bottom 90 per cent), and the one that supplied the researchers with the most extreme instances of inequality's collateral damage, Wilkinson and Pickett's message should have sounded most urgently and rung a red alarm.

Even at this late stage Kristof prefers to introduce the authors of the study to American readers as 'distinguished British *epidemiologists*' (rather than connecting them to *social* studies – storytellers guilty, according to American opinion leaders, of a condemnable and contemptible leftist-liberal bias and for that reason dismissed before they can be heard, let alone listened to). Guided probably by the same prudent caution, Kristof mostly quotes from the reviewed study the data concerning macaques and the relations between low-status and high-status macaques and other, unnamed 'monkeys'. And having quoted in support John Steinbeck's sentence on the 'sad soul' that is able to 'kill you quicker, far quicker, than a germ', he placates the possible alarm of readers likely to spy out another tax-hike menace, and preempts their violent protests, by putting the bad news in a less wallet-threatening order: the toll of inequality, he points out, is 'not just economic but also a melancholy of the soul'. He admits, though, even if in a somewhat roundabout and so innocuous way, that the toll is also 'economic', when he points out that the choice is between less inequality and more prisons and police – both alternatives known all too well to be costly in terms of the tax rate. In Kristof's rendition, inequality is bad not as such, because of its own injustice, inhumanity, immorality and life-destroying potential – but for making the soul bad and melancholic...

As to its morbid connection with biology, now finally scientifically confirmed, Kristof has the following to say: 'Humans become stressed when they find themselves at the bottom of a hierarchy. That stress leads to biological changes' – like the accumulation of abdominal fat, heart disease, self-destructive behaviour and (sic!)...persistent poverty. Now, finally, we know – as endorsed and certified by distinguished scientists unsuspected of wicked sympathies and illicit connections – why some people are sunk in misery and why, unlike us, they can neither avoid sinking into it nor climb out of it once they are there. This scientific finding comes, at long last, as a much-needed sweetener in the bitter reminder of our world record-beating inequality: the silver lining under that particularly nasty and threateningly murky cloud. It's all biology, stupid!

All the same, one could say that speaking up in whatever way is admittedly better than keeping silent, and speaking up late is admittedly better than never. And a truncated, sanitized and blunted message is better than none, so one would be tempted to add. But is it indeed? Has not the intended call-to-arms been surreptitiously transformed, in the process, into a call to lay down the arms? Shouldn't we rather, for the sake of the message we carry and the good it was meant to accomplish, beware surrendering to that temptation?

'The better part of valour is discretion' opined one of Shakespeare's less admirable characters, adding that 'in the which better part I have saved my life'... Faced with a deficit of valour, many would seek that part known to be better – on the authority... of Falstaff.

3 January 2011

On growth: do we need it?

Professor Tim Jackson of the University of Surrey, in his latest book, *Redefining Prosperity*, sounds the alarm: the present-day model of growth produces damage that is irreversible. And this is because 'growth' is measured by the rise in material production, rather than services like leisure, health, education...

Lewis Mumford's memorable juxtaposition of mining and agriculture comes to mind: the first wounds, destroys and uglifies the environment, whereas the second heals it, makes it self-regenerating, beautifies it. The first renders terrain uninhabitable, the second makes it hospitable and inviting to human habitation. The first violates, extracts, removes, empties and leaves a void behind: kills. The second cares, aids and adds, fills up, replenishes: keeps alive. The first exhausts finite resources. The second regenerates and resurrects resources: makes them forever renewable. But let's note that Mumford ruminated on the blessings of agriculture at a time when it still, by and large, served human sustenance, instead of monetary gain. It was made to the measure of human needs kept steady, resistant to stretching and so remaining in principle finite – not to human greed and avarice that are in principle infinite. The planet with its admittedly limited resources may be able to satisfy human needs, while being totally unfit to satisfy human rapacity.

For the irreparable damage being done to the planet's potential, Jackson only indirectly blames greed – singling out as a target 'our culture founded on a continuing appetite for novelty – which is the symbolic aspect of objects' (see his interview in today's *Le Monde*). All the same, we find ourselves continually encouraged to behave egotistically and materialistically – this behaviour being indispensable to keep our kind of economy going. We are prodded, forced or cajoled to buy and to spend, to spend what we have and to spend what we don't have but hope to earn in the future. In the recession, however, Jackson suggests, people abandoned those morbid habits and reverted to saving rather than spending, revealing the other, altruistic side of their nature (I wonder on what facts that supposition rests; there is a lot of evidence that 'in a recession' some people are forcefully, against their wishes and much to their despair, disqualified as credit-worthy and eliminated from the consumer orgy, while others continue unabated; and it would take a lot of spinning, stretching and massaging to interpret these diversified reactions to the recession as evidence surfacing of altruistic inclinations hitherto hidden or suppressed).

In a market, as Adam Smith pointed out, we owe our daily supply of fresh bread to the baker's greed, not to his altruism, charity, benevolence or high moral standards. It is thanks to the all-too-human lust for profit that goods are brought to market stalls and that we can be sure to find them there. Even Amartya Sen, who insists that well-being and the freedom to lead decent human lives needs to be seen as the ultimate objective of the economy (see his essay 'Justice in the global world' in *Indigo*, winter 2011), admits that 'it is indeed not possible to have a flourishing economy without extensive use of markets, so that the cultivation, rather than the prevention, of the development of necessary markets has to be a part of a prosperous and fair economic world'. What follows, first, is that to take away the lust for and chase after profit means making markets disappear, taking the goods with them. Second, markets being necessary for the 'economy to flourish', selfishness and avarice can only be eliminated from human motives at our shared peril. Finally, a third conclusion: altruism is at loggerheads with a 'flourishing economy'. You can have one or the other, but hardly both of them together...

Jackson bypasses this quite serious hurdle by putting his wager on human reason and power of persuasion; both powerful weapons, no doubt, and ones that would indeed be effective in the 'remodelling of the economic system' – if it was not for the unfortunate fact that the dictates of reason depend on the reality being reasoned about, and that those realities, when reasoned about by reasonable agents, dispose of a 'power of persuasion' much stronger than any arguments that ignore them or play them down. The reality in question is a society which can resolve (however imperfectly) the problems it itself creates (social conflicts and antagonisms menacing its own preservation) solely through an uninterrupted beefing up of the 'appetite for novelty' – thereby appealing to the greed and avarice that keep the economy 'flourishing'...

In the early stages of capitalism the major obstacle to the rise of the industrial economy was the 'traditional worker', guided not by greed but by need, and therefore seeing no reason for going to work today if the money he earned yesterday was sufficient to cover his (unchanged) needs of today. At the present stage of the history of capitalism, a figure of the 'traditional consumer' who saw no reason to go shopping today if the goods they had already purchased were in proper working order would be similarly disastrous for the consumerist economy. A reduction of the popular appetite to just those commodities required to satisfy needs would be a mortal blow to the sole economic model currently on offer – that is, to the consumerist economy. The point is, though, that it would also be a mortal blow to the one and only model of *society* currently approved. It is not just a 'flourishing economy' that nowadays depends on the baker's greed, but the only recipe for orderly coexistence among humans that is being deployed and which we are determined to go on deploying.

Against such awesome odds, Jackson proposes a three-point programme: making people aware that economic growth has its limits; convincing (obliging?) capitalists to commit themselves to distributing their profits not only in 'financial terms' but also according to social and environmental benefits in the community; and 'changing the social logic' so that governments favour the stimuli that currently induce people to expand and enrich their lives in other than materialistic ways. There is a snag, though: could all that be seriously contemplated without tackling those aspects of the human condition that prompted people to seek redress in markets in the first place? That is, grievances looking in vain for remedies, genuine or putative, and anxieties unattended to by society: therefore finding no outlets except in offers made by the market, and redirected to consumer markets in an insistent, if vain and deceptive, hope of finding a medicine or solution.

4 January 2011

On sustainability: this time, of social democracy...

Social democrats: do they know where they are going? Do they have a notion of a 'good society' worth fighting for? I doubt it. I believe they don't. Not in the part of the world we inhabit, at any rate.

Chancellor Schröder is on record as squinting at Tony Blair's and Gordon Brown's estates and saying, quite a few years ago, that there is no capitalist or socialist economy, only good or bad ... For a long time now, at least thirty to forty years, the policy of social democratic parties has been articulated, year after year of neoliberalist rule, by the principle that 'whatever you (the centre-right) do, we (the centre-left) can do better'. Sometimes, though even then not very often, one or another particularly outrageous and arrogant initiative taken by the rulers has provoked a pang of the old socialist conscience, and at such times, occasionally and without making a big issue out of it, a bit more compassion and slightly longer lifelines have been demanded for 'those who need it most' – or some 'softening of the blow' for those 'it hits the hardest' – though, more often than not, only borrowing the phrases from the vocabulary of 'the other side', and not before it had been put to the test of potential electoral popularity.

This state of affairs has a reason: social democracy has lost its own separate constituency, its social fortresses and ramparts: the enclosures inhabited by people at the receiving end of political and economic action, people waiting and yearning to be recast or to lift themselves out of the aggregate of victims into an integrated collective subject with interests, political agenda and political agency all of its own.

In short, what remains (at least in our part of the world) of the exploited industrial working class fighting for the vindication of the injustices it has suffered has shrunk to a marginal position in Western societies, repeating the itinerary travelled by agricultural labour a century earlier. As Vladislav Inozemtsev recently pointed out in his profound and comprehensive study of the 'Crisis of the Great Idea' (published in the August 2010 issue of the Russian-language monthly *Svobodnaya Mys'l*), the sharpest and most spectacular social inequalities characteristic of contemporary Western societies are no longer between capital and labour, and the most offensively gigantic fortunes are no longer the fruits of a factory-based exploitation of labour. The defence of the poor is thereby stripped of the elaborate theoretical scaffolding constructed by Marx in his analysis of capitalist industry to support the practice of social democracy. The defence of the poor is not the same as the defence of the working (and thereby robbed of surplus value) class.

Moreover, what has remained of social democracy's 'natural constituency' has been all but pulverized into an aggregate of self-concerned and self-centred individuals, competing for jobs and promotions, with little if any awareness of a commonality of fate and still less inclination to close ranks and undertake solidary action. 'Solidarity' was a phenomenon endemic to the bygone society of producers; it is no more than a nostalgia-bred fancy in the society of consumers, even though members of that brave new society are notorious for swarming to the same shops on the same date and at the same hour, now ruled by the 'invisible hand of the market' with the same efficiency as when they were herded onto factory floors and alongside assembly lines by bosses and their hired supervisors. Recast as consumers first and producers as a distant (and not necessary) second, the former social democratic constituency has been dissolved in the rest of the aggregate of solitary consumers, knowing of no other 'common interest' than that of taxpayers. No wonder the extant heirs of social democratic movements have their eyes focused on the 'middle ground' (referred to not so long ago as the 'middle classes') and rally to the defence of the 'taxpayers' no longer, ostensibly divided by their interests and so the only 'public' from whom it seems feasible and plausible to obtain solidary electoral support. Both parts of the current political spectrum hunt and graze on the same ground, trying to sell their 'policy product' to the same clients. No room here for a 'utopia of one's own'! Not enough room, at any rate, in the space separating one general election from the next...

'The left', so Saramago noted in his diary on 9 June 2009, 'does not appear to have noticed that it has become very much like the right.' But it has indeed become 'very much like the right':

> A movement that in the past succeeded in representing one of the greatest hopes for humanity, capable of spurring us to action by the simple resort of an appeal to what is best in human nature, I saw, over the passage of time, undergoing a change in its social composition... daily moving further away from its early promises, becoming more and more like its old adversaries and enemies, as if this were the only possible means of achieving acceptance, and so ending up becoming a faint replica of what it once was, employing concepts to justify certain actions, which it formerly used to argue against precisely the same actions... It has sold out to the right, and once it realizes this, it can ask itself what has created the entrenched distance between it and its natural supporters – the poor, the needy, but also the dreamers – in relation to what still remains of its principles. For it is no longer possible to vote for the left if the left has ceased to exist.

It is the right, and only the right, that with the left's consent has assumed the uncontested dictatorship over the political agenda of the day. It is the right that decides what is in and what is out, what can be spoken and what ought to/must become/remain unspeakable. It is the right, with the connivance of the left, that draws the line separating the possible from the impossible – and has thereby made self-fulfilling Margaret Thatcher's sentence about there being no alternative to itself...

The message to the poor and needy cannot be clearer: there is no alternative to a society that makes room for poverty and for needs stripped of any prospect of satisfaction – but no room for dreams and dreamers...

5 January 2011

On consumption getting richer and the planet poorer

The 'social state' is unsustainable nowadays; but for a reason that has nothing to do with the specificity of the 'sociality' of the state, but rather with a generalized weakening of the state as an 'agency'. I repeat what I have said many times before – this is, after all, the hub of all the other problems the remnant of the 'welfare state' needs to face up to.

Our ancestors worried and quarrelled about 'what is to be done'; we are worried, though hardly ever quarrel (as the topic seems to be hopeless), about 'who is going to do it'; a point on which our ancestors never quarrelled, being in complete agreement – 'the state, of course'! Once we capture the state, we'll do whatever we think needs to be done – the state, that union of power (that is, the ability to have things done) and politics (that is, the ability to decide which things need to be done) is all we need to make the word flesh, whichever word we choose. Well, it no longer seems to be the case that such an answer is self-evident. Politicians leave us in no doubt, monotonously echoing Margaret Thatcher: 'TINA' ('there is no alternative'). Meaning: we make our choices under conditions not of our choosing. On this latter point at least I am inclined to agree, though for somewhat different reasons. The conditions are 'not of their choosing' in that politicians placidly accept those conditions and stay determined not to try other choices: 'TINA' is a self-fulfilling prophecy, or rather a gloss on willingly embraced and zealously conducted practice.

The state is 'capitalist', as Habermas pointed out thirty years ago, writing in the time of a waning society of *producers*, in as far as it strives to secure a regular, and effective (that is, involving capital buying labour), encounter between capital and labour. For that encounter to be successful, capital must be able to afford to pay the price of labour, and labour must be in good enough shape to entice capital to buy it. Hence, we may say, the 'social state' is seen as indispensable for survival by 'both left and right'. No longer, though... Today, in the society of *consumers*, what makes the state 'capitalist' is servicing the encounter between commodity and consumer (as was vividly shown by the universal governmental reaction to the bank/credit collapse; hundreds of billions were found in the very coffers considered by governmental opinion to lack the few millions needed to salvage social services). For that purpose, the 'social state' is neither here nor there, and hence the issue of its emaciation and the recasting of its residues into a 'law and order' question rather than a social one is currently 'beyond left and right'...

Globalization or not, can we go on indefinitely measuring the rise of happiness by the rise of gross national product, let alone spreading that habit to the rest of the globe and raising their levels of consumption to the heights viewed as indispensable in the richest countries?! There is the impact of consumerism on the sustainability of our shared home, planet earth, to consider. We now know all too well that the resources of the planet have limits and cannot be infinitely stretched. We also know that the limited resources of the planet are too modest to accommodate a rise in the levels of consumption everywhere to the standards currently reached in the richest parts of the planet – the very standards by which the rest of the planet tends to measure its dreams and prospects, ambitions and postulates in the era of the information highway (according to some calculations, such a feat would require the resources of our planet to be multiplied by a factor of five; five planets would be needed instead of the single one we have).

And yet the invasion and annexation of the realm of morality by consumer markets has burdened consumption with additional functions it can perform only by pushing the levels of consumption ever higher. This is the principal reason why 'zero growth' as measured by GNP, the statistic of the quantity of money changing hands in buying and selling transactions, is viewed as little short not only of economic, but also of social and political catastrophe. It is due in large measure to those extra functions – linked to consumption neither by nature nor 'natural affinity' – that the prospect of setting a limit to the rise of consumption, not to mention cutting it down to an ecologically sustainable level, seems both nebulous and abhorrent, and that no 'responsible' political force (read, no party with its eyes glued to the nearest elections) would include such a prospect in its policy agenda. It may be surmised that the commodification of ethical responsibilities, those major building materials and tools of human togetherness, combined with the gradual yet relentless decay of all alternative, non-market ways of bringing it about, is a much more formidable obstacle to the containment and moderation of consuming appetites than the non-negotiable prerequisites of biological and social survival.

Indeed, if the level of consumption determined by biological and social survival is by nature inflexible, fixed and so relatively stable, the levels required to gratify the other needs promised, expected and demanded to be serviced by consumption are, again by the nature of such needs, inherently upward-oriented and rising; the satisfaction of those added needs does not depend on maintaining stable standards, but on the speed and degree of their rise. Consumers turning to the commodity market in a quest to satisfy their moral impulses and fulfil their duties of self-identification (read, self-commodification) are obliged to seek differentials in value and volume, and therefore this kind of 'consumer demand' is an overpowering and irresistible factor in an upward push. Just as ethical responsibility for the Other tolerates no limits, consumption invested with the task of venting and satisfying moral impulses resists any kind of constraint imposed on its extension. Having been harnessed to the consumerist economy, moral impulses and ethical responsibilities are recycled, ironically, into an awesome hindrance when humanity finds itself confronted with arguably the most formidable threat to its survival: a threat only to be fought back against through a lot, perhaps an unprecedented amount, of voluntary self-constraint and readiness for self-sacrifice.

Once set and kept in motion by moral energy, the consumerist economy has the sky as its only limit. To be effective in the job it has assumed, it cannot allow itself to slow down, let alone pause and stand still. It must consequently make the assumption, counter-factually, tacitly if not in so many words, of the limitlessness of the planet's durability and the infinity of its resources. From the beginning of the consumerist era, enlarging the loaf of bread was promoted as the patent remedy, indeed a foolproof prophylactic, against the conflicts and squabbles around the redistribution of that loaf. Effective or not in suspending hostilities, that strategy had to assume there were infinite supplies of flour and yeast. We are now nearing the moment when the falsity of that assumption and the dangers of clinging to it are likely to be exposed. This might be the moment for moral responsibility to be refocused on its primary vocation: the mutual assurance of survival. Among all the necessary conditions for such a refocusing, the decommodification of the moral impulse seems to be paramount.

The moment of truth may be nearer than we might believe when we look at the overflowing shelves of supermarkets and the websites strewn with commercial pop-ups and choruses of self-improvement experts and counsellors on how to make friends and influence people. The point is how to precede or forestall its coming with a moment of self-awakening. Not an easy task, to be sure: it would take nothing less than the whole of humanity, complete with its dignity and well-being, as well as the survival of the planet, its shared home, to be embraced by the universe of moral obligations.

6 January 2011

On justice, and how to know it is there

In the same *Indigo* essay to which I previously referred, and yet earlier in his study *The Idea of Justice* (Harvard University Press, 2009), Amartya Sen does not beat about the bush when he analyses the lessons to be drawn from the global economic slump of 2008. Whereas some very rich persons saw their fortunes somewhat diminished, it was the poorest people, people 'at the bottom of the pyramid', local or global, who were most badly affected by that slump: 'Families who were already worst placed to face any further adversity have often suffered from still greater deprivation, in the form of lasting joblessness, loss of housing and shelter, loss of medical care, and other deprivations that have plagued the lives of hundreds of millions of people.' The conclusion, Amartya Sen asserts, is all too obvious: if you want to correctly evaluate the severity of the current global crisis, examine 'what is happening to the lives of human beings, especially the less privileged people – their well-being and their freedom to lead decent human lives'.

Chronically deprived categories of people tend to learn to accept their lot and precisely because of its 'ordinariness', 'indisputability' and 'normality' suffer it meekly ('underprivileged people without hope of liberation often try to do just that to cope with the inescapability of the deprivation involved'). It is in a time of crisis that the routine, daily, perpetual and habitual inequality (indeed, polarization) in the distribution of privileges and deprivations is abruptly recast as defying 'the norm', as 'extraordinary', a fatal accident, an emergency – and so brutally drawn to the surface and brought into a dazzling light for everyone to note. We may add that because catastrophes as a rule affect different categories of people unequally, it is the degree of vulnerability to all sorts of natural, economic or social earthquakes and the high probability of being hit much more severely than other residents of the country or other members of humanity that are revealed as the defining feature of social *injustice*.

But wouldn't we rather begin with defining the standard of *justice*, so that we are better equipped to spot and isolate cases of injustice whenever and wherever they appear (or rather hide)? Easier said than done. Amartya Sen would not advise us to take this line. Asking what perfect justice would look like is 'a question in the answer to which there could be substantial differences even among very reasonable people'. Obviously, we may add, as reasonable people seasoned in the art of argumentation and rhetoric are to be found in each of the camps determined, in a bizarre reversal of Kant's categorical imperative, to flex the proposed universal standards to make them fit their own anything but universal interests; in other words, to summon the idea of justice to the defence of a particular injustice that rebounds as their privilege. There is little hope, then, that a debate about universal standards of justice will ever bear fruits palatable to everyone involved and so acquire genuine universality.

But there is yet another reason to be doubtful as to the advisability of such a debate. As Barrington Moore Jr pointed out a long time ago, the historical evidence shows beyond reasonable doubt that whereas people are quick to spot injustice in acts changing the prevailing state of affairs or the previously binding rules of the game, they tend to be abominably slow, if not downright inept, in decrying as 'unjust' much more adverse conditions once they have persisted long enough to be accepted as 'normal', intractable, immune to protests and resistant to change. It is similar to the apparently opposite case of 'pleasure', which, as Sigmund Freud observed, only tends to be felt at the moment when displeasure is removed, and is hardly ever produced by the continuous, monotonous presence of even the most pleasurable (that is, free from displeasure) conditions. In the language of semiotics, we may say that 'injustice' along with 'displeasure' are, contrary to appearances, the primary, 'unmarked' terms of the oppositions in which 'justice' along with 'pleasure' are the 'marked' members, that is, concepts deriving all their meaning from their opposition, denial and refutation in relation to the 'unmarked' ones. Whatever we know or imagine about the nature of *justice* is derived from the experience of *injustice* – just as it is from the experience of displeasure, and only from that experience, that we can learn or rather imagine what 'pleasure' might be like. In a nutshell: whenever we imagine or postulate 'justice' we tend to start from the cases of injustice that are currently the most salient, painful and offensive.

Since we start with widely varied experiences and sharply and often irreconcilably differing interests, we are unlikely ever to arrive at an uncontentious model of the 'just society'. Unable to resolve the quandary, we can only agree to the solution of a 'settlement' – reduced to a hard core evident to all, while being staunchly unprejudiced and resisting the temptation to pre-empt the future twists and turns of the continuing (and encouraged) polyvocal debate. I'd suggest the following formula as a 'settlement' of that kind: the 'just society' is a society permanently vigilant and sensitive to all cases of injustice, undertaking to take action to rectify them without waiting for the search for a universal model of justice to be completed. In somewhat different and perhaps simpler terms, a society mobilized to promote the well-being of the underdog; 'well-being' in this case including the capacity to make real the formal human right to a decent life – recasting 'freedom de jure' into 'freedom de facto'.

Implied in this choice of a settlement formula is a preference for Richard Rorty's 'politics of campaign' over its competitor, a 'politics of movement'. A 'politics of movement' starts by assuming an ideal model of, if not a 'perfectly' ('perfectly' meaning the *a priori* impossibility and undesirability of any further improvement), then at any rate a 'comprehensively' or 'fully' just society, and consequently measures and evaluates any proposed move by its impact on shortening the distance separating reality from the ideal, and not by how far it diminishes or increases the sum total of human suffering caused by present injustices. A 'politics of campaign' follows an opposite strategy: it starts by locating an indubitable case of suffering, proceeds to a diagnosis of the injustice that caused it, and then undertakes to correct it – without wasting time on a (clearly hopeless) attempt to solve (the clearly unresolvable) issue of the possible impact of this undertaking on bringing 'perfect justice' closer or delaying its arrival.

7 January 2011

On the internet, anonymity and irresponsibility

Reviewing in the *New York Times* of 3 January a collection of studies edited by Saul Levmore and Martha Nussbaum and called *The Offensive Internet*, Stanley Fish follows the line taken by most of its contributors, mapping the topic of the study being reviewed – the issue of the anonymous slander licensed by the internet versus demands for its legal prohibition or limitation – within the cognitive frame of 'freedom of speech'. Can one stand up against the glorious legacy of the First Amendment, the familiar assumption that freedom of speech cannot be overprotected, and demand that the voicing of certain opinions should be made illegal and a punishable offence? In 1995, Supreme Court Justice John Paul Stevens dismissed the potentially morbid consequences of the anonymity of information, arguing within the same frame and in the same spirit: he insisted that 'the inherent worth of...speech in terms of its capacity for informing the public does not depend upon the identity of its source, whether corporation, association, union, or individual'. Jürgen Habermas, by the way, would certainly, and rightly, disagree with that somewhat stretched and skewed interpretation of the First Amendment: his own theory of (ideal, undistorted) communication rested on the (empirically confirmed) supposition that precisely the opposite is true in offering and perceiving, absorbing and evaluating a message: most commonly, routinely, indeed matter-of-factly, we tend to judge the value of information by the quality of its source. This is why, as Habermas complained, communication tends, as a rule, to be 'distorted': *who* said it matters more and counts for more than *what* has been said. The value of information is enhanced or debased not so much by its content, as by the authority of its author or messenger. What inevitably follows is that in the event the information arrives without the name of its source attached people are likely to feel lost and unable to take a stance; where distorted communication is concerned, naming the source is an *enabling* act, allowing a decision to be made on whether to trust or ignore the message – and all or almost all communication in our type of society belongs in that 'distorted' category. (To be freed from distortion, communication would require genuine equality between participants, an equality not just around the debating table, but in 'real' life, offline or away from the debating chamber. That condition would require nothing less than exploding and levelling out the hierarchy of the speakers' authority; it would not suffice to tell people that the information needs to be judged on its own, not its author's, merits or vices for the condition to be met, and in all probability people would dismiss that advice or instruction as counterfactual, an evident travesty of life's rugged realities. Stanley Fish obliquely, and in an idiom different from Habermas's, admits that fact: 'Suppose I receive an anonymous note asserting that I have been betrayed by a friend. I will not know what to make of it – is it a cruel joke, a slander, a warning, a test? But if I manage to identify the note's author – it's a friend or an enemy or a known gossip – I will be able to reason about its meaning because I will know what kind of person composed it and what motives that person might have had.')

All these suggestions and reservations are, however, only side issues in this case (as I have signalled by putting them in brackets); what really matters is whether the issue of the anonymity of opinion propagated and enabled by the internet needs to be put, judged and resolved within the framework of *freedom of speech* at all, or whether its true social importance, one that needs to become and be kept as the focus of public concern, is its relation to the problem of a *person's responsibility* for her or his actions and for their consequences... The genuine adversary of internet-style anonymity is not the principle of freedom of speech, but the principle of responsibility: internet-style anonymity is first and foremost, and most importantly socially, an officially endorsed licence for irresponsibility and a public lesson in its practice – online and offline alike – an enormously large and venomous anti-social fly allowed to despoil an enormously huge barrel of ointment advertised as, and allegedly being dedicated to, promoting the cause of sociality and socializing...

The more potentially deadly the weapons, the more difficult it should be to obtain permission to possess and carry them (though there should be no blank-cheque permission, whether liberally or sparingly granted, embracing their use). The internet, however, (along with the bygone Wild West and the mythical jungle), is a stark exemption to that rule so widely assumed to be indispensable for a civilized life. Slander, invective, calumny, slur, smear, casting aspersions and defamation belong to the deadliest of weapons: deadly to persons, but also to the social fabric. Their possession and use, particularly their indiscriminate use, is a crime in offline life (commonly called 'real life', though it is far from clear which one, online or offline life, would win a competition for the title of reality); but it has not been recognized and proclaimed to be a crime in the online world. And it can only be guessed which of the two worlds, online or offline, will assimilate to the other and adjust its rules to the other's standards; which will eventually surrender to the pressure, and which will press harder for surrender. For the time being, though, the online world has a considerable advantage over its competitor: in the online world, unlike in the offline one, everybody can be a 007: in the online world, everyone can boast a licence to kill. Better still, everyone can kill without even such a trifling effort as applying for a licence. It's impossible to deny the seductive power of such an advantage. And remember that every kind of seduction pre-selects its seduced...

A 'floating responsibility' (that is, a responsibility detached from its carriers with agents relieved of their responsibility) means, as Hannah Arendt warned a long time ago, the 'responsibility of nobody'. Arendt arrived at that conclusion while closely watching the gruesome practices of bureaucracy, suspected at that time of being an awesome menace requiring our civilization and humanity to find ways to counter it. She did not live to witness the scattering of that invention and long-time speciality of modern bureaucracy across more places than bureaucracy, confined to its technically primitive, cottage-industry appliances, could dream of reaching...

16 January 2011

On collateral damage and casualties of cuts

It takes only a few minutes and a couple of signatures to destroy what took thousands of brains and twice as many hands many years to build.

This is, perhaps, the most awesome and sinister, yet irresistible attraction of destruction at all times – though at no time has the temptation been more indomitable than in the hurried lives lived in our speed-and-acceleration obsessed world. In our liquid modern society of consumers, the eviction, removal and disposal industry built on getting rid of things is one of the very few businesses assured of continuous growth and immune to the vagaries of consumer markets. That business, after all, is absolutely indispensable if markets are to be allowed to proceed in the only way they are able to act: stumbling from one round of overshooting targets to another, each time clearing away the resulting waste together with the facilities blamed for turning it out.

This is, obviously, an exceedingly wasteful fashion in which to proceed; and, indeed, excess and wastefulness are the principal endemic banes of the consumerist economy, pregnant as they are with a large amount of collateral damage and still larger echelons of collateral victims. Excess and waste are the consumerist economy's most loyal, indeed inseparable, fellow travellers – bound to remain inseparable until (shared) death do them part. It happens, though, that the timetables of the excess and waste cycles, normally scattered over a wide spectrum of the consumerist economy and following their own unsynchronized rhythms, synchronize, coordinate, overlap and merge, making it all but untenable and unattainable to simply patch up cracks and clefts with the economic equivalent of the cosmetics of face-lifts and skin transplants. Where cosmetics won't suffice, wholesale surgery is called for, and – however reluctantly – resorted to. The time arrives for 'retrenchment', 'rearrangement' or 'readjustment' (politically favoured codenames for the slowdown of consumerist activities) and for 'austerity' (the codename for cuts in state expenditure) in the hope of bringing closer a 'recovery led by consumers' (codename for using the cash spared from Treasury coffers to recapitalize the agencies nourishing and energizing consumerism, mostly banks and issuers of credit cards).

This is the time span we currently live in, in the aftermath of a massive accumulation and congestion of excess and waste and the resulting collapse of the credit system with all its uncountable collateral casualties. In the credit-supported life strategy of 'enjoy now, pay later' – fostered, nourished and boosted by the joint forces of marketing techniques and governmental policies (drilling successive cohorts of students in the art and the habit of living on credit) – consumer markets found a magic wand with which to transform hosts of Cinderellas, inactive and so still good-for-nothing consumers, into crowds of (profit-generating) debtors; even though, also like Cinderella, only for one ravishing night. The wand did its magic with the help of assurances that when the time to pay up arrived, the needed cash would be easy to extract from the accrued market value of the wonders purchased. Prudently left out of the advertising leaflets was the fact that market values go on accruing *because* of the assurance that the ranks of willing and capable buyers of those wonders will keep on growing; in simpler terms, the reasoning behind such assurances was, just like the bubbles they inflated, circular. If you believed the pushers of credit, you would expect that the mortgage loan you took out for your house would be repaid by the house itself, as it continued to rise in price just as it had through recent years, being bound to go on rising well after the loan was repaid in full. Or you would believe that the loan you took out to finance your university study would be repaid, with huge interest, by the fabulous salaries and perks of office awaiting the holders of diplomas...

The successive bubbles have now burst, and the truth did out – though, as in most such cases, *after* the damage had been done. And instead of the gains tantalizingly promised to be privatized by the invisible hand of the market, the losses are now being forcibly nationalized by a government bent on promoting consumer liberties and eulogizing consumption as the shortest and surest shortcut to happiness. It is the most severely hit victims of the economy of excess and waste who are forced to pay its costs, whether or not they trusted its sustainability and whether or not they believed its promises and willingly surrendered to its temptations. Those who inflated the bubble show few if any signs of suffering. It is not *their* houses that are repossessed, not *their* unemployment benefits that are cut, not *their* children's playgrounds that are condemned to stay unbuilt. It is the people cajoled or forced into dependency on borrowing who are punished.

Among the millions punished are hundreds of thousands of youngsters who believed, or were given no choice but to behave *as if* they believed that the room at the top is boundless, that a university diploma is all you need to be let in, and that once you get in the repayment of the loans you took out the road would be childishly easy, considering the new credit-worthiness that comes together with an address at the top – but who are now facing the prospect of scribbling innumerable job applications hardly ever dignified with an answer, of infinitely lengthy unemployment, and of the need to accept prospect-less and wobbly jobs, miles below the top rooms, as their sole option...

Every generation has its measure of outcasts. There are people in each generation assigned to outcast status because a 'generation change' brings a significant change in life conditions and life demands that is likely to force realities to depart from the expectations implanted by the status quo ante and devalue the skills they trained in and promoted, and therefore to render at least some of the new arrivals, those not flexible or prompt enough to adapt to the emerging standards, ill-prepared to cope with novel challenges – while unarmed against their pressures. It does not happen often, however, that the plight of being cast out stretches to embrace a *generation as a whole*. This may be what is happening now...

Several generational changes have been noted in the course of the postwar history of Europe. A 'boom generation' came first, followed by two generations called respectively X and Y; most recently (though not as recently as the shock of the collapse of the Reaganite/Thatcherite economy), the impending arrival of the Z generation was announced. Each of these generational changes were more or less traumatic events; in each case some break in continuity was signalled, requiring sometimes painful readjustments caused by a clash between inherited and learned expectations and unanticipated realities. And yet, looking back from the second decade of the twenty-first century, we can hardly fail to notice that when confronted with the profound changes brought about by the latest economic collapse, each of the previous passages between generations may well seem to be the epitome of neat and smooth intergenerational continuity...

After several decades of rising expectations, present-day graduate newcomers to adult life confront expectations that are *falling* – and much too steeply and abruptly for any hope of a gentle and safe landing. There was bright, dazzling light at the end of every one of the few tunnels through which their predecessors might have been forced to pass in the course of their lives; now a long, dark tunnel stretches instead behind every one of the few blinking, flickering and fast fading lights vainly trying to pierce the gloom.

This is the first postwar generation facing the prospect of downward mobility. Their elders were trained to expect, matter-of-factly, that children would aim higher and reach further than they themselves had managed (or had been allowed by the now bygone state of affairs) to dare to achieve: they expected the intergenerational 'reproduction of success' to go on breaking their own records as easily as they themselves had overtaken the achievements of their parents. Generations of parents were used to expecting that their children would have a yet wider range of choices, each more attractive than the other; be even better educated, climb even higher in the hierarchy of learning and professional excellence, be richer and feel even more secure. The parents' point of arrival, so they believed, would be their children's starting point – and a point with even more roads stretching ahead, all leading upwards.

The youngsters of the generation now entering or preparing to enter the so-called 'labour market' have been groomed and honed to believe that their task in life is to outshoot and leave behind their parents' success stories, and that such a task (barring a cruel blow of fate or an eminently curable inadequacy of their own) would be fully within their capacity. However far their parents had reached, they would reach further. So, at any rate, they had been taught and indoctrinated to believe. Nothing prepared them for the arrival of the hard, uninviting and inhospitable new world of the downgrading of grades, the devaluation of earned merits, doors shown and locked, the volatility of jobs and the stubbornness of joblessness, the transience of prospects and the durability of defeat; a new world of stillborn projects and frustrated hopes, and of chances ever more conspicuous by their absence.

The last decades were times of the unbounded expansion of all forms of higher education and of an unstoppable rise in the size of student cohorts. A university degree promised plum jobs, prosperity and glory: the volume of rewards steadily rising to match the steadily expanding ranks of degree holders. With coordination between demand and offer ostensibly preordained, assured and well nigh automatic, the seductive power of the promise was all but impossible to resist. Now, however, the throngs of the seduced are turning wholesale, and almost overnight, into crowds of the frustrated. For the first time in living memory, a *whole class of graduates* faces a high probability, almost a certainty, of ad hoc, temporary, insecure and part-time jobs and unpaid 'trainee' pseudo-jobs deceitfully rebranded 'practice' – all considerably below their acquired skills and eons below the level of their expectations; or of a stretch of unemployment lasting longer than it'll take for the next class of graduates to add their names to the already uncannily long job-centre waiting lists.

In a capitalist society like ours, geared above all to the defence and preservation of extant privileges and only as a distant (and much less respected or attended to) second to lifting the rest out of deprivation, this class of graduates, high on goals but low on means, has no one to turn to for assistance and remedy. The people at the helm, whether on the right or the left of the political spectrum, are up in arms in protection of their currently muscular constituencies – against the newcomers who are still slow in flexing their laughably immature muscles, and in all probability are deferring any serious attempt to flex them in earnest until after the next general election. Just as we all, collectively, and regardless of the peculiarities of generations, tend to be all too eager to defend our comforts against the livelihoods of the generations not yet born...

Noting the 'anger, even hate' that can be observed in the 2010 class of graduates, political scientist Louis Chauvel, in his article in *Le Monde* of 4 January, 'Les jeunes sont mal partis', asks how much time it will take to combine the rancour of the French contingent of baby-boomers infuriated by the threats to their pension nests, with that of the class of 2010 denied the exercise of their right to earn a pension. But combine into what, we may (and should) ask? Into a new war of generations? Into a new leap into the pugnacity of the extremist fringes surrounding an increasingly despondent and dejected middle? Or into supragenerational consent that this world of ours, so prominent for using duplicity as its survival weapon and for burying hopes alive, is no longer sustainable and in need of an already grossly delayed refurbishment?

What about the graduate classes yet to come? And what about the society in which, sooner rather than later, they will have to take over the tasks their elders were presumed to perform and for better or worse did? That society whose sum total of skills, knowledge, competitiveness, stamina and guts, its ability to face challenges and capacity to get the better of them and to self-improve, will be determined by them – whether they like it or not, and whether by design or default.

It would be premature and irresponsible to speak of the planet as a whole as entering the post-industrial era. But it would be no less irresponsible to deny that Great Britain entered such an era quite a few decades ago. Through the twentieth century, British industry shared the lot suffered by British agriculture in the nineteenth – industry started the century overcrowded, and left it depopulated (in fact, in all the 'most developed' Western countries industrial workers currently constitute less than 18 per cent of the working population). What has been all too often overlooked, however, is that in parallel with the shrinking in the numbers of industrial workers in the national labour force, there was also a shrinking in the ranks of industrialists among the elite of wealth and political power. We continue to live in a capitalist society, but the capitalists who set the tune and pay the pipers are no longer owners of mines, docks, steelworks or automobile plants. On the list of the richest 1 per cent of Americans, only one in six names belongs to an industrial entrepreneur; the rest are financiers, lawyers, doctors, scientists, architects, programmers, designers, and all sorts of stage, screen and stadium celebrities. The biggest money is now to be found in the handling and allocation of finances and the invention of new technical gadgets, utensils of communication, marketing and publicity gimmicks, as well as in the universe of arts and entertainment; in other words, in new and still unexploited imaginative and catching ideas. It is people with brilliant and useful (read, sellable) ideas who now inhabit the rooms at the top. It is people like that who contribute most to what is currently understood as 'economic growth'. The primary 'deficit resources' from which capital is made and whose possession and management provides the primary source of wealth and power are nowadays, in the post-industrial era, knowledge, inventiveness, imagination, the ability to think and the courage to think differently – qualities which universities were called on to create, disseminate and instil.

About a hundred years ago, at the time of the Boer War, panic struck people concerned with the might and prosperity of the nation at the news of large and growing numbers of undernourished recruits with decrepit bodies or in poor health, and so physically and mentally unfit for factory floors and battlefields. Now is the time to panic at the prospect of the rising numbers of people who are undereducated (certainly undereducated by the world's fast-rising standards), and so unfit for research laboratories, designer workshops, lecture theatres, artists' studios or information networks, that may result from the shrinking of university resources and the falling numbers of high-class university graduates. The government's cuts in the higher education funding manage to be, both at the same time, cuts in the life prospects of the generation now coming of age, and in the future standard and standing of British civilization, as well as in Britain's European and worldwide status and role.

Cuts in government funding come together with the uncommonly steep, indeed savage, rises in university fees. We are used to feeling alarmed by, and fulminating against, a few per cent rise in the cost of train tickets, beef or electricity; we tend to be aghast and baffled, however, in the face of a rise of 300 per cent – incapacitated and disarmed, unsure how to react. In the arsenal of our defensive weapons, there are none we can resort to – just as happened in the recent events when those billions and trillions of dollars were pumped in one go by governments into the strongrooms of banks after dozens of years of penny-pinching and feverish litigation about a few millions that were deducted or should have been added, but were not, to the budgets of schools, hospitals, welfare funds and urban renovation projects. We can hardly imagine the misery and anguish of our grandchildren when they awake to the inheritance of a hitherto unimaginable volume of national debt clamouring for repayment; we are still not ready to visualize it, even now, when courtesy of our con-lib government we have been offered the chance of tasting the first sample spoonfuls of the bitter brew which they, our grandchildren, will be force-fed by the cauldronful. And we can hardly imagine as yet the full reach of the social and cultural devastation that is bound to follow the erection of a monetary version of the walls of Berlin or Palestine at the entry to our knowledge distribution centres. Yet we must, and we should – at our shared future peril.

Talent, insightfulness, inventiveness, adventurousness – all those rough stones waiting to be polished into diamonds by talented, insightful, inventive and adventurous teachers inside university buildings – are spread more or less evenly through the human species, even though artificial barriers erected by humans on the path from *zoon*, the 'bare life', to *bios*, the social life, prevent us from perceiving it. Rough diamonds do not select the lodes in which nature cast them and care little about divisions invented by humans; even though those divisions invented by humans take care of selecting some of them into a class earmarked for polishing, and relegating others to the category of 'might have been' – as well as doing all they can to cover up the traces of that operation. A tripling of fees will inevitably decimate the ranks of the youngsters growing up in the mean districts of social and cultural deprivation, yet determined and daring enough to knock on the university doors of opportunity – and so it will also deprive the rest of the nation of the rough diamonds those youngsters used to contribute year by year. And as success in life, and particularly upward social mobility, tends nowadays to be enabled, prompted and set in motion by the meeting of knowledge with talent, insightfulness, inventiveness and spirit of adventure, a tripling of fees will pull British society at least half a century back in its drive towards classlessness. Just a few decades after being flooded with scholarly discoveries of a 'farewell to class', we may expect, in not so distant a future, a spate of treatises to 'welcome back, class – all is forgotten'.

Expect it indeed we may; and therefore – we, academics, being the socially responsible creatures we need and are expected to be, and sometimes are – should worry about a damage even more damaging than the immediate effect of throwing universities to the mercy of consumer markets (which is what the combination of the state retreating from its patronage and a tripling of fees amounts to): in terms of redundancies, the suspension or abandonment of research projects, and probably also a further worsening of the staff/students ratio, and so also of teaching conditions and quality. And the resurrection of class divisions is to be expected, as more than enough reasons have been created for less well-off parents to think twice before committing their children to burdening themselves in only three years with more debt than they themselves incurred in their lifetimes; and for the children of those parents, watching their slightly older acquaintances lining up in front of the job agencies, to think twice about the sense of it all – the sense of committing themselves to three years of unremitting work and living in poverty only to confront a set of options at the end not much more prepossessing than the ones they currently face...

Well, it takes only a few minutes and a couple of signatures to destroy what took thousands of brains and twice as many hands many years to build.

17 January 2011

On one of many pages torn out from the history of democratic crusade

Half a century ago to the day, the first president democratically elected in the nominally 'post-colonial' Africa, Patrice Lumumba, thirty-five years old, was beaten, tortured and shot – just a few months after his election, certified for its democratic flawlessness by Western observers, envoys from American and Belgian democracies, embarked on spreading the democratic gospel on the lands vacated by colonial garrisons. To be sure, the garrisons had left the country, but Lumumba was left with just a few Congolese graduates in a land of 15 million people, and only three black faces among the 5,000 senior officers in the country's administration who stayed and took to sabotaging the will of the newly born nation, expressed democratically in the ballot boxes, once the polling stations had closed. The highest ranking Belgian officials of that old/new state bureaucracy selected the codename 'Satan' for the new democratically elected president. Can you imagine a fiend more hateful and repellent than someone demanding restitution and return of the opulent country's riches, its diamond, gold, uranium and copper mines, to the people from whom they had been stolen? Adam Hochschild, who visited the Congo capital shortly after these events, recalls in today's edition of the *New York Times* 'the triumphant, macho satisfaction with which two young American Embassy officials – much later identified as CIA men – talked with me over drinks about the death of someone they regarded not as an elected leader but as an upstart enemy of the United States'.

Attempts on Lumumba's life started on the very day after his election. When the plan to poison him by an agent dispatched by the CIA failed, the US and Belgian governments smuggled cash and weapons to Lumumba's local competitors, hastily converted into 'opposition forces', and orchestrated the secession and 'proclamation of independence' of Katanga, a region of Congo richly endowed with mineral treasures. The first task put by their American and Belgian mandatories to the new rulers of the newly 'liberated' country was to put an end to the insubordinate and intractable president, once he was demoted and promptly delivered to them by the Congolese 'democratic opposition'. The rulers of Katanga acquitted themselves of their commission impeccably, following their overseas principals' briefing to the dot.

The next thirty-two years of the 'independent republic' of Katanga, the story of the ruthless, gory and corrupt rule of the thief-butcher Joseph Mobutu, a dictator showered with bribes and praise by the White House and proclaimed by George Bush Sr to be 'one of our most valued friends', are years which many of the leaders of our democratic world would dearly wish to forget, together with the demotion, trial and imprisonment of the democratically elected Mohammad Mossadeq of oil-rich Persia (see the top secret CIA report on Mossadeq's overthrow at www. iranonline.com/newsroom/Archive/Mossadeq) and the subsequent long and still unfinished agony of the country under the Shah's and ayatollahs' dictatorships, as well as the murder of the democratically elected Salvador Allende of manganese-rich Chile and the subsequent ruthless and gory warlordship of Augusto Pinochet; as they have forgotten the fiftieth anniversary of the murder of

Patrice Lumumba, the first democratically elected president in an African country.

18 January 2011

On immoral axes and moral axemen

During the last world war, George Orwell mused: 'As I write, highly civilized human beings are flying overhead, trying to kill me. They do not feel any enmity against me as an individual, nor I against them. They are "only doing their duty", as the saying goes.' A few years later, scanning the vast multi-tiered graveyard called Europe in search of the kind of humans who managed to do that to other humans, Hannah Arendt laid bare the 'floating' habit of responsibility inside the bureaucratic body; she named the consequences of that flotation the 'responsibility of nobody'. More than half a century later, we could say much the same of the current state of the killing arts.

Continuity, then? Oh yes, there is continuity, though true to continuity's habits, in company with a few discontinuities…The major novelty is the effacing of differences in status between means and ends. Or, rather, the war of independence ending in the victory of axes over the axemen. It is now the axes who select the ends: the heads to be axed. The axemen can do little more to stop them (that is, to change the minds they do not have or appeal to the feelings they do not possess) than the legendary sorcerer's apprentice could (this allegory is by no means fanciful: as Pentagon correspondent Thom Shanker and technology correspondent Matt Richtel put it in today's *New York Times*, 'just as the military has long pushed technology forward, it is now at the forefront in figuring out how humans can cope with technology without being overwhelmed by it'. And as the neuroscientist Art Kramer sees the situation, 'there is information overload at every level of the military – from the general to the soldier on the ground.' Everybody in the army, 'from the general to the soldier on the ground', has been demoted from the sorcerer's office to the lowly rank of his apprentice.

Since 11 September 2001, the amount of 'intelligence' gathered by the cutting-edge technology at the US Army's disposal has risen

1,600 per cent. It is not that the axemen have lost their consciences or have been immunized against moral scruples; they simply can't cope with the volume of information amassed by the gadgets they operate. The gadgets, as a matter of fact, can now do as well (or as badly...) *with* or *without* their help, thank you. Kick the axemen away from their screens and you'd hardly notice their absence if you looked at the distribution of results.

By the start of the twenty-first century, military technology had managed to float and so 'depersonalize' responsibility to an extent unimaginable in Orwell's or Arendt's time. 'Smart', 'intelligent' missiles or 'drones' have taken over decision-making and the selection of targets from both the rank-and-file and the highest placed ranks of the military machine. I would suggest that the most seminal technological developments in recent years have not been sought and accomplished in the murderous powers of weapons, but in the area of an 'adiaphorization' of military killing (that is, removing it from the category of acts subject to moral evaluation). As Günther Anders warned after Nagasaki, but still well before Vietnam, Afghanistan or Iraq, 'one wouldn't gnash one's teeth when pressing a button...A key is a key.' Whether pressing the key starts a kitchen contraption making ice-cream, feeds electric current into a network, or lets loose the Horsemen of the Apocalypse makes no difference. 'The gesture initiating the Apocalypse would not differ from any of the other gestures – and it would be performed, like all other identical gestures, by a similarly routine-guided and routine-bored operator.' 'If something symbolizes the satanic nature of our situation, it is precisely that innocence of the gesture,'[4] Anders concludes with the negligibility of the effort and thought needed to set off a cataclysm – *any* cataclysm, including 'globocide'...

What is new is the 'drone', aptly called 'Predator', that has taken over the task of gathering and processing information. The electronic equipment of the drone excels in performing its task. But which task? Just as the manifest function of an axe is to enable the axeman to execute the convict, the manifest function of the drone is to enable its operator to locate the object of the execution. But the drone that excels in that function and keeps flooding the operator with tides of information he is unable to digest, let alone process promptly and swiftly, 'in real time', may be performing another function, latent and not spoken about: that of exonerating the operator from the moral guilt that would haunt him were he fully and truly in charge of selecting the convicts for execution; and, even more importantly, of reassuring the operator in advance that if a mistake happens, it won't be blamed on his immorality. If 'innocent people' are killed, it is a technical fault, not a moral failure or sin – and judging from the statute books most certainly not a crime. As Shanker and Richtel put it, 'drone-based sensors have given rise to a new class of wired warriors who must filter the information sea. But sometimes they are drowning.' But is not the capacity to drown the operator's mental (and so, obliquely but inevitably, moral) faculties included in the drone's design? Is not drowning the operator the paramount function of the drone? When, last February, twenty-three Afghan wedding guests were killed, the button-pushing operators could blame it on the screens turned 'drool buckets': they got lost just by staring into them. There were children among the bombs' victims, but the operators 'did not adequately focus on them amid the swirl of data' – 'much like a cubicle worker who loses track of an impor-tant e-mail under the mounting pile'. Well, no one would accuse that worker in an office cubicle of moral failure...

Starting off a cataclysm (including, as Anders insists, 'globo-cide') has now become even easier and more plausible than it used to be when Anders wrote down his warnings. The 'routine-bored operator' has been joined by his colleague and his probable replacement and successor – the chap with his eyes fixed on a 'drool bucket', and his mind drowning in a 'swirl of data'...

20 January 2011

On Berlusconi, and on Italy

Preparing a special issue dedicated to the evaluation of Berlusconi's continuing rule, *Macromega* asked me to add my opinion on how it looks when it is seen 'from far away'. What follows is my reply:

Rather than try to compose my own indictment of the 'Berlusconi phenomenon' and add a few more pages to the already unmanage-ably thick files amassed for his – unlikely to be held in the foresee-able future – trial, let me remind your readers of the verdicts of the great Portuguese man of letters José Saramago, who, frustrated by the stultifying dilatoriness of Italian *legal justice*, would not meekly wait for the court of the Italian *conscience* to be called into session. Saramago, alas, won't be able to respond to your questionnaire in person, so let me serve as his messenger, or self-appointed spokesman. I'll select all my quotations from *O Caderno*, a sort of a diary conducted by Saramago in 2008–9 and published in 2010 in Lisbon by Editorial Caminho.

Saramago, a supreme master of word-craft, is known to select his words with truly Benedictine care and uncanny precision. He knew that in Italian 'the term for criminal (delinquenza) has a negative weight far stronger than that in any other language spoken in Europe'. All the same, he did not hesitate to apply that term to Berlusconi (see his entry dated 9 June 2009): Berlusconi 'has been seen to commit a variety of crimes, always of demonstrable seriousness. That said, he not only disobeys the law but, worse still, manufactures new laws to protect his public and private interests, which are those of a politician, businessman and an escort of minors.' Nor does Saramago hesitate to conclude that Berlusconi 'has sunk into the most abject and utter depravity'. In a note entered a month earlier, on 9 May 2009, Saramago called Berlusconi 'the Catiline of present-day Italy', with the proviso that, unlike his ancient prototype, Berlusconi 'has no need to seize power, for it is already his, and he has more than enough money to buy all the accomplices he could possibly need, including judges, members of parliament, deputies, and senators'. But he sought in vain for an 'Italian voice' repeating almost verbatim after Cicero, only changing the name of the addressee: 'How long, Berlusconi, will you abuse our patience thus?' And it was that absence of voice that remained the most frightening mystery to Saramago – yet for him (just as it is for me) it was not a mystery of *Berlusconi*, but of *Italy*. Because Berlusconi, as Saramago noted on 15 May 2009, 'seems to have accomplished the feat of dividing the Italian population into two camps: those who wish to be like him and those who already are like him'. But Saramago still had hopes for that 'seems', and that the nightmare would (sooner rather than later) disperse.

The history of Italy, in Saramago's eyes, as in the eyes of so many Europeans, looks 'like an enormously long rosary of geniuses, including painters, sculptors and architects; musicians, philosophers, writers, and poets...an endless list of sublime individuals who produced a large share of the best that humanity has ever thought, imagined or achieved'. There has never been a shortage of noble spirits in Italian history. So – Cicero, where are you, why have you deserted your post when Italy as we know and love it is once more in danger?!

In an entry dated 18 February 2009, Saramago complains, as so many European lovers of Italy would repeat after him: 'The most offended party in all this is me. Yes, specifically me. My love for Italy is offended, along with my love for Italian culture and Italian history. Even my tenacious hope that the nightmare will somehow end and Italy will return to the exalted spirit inspired by Verdi, who was in his time its best manifestation, is offended.' Having twice – twice! – elected 'this disease, this virus that threatens moral death to the land of Verdi', this 'deep sickness that needs to be wrested from the Italian consciousness before its venom ends up running through the veins and destroying the heart of one of the richest of European cultures', the Italian people have entered 'the road to ruin', 'dragging through the dirt the values of liberty and dignity...'

'Are the Italians really going to permit this to happen?' asks Saramago, in the utmost bafflement and despair. And I share his concern in full.

On another, though in a few respects similar historical occasion, Karl Marx opined that no nation, just as no woman, can be forgiven a moment of weakness in which any rogue can rape her...

28 January 2011

On keeping him in by being kept out

A few months before the last US presidential elections, I said the following in a conversation with Giuliano Battiston in response to his query: 'Could [Obama's] election be interpreted as a sign that the American political system has definitively broken the link between demos and ethnos and that America is going toward a more conscious post-ethnic society?':

Obama has to be careful not to bid for power in the name of the 'downtrodden and oppressed' masses, who are for that reason proclaimed inferior – and whose imposed and stereotyped ineptitude, indignity and infamy rubs off on him because of his ethnically/racially inherited/ascribed classification. And he is not running for power on a wave of rebellion by the 'downtrodden and oppressed' or by a 'social/political movement', as their spokesman, plenipotentiary and avenger. What his advance and elevation is intended to prove – as in all probability it will – is that a collective stigma can be washed away from *selected* individuals; in other words, that *some* individuals among categories oppressed and discriminated against possess qualities that 'outweigh' their participation in a collective, categorial inferiority; and those qualities may equal, or even surpass those boasted of by competitors unburdened by the categorial stigma. Such a phenomenon does not necessarily invalidate the assumption of the categorial inferiority. It should rather be perceived (and is by many) as a perverse reassertion of the assumption: here is an individual who, almost in Baron Münchhausen's style, has lifted himself out of the bog by his own bootstraps: through his individual talents and stamina, not thanks to his belonging but despite it – and proving by the same token not so much the grossly underestimated valour and virtues of 'his people', as the tolerance and generosity of their social superiors, whose superiority manifests itself in their readiness to allow ambitious and talented individuals from the inferior category to join them and attempt to climb to the top, as well as in their readiness to quash many of the widespread objections to social and political acceptance of those who succeed. This does not mean, though, that the advance of the individuals who jumped at such an opportunity will lift the category as a whole, the 'category as such', from its inferior social position and open up wider life prospects to all its members. The long semi-dictatorial rule of Margaret Thatcher did not bring the social equality of women; what it proved was that some women may defeat men at their own macho game. Many of the Jews who managed to emerge from the ghettos in the nineteenth century and could pass for Germans (or so they tried to believe) did pretty little for the ascribed or imputed brethren they left behind to lift them out of poverty and protect them from legal and social discrimination. And just as the personal promotion of Margaret Thatcher did not make the British establishment less 'masculine', the career of the escapees from the Jewish ghetto did not make Germany less nationalistic. Nor did it shorten the distance separating the discriminating from the discriminated. If anything, the opposite happened...

Many of the most vociferous and dedicated ideologues and practitioners of the most radical varieties of the up and coming nationalisms in the twentieth century were newcomers from 'ethnic minorities', or 'naturalized' foreigners (Stalin and Hitler included). A Jew, Benjamin Disraeli, solidified and fortified the Empire of the British. The war-cry of the 'assimilated' was 'anything you can do, I can do better' – a promise and determination to be more Catholic than the Pope, to out-German the Germans, out-Pole the Poles or to out-Russian the Russians in enriching their respective cultures and promoting their respective 'national interests' (feats which all too often were held against them, and taken to be proof of their duplicity and insidious intentions). Among all those things they were bent on 'doing better' than the natives were also (for many of the assimilated) the indifference to the plight and the interests of their own 'community of origin' that marked the thoughts and deeds of the 'natives'...

About a year after Obama's move into the White House, when my earlier premonitions had turned into observations, I added (in one of the letters published in *La Repubblica*) the following comments by Naomi Klein:

> Non-elite blacks and Latinos are losing significant ground, with their homes and jobs slipping away from them at much higher rate than from whites. So far, Obama has been unwilling to adopt policies specifically geared toward closing this ever-widening divide. The result may well leave minorities with the worst of all worlds: the pain of a full-scale racist backlash without the benefits of policies that alleviate daily hardships.

Another year has passed and much more water has flowed under the bridges of the Potomac River, but much the same messages flow from the Oval Office to America's black urban ghettos. Messages in words, as well as messages of silence...As Charles M. Blow observes in today's *New York Times*, 'It was only the second time since Harry S. Truman's State of the Union address in 1948 that such a speech by a Democratic president did not include a single mention of poverty or the plight of the poor.' Little doubt remains: the hope of the deprived, downtrodden and humiliated turned his back on those who sent him to his office (that is, 95 per cent of black voters and 67 per cent of Hispanic voters; 73 per cent of those earning below $15,000 a year, 60 per cent of those earning $5,000–$30,000, and 55 per cent of the $30,000–$50,000 a year earners). He kicked away the ladder by which he climbed to that office in which State of the Union addresses are annually composed. Brian Miller, the executive director on the United for a Fair Economy research group, comments on the message which Obama left out of his address, even if his way of ruling America all too clearly conveyed it to those who helped him into power: 'With 42 per cent of blacks and 37 per cent of Latinos lacking the funds to meet minimal household expenses for even three months should they become unemployed, cutting public assistance programs will have devastating impacts on black and Latino workers.'

'My faith in him [the President] as a fervent crusader for the poor and disenfranchised has taken yet another nose dive...[The President] appears to be moving, often at a full sprint, away from the people who once carried him' is how Charles Blow sums up his own comments. And, saddened, he asks the questions which he must now see as purely rhetorical, just as I do:

> For the poor, this is the Obama conundrum. He was obviously the best choice in 2008. And judging by the current cast of Republican presidential contenders, he could well be the best choice in 2012. But does that give him license to obviate his moral responsibility to his electoral devotees? Can and should they take his snubs as a necessary consequence of political warfare as he makes every effort to tack back to the middle and reconnect with those whose opinion of him vacillates between contempt on a bad day and sufferance on a good one? Does keeping him in the White House dictate keeping them in the shadows?

30 January 2011

On people on the streets

Under the date of 14 July 1789, the king of France, Louis XVI, entered in his diary just one word: *Rien*. On that day a crowd of Parisian sans-culottes flooded onto the kind of streets which were not in the habit of being visited by *les misérables*, not *en masse* at any rate – and certainly not to linger. This day they did, and would not leave until they had overwhelmed the guards and captured the Bastille.

But how was Louis XVI to know? The thought of a crowd (that 'great unwashed', as Henry Peter Brougham was to dismiss some other people taking to some other streets a good few decades after the fall of the Bastille) turning history back to front or front to back, depending which side you were looking from, was not yet an idea to be taken seriously. Much water needed to flow under the Seine, Rhine or Thames before the arrival and the presence of the 'mob' (a sobriquet coined from 'mobile vulgus', 'rabble on the move') on the historical stage was noted, acknowledged – and feared, never to be dismissed again. After the warnings and alarms raised by the likes of Gustave le Bon, Georges Sorel or Ortega y Gasset, writers of diaries would not write *'rien'* when they heard of crowds roaming the squares of the city centre; most likely, however, they would replace it with a huge question mark. All of them: those who contemplate, like Hillary Clinton, a vision of a democratically elected parliament rising from the ashes of popular fury; those who nervously scan the crowd flooding Tahrir Square for the would-be founder of the next Islamic republic; and those who dream of the crowd righting the wrongs of wrongdoers and doing justice to the makers of injustice...

Joseph Conrad, a man of the sea by choice, is remembered as proclaiming that 'nothing is so seductive, so disillusioning or so enthralling as life on the sea'. Whereas, some years later, Elias Canetti was to choose the sea (alongside fire, forest, sand, etc.) as one of the most poignant and illuminating metaphors for the human crowd. It was especially fitting perhaps for one of the several varieties of crowds he named, the *reversal* crowd, that, so to speak, *instant re-volution* that turns things momentarily into their oppositions: jailed into jailers, jailers into jailed, herd into shepherd, (lonely) shepherd into sheep – and squeezes and congeals a bagful of crumbs into a monolithic whole, while recasting the crowd into an individual: an indivisible subject of 'Nous ne sommes rien, soyons tout!' sort. One could stretch that 'reversal' idea to embrace the act of reversal itself: 'In the crowd,' wrote Canetti, 'the individual feels that he is transcending the limits of his own person.' The individual does not feel he is dissolving, but expanding: it is he, the negligible *loner*, who is now reincarnated as *the many* – the impression the hall of mirrors tries to reproduce, with limited and inferior effect.

The crowd also means an instant liberation from phobias: 'There is nothing that man fears more than the touch of the unknown,' says Canetti. 'He wants to see what is reaching towards him, and to be able to recognize or at least classify it. Man always tends to avoid physical contact with anything strange.' But in the crowd that fear of the unknown is paradoxically quashed by being reversed; the fear of being touched dissipates in a public rehearsal of squeezing out inter-individual space – in the course of the many turning into one, and the one into the many, the space recycles its role of separating and isolating into one of merging and blending...

The formative experience that led Canetti to that reading of crowd psychology was when in 1922 he joined a mass demonstration protesting the assassination of Walter Rathenau, the German-Jewish industrialist and statesman. In the crowd, he discovered 'a total alteration of consciousness' that is both 'drastic and enigmatic'. As Roger Kimball has suggested (see his 'Becoming Elias Canetti', *New Criterion*, September 1986), he described his first encounter with a crowd as little short of the kind of experience one finds recounted in certain species of mystic literature:

> an intoxication; you were lost, you forgot yourself, you felt tremendously remote and yet fulfilled; whatever you felt, you didn't feel it for yourself; it was the most selfless thing you knew; and since selfishness was shown, talked, and *threatened* on all sides, you needed this experience of thunderous unselfishness like the blast of the trumpet at the Last Judgment...How could all this happen together? What was it?

Now we can guess why the crowd is, like the sea, seducing and enthralling. Because in a crowd, as in the sea but unlike on hard ground, built up and criss-crossed with fences and fully mapped, anything or almost anything can happen, even if nothing or almost nothing can be done for sure.

But it might be also disillusioning. Why? For much the same reasons. In the sea, ships may sink to the bottom. From a crowd's fury, revolutions may arise.

In *Under Western Eyes*, a novel published in 1911, Joseph Conrad makes one of his central characters observe that in a 'real revolution'

> the best characters do not come to the front. A violent revolution falls into the hands of the narrow-minded fanatics and of tyrannical hypocrites... The scrupulous and the just, the noble, humane, and devoted natures; the unselfish and the intelligent may begin a move-ment – but it passes away from them. They are not the leaders of a revolution. They are its victims; the victims of disgust, of disen-chantment – often of remorse.

The speaker of those words counted himself among the scrupu-lous, just, noble and humane – and he addressed his warnings to others like him. I can't say whether Hosni Mubarak or any of his counsellors studied those words, but they seem to have decided to pass the same warning on to well-off and well-wishing middle-class Egyptians who joined the feverish crowds on the streets – though this time to convey the portents in the form of (much more persuasive) brutal deeds rather than in that of an elegant literary locution. As Anthony Shadid and David D. Kirkpatrick report from Cairo in today's *New York Times*,

> In a collapse of authority, the police withdrew from major cities on Saturday, giving free rein to gangs that stole and burned cars, looted shops and ransacked a fashionable mall, where dis-membered mannequins for conservative Islamic dress were strewn over broken glass and puddles of water. Thousands of inmates poured out of four prisons, including the country's most notorious, Abu Zaabal and Wadi Natroun. Checkpoints run by the military and neighborhood groups, sometimes spaced just a block apart, proliferated across Cairo and other cities. Many have darkly sug-gested that the government was behind the collapse of authority as a way to justify a crackdown or discredit protesters' calls for change.

The dress rehearsal of mob rule staged in public by the authori-ties did make, it seems, the intended impression. In another report, also in today's *New York Times*, Kirkpatrick and Mona El-Naggar note an instant change in the mood of the Egyptian intelligentsia:

On Friday night, the police pulled out of Egypt's major cities abruptly, and tensions between rich and poor exploded. Looters from Cairo's vast shantytowns attacked gleaming suburban shopping malls, wild rumors swirled of gunfights at the bridges and gates to the most expensive neighborhoods and some of their residents turned wistful about Mr. Mubarak and his authoritarian rule. 'It is as if a domestic war is declared,' said Sarah Elayashi, 33, from an apartment in the affluent neighborhood of Heliopolis, not far from Mr. Mubarak's palace. 'And we have nothing to defend ourselves but kitchen knives and mop sticks.' 'The protesters are against us,' she added. 'We hope President Mubarak stays because at least we have national security. I wish we could be like the United States with a democracy, but we cannot. We have to have a ruler with an iron hand.'

The intention of the discredited leader of the nation, shared for quite some time by his 'global' protectors who preferred 'rulers with an iron hand' to rulers bent on serving the interests of the people they ruled, was to pave the road to a choice between the military-backed National Democratic Party's secular or the Muslim Brotherhood's religious tyrannies – there was no third option, *tertium non datur*. But *tertium*, it becomes clearer by the day, is *datur*... Though the *non* was not deleted from that time-hallowed Latin precept either by the 'rulers with an iron hand' or by those who helped them into power.

February 2011

2 February 2011

On glocalization coming of age

One is tempted to say that social inventions or reinventions – such as the newly invented or discovered possibility of restoring to the city square its ancient role of the agora in which rules and rulers were made and unmade – tend to spread 'like a forest fire'. One would say that if it were not for the fact that globalization has finally invalidated that time-honoured metaphor. Forest fires proceed by *spreading*. Today's social inventions progress by *leaping*.

Geographical distances no longer matter. Distances are no longer obstacles, and their lengths no longer determine the distribution of probabilities. Nor do neighbourhoods and physical proximity – this is why the metaphor of the 'domino effect', implying close proximity, indeed contiguity of cause and effect has lost much, perhaps even most, of its accuracy. Stimuli travel independently of their causes: causes may be local, the reach of their inspirations is global; causes may be global, their impacts are shaped and targeted locally. Entangled in the world-wide web, copycat patterns fly almost randomly in extraterritorial space – without scheduled itineraries and encountering few if any barriers or checkpoints – but they invariably come down on locally built landing strips. You can never be sure in advance on which strip they will land, by which of the innumerable control towers they will be spotted, intercepted and guided to a local airfield, and how many crash landings they will suffer and where. What renders time spent on predictions wasted, and prognoses unreliable, is the fact that the landing strips and control towers share the habits of things that float – they are constructed ad hoc, to catch a single selected trophy, hunt a single quarry, and tend to fall down the moment the mission is accomplished. Who is that 'al-Shahid' ('martyr' in Arabic) who single-handedly summoned the crowds to transform the Tahrir Square for a few days into a (temporary, ad hoc) agora? No one had heard of her or him before (read, she or he was not there before), and no one recognized the man or woman on the square beyond the nickname (read, she or he was not there) when the crowds answered the call... The point is, though, that this hardly matters.

The distinctions between far away and close by, or here and there, are made all but null and void once they are transferred to cyberspace and subjected to online or on-air logic; if not yet in the notoriously inert, lagging and sluggish imagination, then in their pragmatic potency. This is the condition towards which *glocalization*, the process of stripping locality of its importance while simultaneously adding to its significance, was aimed from its very start. The time has come to admit that it has arrived there: or, rather, that it has brought (pushed or pulled) us there.

Stripping place of its *importance* means that its plight and potency, fullness or emptiness, the dramas played in it and the spectators they attract can no longer be considered as its private matter. Places may (and do) propose, but it is now the turn of the unknown, uncontrolled, intractable and unpredictable forces roaming in the 'space of flows' to dispose. Initiatives continue to be local, but their consequences are now global, staying stubbornly beyond the powers of the initiative's birthplace to predict, plan or steer, or the powers of any other place for that matter. Once launched, they – like the notorious 'intelligent missiles' – are fully and truly on their own. They are also 'hostages to fate', though the fate to which they are hostage is nowadays composed and perpetually recomposed from the ongoing rivalry between landing strips locally laid out and hastily paved for ready-made copycats. The current map and rankings of established airports are of no importance here. And the composition of a global air-traffic authority would be similarly unimportant were such an institution to exist – which it does not, as the pretenders to such a role currently learn the hard way.

'Every time the administration uttered something, its words were immediately overtaken by events on the ground,' said Robert Malley, Middle East and North Africa programme director for the International Crisis Group. 'And in a matter of days, every assumption about the United States' relationship with Egypt was upended', – according to today's issue of the *New York Times*. And according to the latest information on Egypt from Mark Mardell, the BBC's North America Editor,

> US Secretary of State Hillary Clinton has telephoned the new vice-president and intelligence chief of two decades, Omar Suleiman, to tell him immediately to seize the opportunity for a transition to a more democratic society. That transition must start now. She said that the violence was shocking and told him that they must investigate the violence and hold those responsible accountable.

A few hours later, leaders of the countries believed to be the most important places in Europe – Merkel, Sarkozy, Cameron, Zapatero and Berlusconi – in an uncharacteristically unanimous declaration, repeated Hillary Clinton's appeal/demand. They all said what they did at roughly the same time that Al-Jazeera's cameras caught a demonstrator carrying a placard saying 'Obama, shut up!' The *significance* of place, rising independently of its importance, is precisely in its ability to accommodate the carrying of such placards and the people who carry them. Hands too short to meddle with things in global space are just long enough (or at least seem to be long enough) to embrace the locality and press it close, while (hopefully) fending off intruders and false pretenders.

One day after Hillary Clinton's announcement, the *New York Times* informs us of the full recasting of American foreign policy: 'The Obama administration seemed determined Wednesday to put as much daylight as possible between Mr. Obama and Mr. Mubarak, once considered an unshakable American supporter in a tumultuous region.' Well, that global power would hardly have made such an acrobatic volte-face had not the distant locality decided to make use of its new-found significance. As Shawki al-Qadi, an opposition lawmaker in Yemen, suggests, it is not the people who are afraid of their governments, which surrendered their powers to 'global forces' in exchange for shedding their obligations to their own people. As he puts it: 'It is the opposite. Governments and their security forces are afraid of the people now. The new generation, the generation of the internet, is fearless. They want their full rights, and they want life, a dignified life.' The knowledge that governments in the form in which they have been squeezed by 'global forces' are not a protection against instability but instability's principal cause has been forced into the heads of the self-appointed 'world leaders' by the spectacular display of glocalization's illogical logic in action.

'Glocalization' is a name given to a marital cohabitation that has been obliged, despite all the sound and fury known only too well to the majority of wedded couples, to negotiate a bearable modus co-vivendi, as separation, let alone divorce, is neither a realistic nor a desirable option. Glocalization is a name for a love–hate relationship, mixing attraction with repulsion: love that lusts for proximity, mixed with hate that yearns for distance. Such a relationship would perhaps have collapsed under the burden of its own incongruity had it not been for a pincer-like duo of inevitabilities: cut off from global supply routes, place would lack the stuff from which autonomous identities, and the contraptions keeping them alive, are nowadays made; and without locally improvised and serviced airfields, global forces would have nowhere to land, restaff, replenish and refuel. These are inevitabilities doomed to cohabit. For better or worse. Till death do them part.

4 February 2011

On what to do with the young

'Increasingly viewed as yet another social burden, youth are no longer included in a discourse about the promise of a better future. Instead they are now considered part of a disposable population whose presence threatens to recall repressed collective memories of adult responsibility': so writes Henry A. Giroux in an essay of

3 February 2011 titled 'Youth in the era of disposability' (see http://bad.eserver.org/issues/2011/Giroux-Youth.html).

As a matter of fact, the young are not fully, unambiguously disposable. What salvages them from straightforward disposability – if only just – and secures a measure of adult attention is their present and still more their potential contribution to consumer demand: successive echelons of youth mean a perpetual supply of 'virgin land', unspoilt and ready for cultivation, without which even the simple reproduction of the capitalist economy, not to mention economic growth, would be all but inconceivable. Youth is thought of and paid attention to as 'yet another market' to be commodified and exploited. 'Through the educational force of a culture that commercializes every aspect of kids' lives, using the Internet and various social networks along with the new media technologies such as cell phones', corporate institutions aim at 'immersing young people in the world of mass consumption in ways more direct and expansive than anything we have seen in the past'. A recent study by the Kaiser Family Foundation found that 'young people aged 8 to 18 now spend more than seven and a half hours a day with smart phones, computers, televisions, and other electronic devices, compared with less than six and a half hours five years ago. When you add the additional time youth spend texting, talking on their cell-phones or doing multiple tasks, such as watching TV while updating Facebook, the number rises to 11 hours of total media content each day.'

One can go on adding ever new evidence to that collected by Giroux: a gathering volume of evidence of 'the problem of youth' being cast fairly and squarely as an issue of 'drilling into consumers' and of all other youth-related issues being left on a side shelf – or being effaced altogether from the political, social and cultural agenda. On the one hand, as I already noted a few days ago, severe limitations imposed on governmental funding of higher education coupled with equally savage rises in university fees (indeed, the state deciding to wash its hands of its obligation to 'educate people', blatantly so in the case of 'cutting edge', bridgehead or frontline areas, but also somewhat more obliquely – as shown by the idea of replacing state-run secondary schools with 'academies' run by the consumer market – at the levels destined to determine the overall volume of knowledge and skills at the nation's disposal as well as their distribution among categories of the population) testify to the fading of interest in youth as the future political and cultural elite of the nation. On the other hand, Facebook, for instance, and also other 'social websites' are opening quite new vistas for agencies bent on focusing on youth and on tackling them primarily as 'virgin land', waiting to be conquered and exploited by the advancing consumerist troops.

Thanks to the happy-go-lucky and enthusiastic self-exposure of Facebook addicts to thousands of online friends and millions of online flâneurs, marketing managers can harness to the consumerist juggernaut the most intimate and ostensibly the most 'personal' and 'unique', articulated or half-conscious – already simmering or only potential – desires and wants; what will pop up on the screens fed by Facebook will now be a *personal* offer, prepared, groomed and caringly honed 'especially for you' – an offer you can't refuse because you are unable to resist its temptation; after all, it is what you fully and truly needed all the time: it 'fits your unique personality' and 'makes a statement' to that effect, the statement you always wanted to make, showing you to be that unique personality that you are. This is, indeed, a genuine breakthrough, if ever there was one, in the fortunes of marketing.

It is well known that the lion's share of the money spent on marketing is consumed by the exorbitantly costly effort of detecting, instilling and cultivating in prospective shoppers suitable desires to be reforged into a decision to obtain the particular product on offer. A certain Sal Abdin, a marketing adviser active on the web, grasps the essence of the task to be confronted when he addresses the following advice to adepts of the marketing art:

> if you sell drills, write an article on how to make better holes, and you'll get lots more sales leads than merely advertising information about your drills and drill specifications. Why does that work? Because nobody who bought a drill wanted a drill. They wanted a hole. Offer information about making holes and you'll be much more successful. If you're selling a course on losing weight, sell the benefits of being slim, of being more healthy, of feeling better, the fun of shopping for clothes, how the opposite sex will respond... know what I mean? Sell the benefits of the product and the product will sell itself when buyers reach the sales page. Mention its features but really emphasize what it can do for the buyer to make life better, easier, faster, happier, more successful... get my drift?

This is not a promise of an easy life, to be sure. Nor of a short, smooth and fast road to the target, which is a meeting between a customer wishing to buy and a product wished to be sold. Developing a desire for beautiful holes, and linking it to the drill promising to make them, is not an impossible task, perhaps, but it will take time and a lot of skill to settle it in the reader's imagination and lift it close to the top of the reader's dreams. The wished-for encounter will probably happen, but the road leading to that glorious moment of fulfilment is long, rough and bumpy, and above all there is no guarantee of reaching the destination until you've got there. And in addition, that road needs to be well paved and wide enough to accommodate an unknown number of walkers, although in all probability the number of those actually deciding to take it won't justify the huge expense of making it so broad, pleasurable to walk on, tempting and inviting.

This is precisely why I called the Facebook opportunity 'a genuine breakthrough'. It is an opportunity to do nothing less than cut out the costs of road-building from the marketing budget altogether – or almost. As in the case of so many other responsibilities, it shifts the task of developing desires in prospective clients from the (marketing) managers to the clients themselves. Thanks to the databank which Facebook users volunteer (unpaid!) and expand daily, marketing offers can now unfailingly spot customers who are already 'prepared', mellowed and matured, complete with right kind of desires (and who therefore hardly need lecturing on the beauty of holes); they can reach them directly in a doubly attractive disguise – flattering in addition to being welcome – offering a blessing that is 'your own, made especially for you, to meet your own, personal needs'.

Just an inane question for our inane times: perhaps the last barrier standing between youth and its disposal is its newly discovered and enabled capacity to serve as a disposal tip for the excesses of the consumer industry in our era of disposability?

8 February 2011

On the virtues not for everyone

The credit collapse, bank giants on the verge of bankruptcy and pushing their clients over that verge, must have shocked savers and happy-go-lucky borrowers alike – but, as the latest figures show, not for long.

Lessons, even shocking ones, seem to be forgotten well before they manage to settle in the memory, let alone sediment into habits and predispositions. Whereas in the third quarter of 2009 Americans set aside 7 per cent of their incomes in saving accounts (a huge, 400 per cent rise compared to their pre-shock custom), by the end of 2010 their savings had fallen again, to just 5.3 per cent. In the same period, borrowing started climbing again, and so did shopping and spending. Hopes of a cultural revolution, or a mini-revolution at least, in the life patterns of the society of consumers seem to have come to nothing – no sooner aroused than quashed. The way to a resurrection of at least some of those puritan values that, as Max Weber kept repeating, ushered the world into the modern, capitalist adventure, from rags to riches and from good to better, has proved to be barricaded and blocked much more solidly than many an observer would have deemed likely. From top to bottom, Americans are returning in throngs to their second nature – contrived and acquired – as spenders, fast shutting the door on their past as savers. Or so at least the statistics of savings books and credit cards, respectively, suggest.

How to explain this? By invoking the demise of virtues and the stubbornness of appropriated and instilled personal vices among the savers turning into debtors who are sticking to their choice through thick and thin? Or blaming people's learning difficulties? Or laying the blame at the door of the deceitful and unscrupulous, yet insidiously, cunningly, craftily seductive marketing agencies? There seems to be some truth in all these explanations. Some truth, but not the whole truth. Merging the statistics of falling savings and growing consumer credit hides two different social realities. Those people who have stopped saving are not the same ones as the people who have started reaching for their credit cards again: those people can afford *neither* to save *nor* to live on credit, both for much the same reason.

No doubt there are plenty of people between the Atlantic and the Pacific shores of the United States who feel firmly enough settled and provided for securely enough to allow themselves and their nearest and dearest to be rewarded with a bit more cossetting and self-indulgence. But there is no doubt either that there are plenty of others who are not creditworthy *and* are unable to save.

According to the most recent survey conducted by the American Payroll Association, around 67 per cent of Americans are dependent on their next paycheck to meet current living expenses, and the majority of US employees would be hard-pressed to meet their financial obligations if their next paycheck came even a week late ... No room for savings here.

A labour lawyer from Chicago, Thomas Geoghegan, suggests in today's *New York Times* that 43 million Americans living in poverty (proportionally equivalent to the number of poverty-stricken in Egypt) are unlikely ever to be able to save however hard they try; and then he adds a few observations of his own, drawn from his protracted and extensive practice among Illinois workers – active, retired and unemployed – to explain why this is the case. Thirty years ago, two-thirds of workers were in pension plans with guaranteed lifetime benefits; now the proportion is one in five, and rapidly falling. Well, in the 1960s and 1970s labour unions 'had their glory days – before they were smashed'; they served as 'the nation's financial planners'. But the world of those 'glory days', Geoghegan says, 'has turned upside down'. And he observes, caustically, that after 'US style banking' 'has destroyed social democracy' in certain countries, 'our pundits' would be likely to go on insisting that 'we can all save – even the poor'. They could point out that in C. L. R. James's classic *The Black Jacobins*, even some slaves from San Domingo managed to save enough to buy freedom – and then would say, 'See, you can do it.' Just save your money. That's the only hope... To which Geoghegan responds:

For most people at the median or below, savings is a matter of luck. Yes, I can pick up the self-help books and figure out a budget. But that requires me to lead a charmed life and not to have any kids. I have represented lots of workers who – with no defined benefits, no union to help – did save money. And it can work – if nothing goes wrong. But something always does go wrong: a wife has a stroke, a boarder you took in to help suddenly lost a job, or ... you lose your job. Then it's on the Visa card, and 20 percent of your income is going to interest of the bank, because of one little accident over which you had no control. Poof: there goes the house, if it was not under water already. Or there go 30 years of savings on an IRA [individual retirement account], for which your bank out of the goodness of its heart had been paying interest under 1 percent.

The conclusion is not difficult to reach: 'The self-help books live in a dream world...But it's really a nightmare world...It's a country where at the median income or lower even Silas Marner would find it hard to save.'

9 February 2011

On the blessings and curses of not taking sides

The internet takes no sides. The internet is neutral. It's a tool – and tools can be used by everyone and for a wide range of purposes. The internet can be used to call lovers of democracy to Liberation Square, as much as to summon lovers of tyranny.

This is good – something to be proud of. Were there no internet, it'd need to be invented, as any protagonist of liberal democracy would readily agree. The neutrality of the internet is another pillar to support equality of chances, the cause so dear to each and every heart beating for the cause of freedom. Tyrants or would-be tyrants of all denominations know only too well that this is the case; no wonder they tend to eye the internet with deep antipathy and suspicion, like a poison surreptitiously sprinkled into a well, or a time bomb. No wonder, either, that they heartily wish it would disappear – while doing everything they possibly can to try to make sure it does. The internet augurs visibility for the invisible, audibility for the dumb, action for those unable to act. To cut a long story short: barring a few abuses that need to and can be nipped in the bud, the internet equals freedom. Perhaps even the freedom of the unfree. Potentially at least it can become even more than that: the power of the powerless. More exactly: while it imposes constraints on the might of the power-holders, the internet adds might to the demands and undertakings of those on power's receiving end.

All that is evidently true, as proof of its truth is abundant while proofs to the contrary are few and far between. Or, rather, that truth was believed to be evident and confirmed, an open and shut case – until recently...

Almost unnoted by the press, and by the public opinion the press is supposed to alert and keep up to date, Stuxnet arrived to shake, perhaps even play havoc, with that belief. 'Stuxnet', as I read in the article by the well-informed Richard A. Falkenrath in the 26 January issue of the *New York Times*, is the codename of 'the computer worm that last year disrupted many of the gas centrifuges central to Iran's nuclear program'. Well, Stuxnet is blatantly and unashamedly a weapon, and a weapon of enormous destructive power. A highly effective, if inconspicuous and stealthy weapon: just half a megabyte in size, but attaining in just a few seconds what years of international diplomatic efforts abominably failed to achieve. It does not pretend to be an electronically enhanced replica of the speaker's soapbox at Hyde Park Corner. And so it is not immediately clear in what way, if any, its appearance undermines the belief in the internet as a non-partisan promoter of freedom and autonomy, and the conviction that not taking sides and being available to everybody, everywhere, is the major reason why. And this wouldn't be a worry were it not for the fact that 'Stuxnet attacked the Iranian nuclear program, but it did so by maliciously manipulating commercial software products sold globally by major Western companies. Whoever launched the assault also infected thousands of computers in several countries, including Australia, Britain, Indonesia and the United States.' Let me put it simply: Stuxnet is a weapon whose effectiveness (read, power of destruction) depends on the wide, and in principle indispensable and thus irremovable, scale and reach of the collateral casualties of its use. And collateral casualties, as we all know, cannot by their nature rely on boundaries or such trifles as proof of innocence and declarations of neutrality. They efface the distinction between combatants and non-combatants, and between taking and not taking sides.

Because it has collateral casualties as its inseparable companion, the entry of Stuxnet on the internet (and no doubt Stuxnet is just an avant-garde, a reconnaissance unit, a test probe, there to blaze open a trail for the main army body to follow) effaces another distinction as well: between defensive and offensive weapons. One can quarrel endlessly about whether the assault on Iranian nuclear stations was a defensive or an offensive act, but there is hardly any doubt that arguing, let alone proving, the defensive intention or meaning of the damage done to Australia or Britain would be

a tall order. And besides, as Falkenrath makes it clear, 'the exper-
tise to defend against a cyberattack is essentially indistinguishable
from that needed to make such an attack'. As the know-how
required and its technical arms are identical in both these otherwise opposite cases, there is no difference between aggression and
self-defence on the internet; if anything, the internet's declared and
practised neutrality is not far from that of illegal arms traffickers,
equally keen to supply tools of murder to both sides of a tribal
war and untroubled by the relative ethical or ideological advan-
tages and disadvantages. The same company, Siemens, supplied
the same data-and-control programs for use in nuclear power
facilities (including Iran's) and for the constructors of Stuxnet –
ostensibly to allow the latter to defend the United States against
cyber-attacks!

All in all, the posture and the practice, as well as the media-is-
the-message effect of the internet's variety of 'not taking sides' has
the effect primarily of casting doubt on the very notion of 'taking
sides', as well as of legitimate defence, or indeed, in a not so
distant future, on the distinction between 'just wars' and 'unjust
ones'. This is, I guess, why Falkenrath admits that warfare conducted on the internet 'is far less controllable than traditional
military and intelligence operations'; extensive new legislation,
internal and possibly also 'international' (whatever that notoriously unpinpointable phantom idea may mean), is called for to
mitigate the present 'legal ambiguity', but even that 'wouldn't
answer all the questions'.

Having admitted that much, Falkenrath – true to his standing
as the former deputy homeland security adviser to President
George W. Bush – ends up with a call not to reason and good will,
but to arms: 'One thing is sure: as bad as this arms race will be,
losing it would be even worse.'

12 February 2011

On a human tsunami, and thereafter

Ancient Chinese wisdom considers the wish 'to live in interesting
times' to be a curse. Contemporary wisdom is of two minds. Many
would see that wish as a blessing.

A human tsunami of unheard of – unremembered or already forgotten – proportions swept away, in a mere fortnight, a dictator perched for thirty years at the top of a huge network of patrons and clients, corrupted bureaucrats and corruptible judges, stool-pigeons, informers and torturers. On hearing the news and for days thereafter, *everybody* in Tahrir Square in Cairo seemed to be rejoicing: dreamers of middle-class freedoms (that is, people finally allowed to match the political clout they hadn't yet had to the economic muscle they already had), dreamers of an Islamic republic (that is, mullahs and imams allowed to announce 'L'État, c'est nous!' – we are the state), or dreamers of a just, caring society (that is millions of the unemployed hoping to become able to earn their living, and dozens of millions of the impoverished dreaming of being able to live on their earnings). Those who might have been nonplussed kept mum. Or their voices were stifled amidst the hubbub of the victors' choral singing and the crackle of fireworks.

Occasionally, though, one can hear sceptical voices, even though thus far they are scattered and sung solo, a capella, sotto voce and pianissimo. Those who voice scepticism look around and see that the pyramid of powers on which the now toppled dictator (as well as his predecessors) was perched has emerged from the turmoil unscathed and intact; and they doubt what else the tightly knit power network, so far showing no sign of coming unstitched or of being ripped up, can support.

Ayaan Hirsi Ali, for instance, the founder of the AHA Foundation dedicated to the defence of Muslim women, points out in her article in today's *Le Monde* ('Non, le monde arabe n'est pas l'Europe de l'Est en 1989!') that Islam, a religion more skilful, seasoned and expedient in the art of mass mobilization than any other faith, can hardly tolerate, let alone sustain, a leaderless existence and a non-authoritarian regime. Mubarak and Gaddafi did not fall from the moon; they are legitimate products of the Islamic civilization, marked as it has always been by the absence of individual liberty. In that civilization, which 'forbids one to respond to one's father or mother or to an imam, the surrender to the dictatorship of the State becomes almost second nature'. And she reminds her readers that until now 'men who arrived as liberators' 'changed into dictators', emboldened by the deafening silence of somnolent masses, 'until such time that someone else came to mobilize the masses to liberate the nation from its former liberator'. Invariantly and inexorably, 'the new ruler restored the old infrastructure of denunciation and torture'. Ali fears a tide of chaos and instability (Pakistan-style) followed by a new dictatorial era...Nothing short of a veritable *cultural* revolution, so she believes, is able to cut through that vicious cycle.

Others sense that the most awesome dangers nest not in culture but in politics, and not in the politics of present or would-be Arab dictators, but in the egotistic and selfish politics of the West. And so Tariq Ramadan of Oxford suggests that 'behind all that talk celebrating democracy, liberty and human rights, cold-blooded and most cynical calculations hide...How to control that movement, how to profit on it?' He reminds his readers that Obama, Merkel, Cameron and others like them, currently pontificating to Egyptians about the ethical superiority of democracy and waxing lyrical about the blessings of the democratic way of life, 'never hesitated to hobnob with the worst of dictators, including Mubarak'. Ramadan asks 'who is so naive to believe in those people's sudden conversion?' (Though on this point Ramadan probably errs: there are many people, not necessarily naive yet all the same eager to believe – if the price is right.)

The record of the United States and Europe in 'promoting democracy' away from home could hardly be worse. Ramadan most certainly does not err when he charges us here, in the 'North', with hypocrisy. Most of us would recognize as purely rhetorical his question 'has not the United States a long history of collaborating and scheming with Islamic and most traditionalistic, retrograde and extremist Islamism forces, from Afghanistan to Saudi Arabia?' Well, he could and should have added that such a long, sad, democracy-discrediting history has been by no means limited to the enchanted circle of Islam. The powers of the 'North' have a long record of disservice to the cause of democracy and freedom – a record that came nowhere near to ending with the end of the colonial era. Mossadeq was indeed a Muslim, but Salvador Allende most certainly was not, which did not save either of them (as well as a long line of others like them) from falling victim to the CIA's unconditional and possibly incorrigible preference for USA-friendly tyrants over democratically elected incorruptible independents...Those cases should also be subject to Ramadan's injunction: 'It should be never a question for the "democrats of the North" whether to accept dictatorship, repression and torture for the sake of security and economic or geostrategic interests.' Ramadan's observation – that what is needed is not only to demand Mubarak's head, but also the dismantling of 'the corrupted system based on clientelism, torture and systematic theft' – also needs be extended: a dismantling of the hierarchy of values practised, if not preached, by the 'North' should share the fate of the 'corrupted systems' operated by Mubarak and his ilk. With such friends as the CIA, democracy hardly needs enemies...

Indeed, Georges Corm, former finance minister in Lebanon, adds in the same issue of *Le Monde* a handful of his own arguments from history to those of Ramadan. For instance: 'Invasion by the American army in 2003 under the pretext of toppling the tyrant and establishing democracy led, on the contrary, to Iraq's descent into outrageous communitarianism and tribalism, and to people's pauperization yet more profound than that perpetrated by the UN sanctions'; or, approved and supported by the West, the 'cedar revolution' in Lebanon managed only 'to worsen the internal communitarianism and sectarian enmity'. The design to 'reinfantilize' the Middle East, put into operation under the aegis of George W. Bush and Condoleezza Rice, and their attempts to impose democracy from outside, could have no other effect except the deepening of tensions and the overall instability of the region.

But Corm adds to the debate an exceptionally important issue missing from the analyses of the other two:

> Supporting solely the political claims of the middle class while forgetting about socio-economic justice and equitability for the most deprived and impoverished classes can only result in gross disappointments. What brought those classes to despair and rebellion was 'kleptocracy', tying local oligarchic interests to big European companies, as well as to the Arab financial interests originating in the petrol-exporting countries. It is this grievance that feeds the Islamist currents in social protests.

What is there left to say? Only that we have been warned. But we were warned so many times in the past. Each time, or almost, to no avail... Alas, history may repeat itself once (?) more. You can gather why from today's comment by Bob Herbert in the *New York Times*:

As the throngs celebrated in Cairo, I couldn't help wondering about what is happening to democracy here in the United States. I think it's on the ropes. We're in serious danger of becoming a democracy in name only. While millions of ordinary Americans are struggling with unemployment and declining standards of living, the levers of real power have been all but completely commandeered by the financial and corporate elite. It doesn't really matter what ordinary people want. The wealthy call the tune, and the politicians dance...

The poor, who are suffering from an all-out depression, are never heard from. In terms of their clout, they might as well not exist. The Obama forces reportedly want to raise a billion dollars or more for the president's re-election bid. Politicians in search of that kind of cash won't be talking much about the wants and needs of the poor. They'll be genuflecting before the very rich.

13 February 2011

On the bottoms beneath the bottoms

The American federal debt is currently growing by $4 billion a day. At the time I write these words, 40 cents of every dollar spent in the shops by an American shopper is borrowed; in other words, unearned. This is a debt that, short of a world war or a giant meteor knocking the planet out of orbit, will eventually need to be repaid. By someone. By whom? You may ask. 'Not by us,' say American Congressmen consolingly to themselves as they push through Capitol Hill a budgetary deficit to the tune of $1,480 billion – that is, if they deign to stoop to answering at all. But it does not look as if they will, or be pressed sufficiently hard to, change their mind – and so by April or May total American debt is forecast to trespass on the legal limit of federal debt set by Congress at $14,290 billion. That last point, unlike the previous points, has kicked Congressmen into a flurry of activity: they have just two to three months left to obtain both Houses' endorsement to...raise that limit still higher, and push America down beneath another of the bottoms it set itself for its financial fall. America is a country famous for breaking records in all fields, and the field of financial inanity is no exception. American legislators have become past masters in the skill of breaking through the bottom in the hope (certainty rather) that another bottom further down could be brought into service, until its turn comes to be broken through as well: only last Christmas they presented American buyers and sellers with $858 billion in tax cuts for the rich. Another record was then broken: as George W. Bush's administration managed to scrape together only around $700 billion to save the American banking system from free fall; a sum that in its time, less than two years ago, was greeted with astonishment, bewilderment, and incredulity mixed with adoration – but now would arouse no more interest, and most probably less than pre-First World War Olympic records.

Most certainly, I am not an economic expert, and so I need to look for advice to those who say that they are and are treated as if they were. One French banker, according to Marie de Vergès writing in today's *Le Monde*, makes light of the whole affair; the American Treasury, he says, can repay debts by printing as many dollars as it wants to. I was, I admit, somewhat baffled to read those words, but it seems that my confusion was shared by at least some people who, unlike me, are not short of economic credentials. One of them, Antoine Brunet, opines that if it continues its present policy, the Fed will pull the American currency down to the status of *la monnaie de singes* – a French idiom for fobbing someone off with empty promises…Whom should I to trust? And who am I to decide about economists' trustworthiness? But I trust Hans Jonas and what he writes on the 'ethics for the era of uncertainty', with his updated version of Pascal's wager (rather than the Kantian categorical imperative, made to serve an age of certainty and self-confidence): if some people predict a catastrophe and some others deny their prediction, it is safer to side with the prophets of doom…

19 February 2011

On being out inside, and inside but out

On 26 September 1940, Walter Benjamin was stopped and turned back at the French–Spanish frontier by the Spanish police because he was not in possession of the 'exit visa' that was then a condition of admission into Spain. Caught between a country that refused him the right to live and a country that refused him a lifeline, Benjamin chose the only direction he could take without being stopped by the guardians of law and order: death. As Spain waived the requirement of exit visas a few days later, Hannah Arendt retrospectively called Benjamin's suicide 'a singular case of bad luck'. But Benjamin couldn't know, could he, what step the powers-that-be would take next. Drawing the line between good and bad luck was not in his hands. The games on the chessboard on which he was a pawn were played by others. This, in a nutshell, is what makes a refugee a refugee.

In his latest book summing up his ten-year field study in refugee camps scattered across Africa and South America, as well as European 'detention centres' for immigrants defined as 'illegal' or suspended in the 'no laws – no rights' status of 'asylum seekers', Michel Agier concludes that seventy years later Benjamin's 'bad luck' has all but lost its singularity.[5] In 1950, one million refugees were counted in official statistics. Today, a conservative estimate of the numbers of 'people in transition' is 12 million, but as many as 1 billion refugees-turned-exiles, ensconced in the nowhere-land of camps, are predicted for 2050.

'Being in transition' is of course an ironic expression if it is applied to the lot of Walter Benjamin or its mimeographed replicas. By definition, the idea of 'transition' stands for a finite process, a time span with clearly drawn starting and finishing lines – a *passage* from a spatial, temporal, or spatial *and* temporal 'here' to 'there'; but these are precisely the attributes denied to the condition of 'being a refugee', having been defined and set apart from and in opposition to the 'norm' by their absence. A 'camp' is not a mid-station, or an inn, or a motel on the voyage from here to there. It is the terminal station, where all the roads on the map peter out and all movement grinds to a halt. Camps ooze finality; not the finality of destination, though, but of the state of transition petrified into the state of permanence. The name 'transition camp', commonly selected by power-holders for the places where refugees are ordered to stay, is an oxymoron: 'transition' is the very quality whose denial and absence defines the status of a refugee. The sole defined meaning of being assigned to a place called a 'refugee camp' is that all other conceivable places are made off-limits. The sole meaning of being an insider of a refugee camp is to be an outsider, a stranger, an alien body, an intruder in the rest of the world; in short, evicted from the world shared by the rest of humanity. 'Having been evicted', being fixed in a condition of *exile*, is all there is, and needs to be, in the identity of the refugee. And as Agier repeatedly points out, it is not an issue of *from where* one arrived at the encampment, but it is the absence of a *where to* that sets an exile apart from all other humans – the declared prohibition against or practical impossibility of arriving anywhere else. Being set apart is what counts. Exiles don't need to cross state borders, to arrive from another country. They may be, and all too often are, born and bred inside the country in which their life of exile is lived. They need not even have moved an inch from the place where they were born. Agier has every right to collapse refugee camps, encampments of the homeless and urban ghettos in the same category – of the 'corridors of exile'. Legal or illegal residents of all these places share one decisive trait: they are all redundant. Rejects or the refuse of society. In a nutshell, waste. 'Waste', by definition, is the antonym of 'utility'; it denotes objects without any possible use. Indeed, the sole accomplishment of waste is soiling and cluttering space which could otherwise be usefully employed.

The production of 'wasted humans' on an industrial scale is an eminently modern phenomenon, as is the concept of 'waste' itself and its opposition, the concept of 'utility'. In the peasant economy dominant in the premodern era, there was no room for the idea of 'waste', with the associated practices of its production and removal and destruction; no room for 'litter', 'refuse', 'garbage' or 'rubbish'. Everything had its utility, being used and reused. All organic leftovers created by a peasant farm and household were promptly returned to the food chain in the form of animal food or fertilizers. *Avant la lettre*, comprehensive 'recycling' was endemic to the peasant economy, and neither inanimate nor animate objects, including humans, were exempt from it: it was *a priori*, even if tacitly, assumed that a newly born child would be assigned a role in the field or farmyard, and a place at the family table; it was only with the development of hired labour and the appearance of the labour market that the demand and supply of labour could fall out of balance and, accordingly, the idea of 'human redundancy' could take hold and a concept of 'structural unemployment' emerge. Once that had happened, however, massive and systematic production of 'redundant humans' became a permanent feature of modern life. Redundant humans were the waste, or collateral casualties, of two exquisitely modern preoccupations (indeed, they were all too often perceived as the defining features of the modern way of life): order-building and economic progress.

First, order-building. This is measured by the degree of 'orderliness': namely, the rising predictability of events and falling volume of their contingency, randomness, accidentality and irregularity. Replacing the extant state of affairs, decried as 'insufficiently orderly', intolerably 'disorderly' or descending into 'chaos', by a newly designed model of order made to the measure of new preferences and capabilities boils down in the end to redefining certain ways of life and the categories of people practising them as 'unsuitable for' the intended scheme of things and therefore denying them room in the order about to be built. 'Order' means a state of affairs in which certain, desirable kind of events are more likely to occur than other events, classified as 'undesirable'. All 'structuring' and 'restructuring' (other names for 'order-building') therefore consists of the manipulation of probabilities, which is pursued through separating, disabling and preferably eliminating those categories of human subjects that are, for one reason or another, suspected of resisting that manipulation, or that openly refuse to surrender to the norms being promoted; in other words, the categories accused of generating uncertainty, and thereby disturbing and undermining the future order. 'Structuring' boils down, in the last resort, to an effort to excise from the 'system' the categories of population threatening to become seats, sources or causes of uncertainty. Once cut out and disconnected from the system, however, these categories need to be effectively prevented from re-entering or reconnecting: they have to be deported, forced, induced, pressed or persuaded and encouraged to depart. Alternatively (or in parallel), they might be relegated to various kinds of internment: a place of incarceration, whether or not surrounded with walls and armed guards, but always encircled by osmotic borders (to differentiate the cross-border traffic: allowing entry, yet rendering exit exceedingly difficult, if not impossible).

Second, economic progress. This is measured, first and foremost, by the speed and volume of the rise in the efficiency of labour and investments. 'Progressing', in the sense imbued into the word by the market economy, means being able to produce the same or greater effects with less expenditure and less labour; consequently, it can be measured by the number of labourers made redundant – that is, no longer needed to keep production of those effects at the level already attained or still rising. In the course of economic progress, successive swathes of the population engaged in productive activity are laid aside as 'useless' or 'unprofitable' – two disqualifying reasons made synonymous by the logic of the market economy. They are the waste – the refuse, the collateral casualties, of economic progress.

The two tendencies, preoccupations or activities discussed above combine in the phenomenon of 'modernization'. Contrary to opinions that once prevailed and still linger, misleading though they still are, modernization – in fact, a compulsive and addictive reforming or replacing of everything, including normative rules, tools and patterns of action themselves modernized only a moment ago, or even those that have not even completed the previous round of modernization – is not a temporary process leading to modernity, but modern society's immanent and permanent existential mode: the defining attribute of the modern form of life. Indeed, modernity *is* the state of compulsive, obsessive, and thus unfinishable, modernization; modernization in the sense spelled out above can only grind to a halt, if it ever does, with the end of modernity. The idea of a modernity that has stopped modernizing is no less absurd than the notion of a wind that does not blow or a river that does not flow. What follows, however, is that modernity is, endemically and (at least thus far) incurably, a waste-producing form of life; and in this branch of production, as in all other branches, the modern form of life is uniquely and exceedingly fertile and efficient. The price of modernity's exceptional creativity, inventiveness and productivity is human vulnerability to redundancy – rising rather than falling.

There is no modernization (and therefore no modern way of life either) without a massive and continuous production of waste, including wasted humans proclaimed redundant. For a couple of centuries or so, the north-western peninsula of the Asiatic continent, called 'Europe', was a solitary island of modernity in a vast, planet-wide premodern sea, and so enjoyed a worldwide monopoly of modernization; it was therefore the sole part of the globe afflicted with the bane of human redundancy. Enjoying a power advantage over the rest of the planet, however, and for a considerable length of time (an advantage offered and assured by that monopolistic status), Europe was also historically unique in being able to put its 'wasted humans', the 'redundant' part of its population, to profitable use: in conquest and colonization. The imperialist episode in European history was the outcome of *a unique concatenation of circumstances unrepeated and probably unrepeatable by other areas of the globe*: a one-off conjunction of the need to dispose of the systematically growing redundant part of the population, and the opportunity to deploy them in the role of conquistadors, expanding European territorial possessions and also gaining new markets open to Europe's undisturbed and potentially unconstrained exploitation. In that and probably only that case, exile could be, and was, recycled into colonization; European overseas empires could be, and were, deployed as workshops in which that recycling was conducted to great effect, and to a large extent accomplished. The curse of exclusion was recycled into the 'white man's mission' (or, as Rudyard Kipling would prefer it, with an undertone of self-approval mixed with self-apology, the 'white man's burden').

With the rising heaps of waste safely transported overseas, the most menacing and potentially most toxic effects of accumulated waste were effectively pre-empted. Whatever fraction of the redundant population remained in the homeland after the overseas garrisons were filled, the offices of the colonial administration and overseas trade outposts were manned, and the lands of annexed territories were redeployed for colonization could, by and large, be made manageable – admittedly not without considerable and occasionally explosive social tensions and friction. In a nutshell, *a global solution was found to locally produced problems*, and for about a couple of centuries it could be energetically and successfully pursued. This was, however, I repeat, a unique and time-limited chance for Europe – in all probability never to be replicated, in Europe or anywhere else on earth.

Well, you can say that by the end of the twentieth century the 'white man's mission' had been accomplished, or if you prefer that the 'white man's burden' had been delivered – even if not in the form the missionaries and ostensible burden-carriers anticipated: the compulsive and obsessive modernization, modernization by necessity even if not by choice, had indeed reached the most distant and isolated nooks and crannies of the planet – or almost. The seeds of the new brave world, coated in poison intended to destroy the residues of the old and not-so-brave world, had been sprinkled planet-wide. The 'modernities' that have grown out of those seeds might be, as some observers insist, many and different – but each and every one of them is, is forced to be, and cannot but be, addicted to perpetual, compulsive and obsessive modernization; which means that wasted humans are produced everywhere – or almost. Human redundancy is no longer a locally generated nuisance that can be mitigated or chased away altogether through seeking, finding and applying global solutions. It is exactly the other way round: it is the local powers, or whatever is left of them, that face the daunting task of seeking, *finding and applying local solutions to the globally generated, universal problem.* In its essence, this problem boils down to the management of the waste-and-refuse removal-and-recycling industry.

An interesting and telling point: alarm about the awesome threat of the overpopulation of the planet burst into 'world opinion' simultaneously with the folding up of European overseas empires and the end of the colonialist era. It gathered force throughout the rest of the twentieth century and shows no sign of abating in the twenty-first. Today, some of the most prestigious scholars – like, for instance, in *Le Monde* of 15 February, Henri Leridon, who was commissioned by the French Academy to analyse and interpret current population trends – warn that as the earth is incapable of feeding more than a population 9 billion strong, anything above that is bound to trigger a social explosion, perhaps even the extinction of the human species; yet, Leridon says, the data collected most recently by the Economic and Social Council of the United Nations, despite the authors' efforts to make their glosses sound maximally optimistic and placate rather than boost the fears of a 'demographic bomb', show that if the rate of fertility is not significantly reduced, that threshold of catastrophe will soon be reached – and passed. The UN report suggests that the feared number of 9 billion humans will be the peak of population growth, to be reached by 2050, after which the planet's population will start to decline. Other scholars refuse to be calmed, however. They point out that, with the earth's population expected to reach 7 billion by the end of August, a simple calculation shows that whereas the first billion took innumerable years to be reached, the second billion took only 180 years, while the seventh billion needed no more than 12...They also question the veracity and trustworthiness of the UN's official optimism, suggesting that with a rise in the birth-rate as small as half a percentage point, the world's population would overshoot the expected peak in 2050 by another 1.5 billion, while growth of merely one-quarter of a percentage point would be enough to bring the population to 14 billion by 2100 (though how that could happen if reaching 9 billion triggered the extinction of the human race, the authors of that prognosis fail to explain). A tone of despair can sometimes be detected in the most alarmist scenarios (though it is hardly ever articulated, and reports prudently keep short of spelling it out): with 'family planning' becoming the sole method of fertility control, we are deprived of effective means to prevent the over-population from happening...

And another interesting and revealing point: invariably, regard-less of the colour of the alert they recommend, the suppliers of the data and commentaries perceive the danger as coming mostly, nearly exclusively, from the poor countries (and, on the whole, those least densely populated).

Let's note that between 1798 and 1826, at the threshold of intensive modernization but before the division of the planet between emergent European empires and massive colonization took off, Thomas Robert Malthus published and updated his *Essay on the Principle of Population*, in which he argued that humanity is bound to face overpopulation, manifested in cata-strophic food shortage, without either a limitation of the birth-rate or an increase in the death-rate, or both:

> The power of population is so superior to the power of the earth to produce subsistence for man, that premature death must in some shape or other visit the human race. The vices of mankind are active and able ministers of depopulation. They are the precursors in the great army of destruction, and often finish the dreadful work them-selves. But should they fail in this war of extermination, sickly seasons, epidemics, pestilence, and plague advance in terrific array, and sweep off their thousands and tens of thousands. Should success be still incomplete, gigantic inevitable famine stalks in the rear, and with one mighty blow levels the population with the food of the world.[6]

Malthus's suggestion stayed at the centre of scholarly attention for several decades; its reception was mixed, but powerful voices were raised in opposition (among the most passionate and influential of them were those of William Godwin, Robert Owen, William Hazlitt, Nassau William Senior, William Cobbett, Karl Marx, Friedrich Engels and Thomas Doubleday): the counterarguments raised in the debate were manifold, but they all circled around the idea that the alleged 'overpopulation' detected behind the shortages of food and other means of existence was the fault of human society, and not a verdict of nature, and that, with human reason, inventiveness and rising powers, a proper balance between supply and demand could be perpetuated ad infinitum. In the course of the nineteenth century and through the better part of the next the debate gradually ran out of steam, times being busy with attempts to expand the reserves of labour and the military, viewed as reliable sources and foolproof guarantees of national wealth and power, rather than with worries that the size of the population would grow out of control. The debate was reborn in a somewhat modified version as 'neo-Malthusianism', and has gained force again, in the last thirty to forty years, with the imperialist/colonialist era already in the past and the era of the 'empire emigrates back' having arrived.

The present-day resurrection of the 'overpopulation' bugbear was to be expected now that the modern way of life – two centuries ago the exclusive privilege of a small sector of the planet whose fortunes determined the ups and downs of the popularity and prestige of the Malthusian vision – has reached every, or almost every, nook and cranny of the globe. With the 'end of history' in the form proclaimed by Francis Fukuyama (a once-and-for-all universalization of capitalist-run markets), outlets for the disposal of 'wasted humans', those inescapable by-products of modernization, all but disappeared, while the volume of human redundancy rose sharply, and continues to grow as all parts of the planet join in its production.

The alarms about 'overpopulation' at the beginning of the twenty-first century reflect, ultimately, the ever more evident inadequacy of the waste-disposal and waste-recycling industry in its orthodox form, initiated at the beginning of the modern era and refined in the course of that era's history. Above all, they reflect the impossibility of the task never encountered before of providing global solutions to locally produced problems. The 'problem', that is human redundancy, is produced globally nowadays, not locally; all, or almost all, of the lands of the planet today fall into the category of producers of net redundancy and crave to export the excess of their population, while none, or hardly any, of the lands is able to absorb, or can be forced to admit, the excess population produced elsewhere. In our era of unprecedented ease of travel and unheard-of mobility, the population surpluses are fixed in the places of their production, which are blatantly incapable of accommodating them – and criminal gangs specializing in cross-border contraband are their only chances of appealing against the verdict of fate.

As Milan Kundera observed, the sole meaning thus far of the unification of humankind is that there is nowhere to escape…

22 February 2011

On miracles, and not quite miracles

A 'miracle' is what we tend to call a *one-off breach in the order of nature*. As to the 'order of nature', it is another name for whatever is not in human power to change or suspend: what would happen if human beings did nothing about it, but also if they tried hard to divert it or stop it in its tracks – and so also something they can ignore only at their peril. As William Adams noted in 1767, a 'miracle' is a relative notion: 'There must be an ordinary regular course of nature, before there can be anything extraordinary. A river must flow, before its stream can be interrupted.'

The 'order of nature' is ruthless, indomitable, ineluctable – and deaf to appeals, begging and immolation; in other words, oblivious to dissent and immune to resistance. It is pointless and misleading, in fact ludicrous, to speak of Nature and natural phenomena using concepts like 'intention', 'motive', 'goal' or 'purpose' (an injunction which Max Weber, one of the founders of modern humanities, regarded as the founding precept of modern scientific reason, branding it the 'disenchantment of the world'). Unlike us, human beings, nature does not 'want', or 'aim at'; natural events follow causes, not purposes: they happen 'because of…', not 'in order to…' Nature being numb and dumb, it is pointless to ask it for favours or mercy, or indeed to try to ingratiate oneself in its eyes (which, manifestly, it does not possess, just as it is stripped of all the other senses). The laws of nature are by definition invulnerable and invincible; nothing that humans can do will change their relentless unfolding. All in all, the order of nature divides conceivable events into the *inevitable* and the *impossible*.

The modern ambition to put nature (that obviously superhuman, and possibly divine creation) under human management could not and did not include an intention to reform, and even less to suspend or abolish, the natural order and its laws; it did not intend to question what nature declared (and made) impossible. Nature was to be taken under human management as a going concern – in a shape established once and for all, whether designed and decreed to last forever by God, or self-born and self-entrenched, but at any rate put and kept in place by a power able to accomplish what humans evidently would be incapable of doing. 'One needs to surrender to Nature in order to master it' was the guiding principle of the modern strategy, aiming at the employment of natural forces in the service of human needs.

Hegel, considered by many as the greatest of modern philosophers, proclaimed that in order to be *free*, one needs to be aware of *necessity*: to achieve success and avoid defeat, one needs to learn diligently the immutable laws on nature (that is, the difference between the inevitable and the impossible). Once the limitations imposed by Nature – the line drawn between the possible and the impossible – came to be known, that acquired knowledge would enable humans to choose goals that could be implemented and designs that could bring them about – instead of human designs being confounded and human expectations being dashed. In short, *surrendering* to intractable 'laws of nature' enhances the human capacity for effective action, and so also expands human *freedom of choice*.

What about the 'miracles' then? Miracles found in the modern spirit their most passionate and formidable enemy to date: an enemy bent on their extirpation, expulsion and exile – from the world and from the human mind. Miracles were deemed by modern science to have been perceived as extraordinary, inexplicable and beyond comprehension only because of humans' (temporary and rectifiable) ignorance of the natural order of things;

and they could go on being believed to be miracles only as long as the laws of nature remained mysterious and inscrutable. As Hume famously (and wittily) declared at the threshold of the modern era, 'no testimony is sufficient to establish a miracle unless the testimony be of such a kind that its falsehood would be more miraculous than the fact which it endeavours to establish'. Anything taken as 'miraculous' by an unenlightened mind will sooner or later be found to have regular causes. Modern science stoutly denied the miraculous nature of apparent and alleged 'miracles'. It refused to accept that any verdict that said 'this is a miracle' could be final, and ensured that it could be quashed: it insisted that any event taken for a 'miracle' in the past would be either revealed retrospectively to have a fully natural cause, or disqualified as a figment of an overexcited imagination or a product of a confidence trick.

In fact, modern science declared a war of attrition not just on alleged miracles, but on all randomness, accidents, opacity, ambiguity – and indeed any kind of irregularity and any case of incomprehensibility – and pronounced them to be only temporary irritants, bound to recede with the – certain – advance of science (stealing secrets from nature), arm-in-arm with technology (pre-empting any undesirable or just unanticipated effects of purposeful acts). In the world which modern science and technology set out to create, there was meant to be no room for miracles. By the same token, though, once the job of science was done, there would be no room left for God...

The explicit or tacit, but irremovable and invariable assumption underlying the modern project confined the role of God in the Universe to the act of creation. It was assumed that, having created nature with all its laws, God refrained from further interference in their operation; in fact, the idea of *deus absconditus* – an absent God – can be seen as the birth-act of the modern worldview. Reporting the mentality that was bound to be shaped by such an idea, José Saramago noted in his *Lanzarote Notebooks* that 'God is the silence of the universe and man is the cry that gives meaning to that silence.'

Theologians may have quarrelled about whether his retreat from daily management of his creation was God's own wilful decision, or the consequence of the completeness and perfection of his design, which rendered any other intervention redundant, undesirable, or even downright impossible (after all, the state of 'perfection' means that any change would only make it worse). But they are obliged to resent any imputation of limitations on God's omnipotence, because the admission of any limit would be bound to have the same effect: it would put theologians in a quandary which they'll have to struggle hard, even though vainly, to resolve. Every limit would question and cast in doubt the canon of God's omnipotence – whether it is the ultimate perfection of his design that is denied, or God's ability to tinker with the universal laws he himself designed. (Leibniz, for instance, went as far as suggesting that eternal truth entered the mind of God without asking his permission, implying by the same token that it wouldn't leave his mind by his command…) The unresolvable ambiguity of that situation is reflected in the ambivalent attitude taken by churches towards miracles nowadays: on the one hand, God's miracle-making capacity is not questioned; on the other hand, any new claim of a miracle being actually witnessed is *a priori* treated with the utmost suspicion, and whatever can be done to officially disavow it is done.

A proposition in stark opposition to the concept of God as the creator and guarantee of the orderliness and rigid, inexorable logic of the world (a concept sometimes explicitly articulated and at other times tacitly assumed, but always endemic in modern thought) was made by the Russian-French Christian-existentialist philosopher Leon Shestov. We postulate God, he insisted – we *need* God, we *turn to* God – in order 'to obtain the impossible. As far as the possible is concerned, humans are self-sufficient.' In other words, we need God to do miracles – doing miracles is God's *raison d'être*. The greatness of God is his inconsistency. No 'absolute' there, no 'once and for all', nothing *sub specie aeternitatis vel necessitatis*. God means: nothing is inevitable; and nothing is impossible.[7] Nothing is exempted from the divine power to make exemptions from the rule; the past is subject to annulment just as the future is; for instance, 'the shameful act of poisoning Socrates' can be made 'never to have existed'. So miracles may happen even *ex post facto*, retrospectively: the 'undoing' of what has been done, effacing it from the chronicle of being, striking it out not just from historical records but from history itself, is a miracle fully in God's power; it is, in fact, the very substance of God's divinity. In Shestov's own words:

The history of humanity – or, more precisely, all the horrors of the history of humanity – is, by one word of the Almighty, 'annulled'; it ceases to exist, and becomes transformed into phantoms and mirages... The 'fact', the 'given', the 'real' do not dominate us; they do not determine our fate either in the present, in the future or in the past. What has been becomes what has not been; man returns to the state of innocence.

The capacity of miracle-making: this is what humans seek in God. If humans need a 'personal God' – superhuman yet human-like, hearing, listening, choosing and deciding with discretion just as humans do – they need him precisely for that capacity. The ultimate test of God's omnipotence is precisely his ability to dismiss, ignore and neglect the rules, laws, regularities, routine he himself created for lesser beings – primarily human – to obey. God bound by the rules, even by the rules of his own creation, would be an oxymoron: a contradiction in terms. It is because they assume he has the ability to *break* the routine, to do the *un*expected and the *in*explicable, that humans simultaneously fear him, trust him, and turn to him whenever they bump into the limits of their own ability to cope. Awe and fear blend into the phenomenon of the 'tremendous' – that, as Rudolf Otto suggested, always was and continues to be the essence of 'divinity'. When Moses tried to convince the Pharaoh that Jahveh who sent him was 'the true God', unlike the gods endorsing the Pharaoh's self-confident obstinacy, he did not resort to reminding the Pharaoh of the orderliness and consistency of the universe, God's creation – but presented him with sights that defied all logic and human power of understanding. When commanded by God to take his mission, Moses had doubts: 'They will never believe me or listen to me; they will say: "The Lord did not appear to you".' To placate his apprehensions, God offered Moses a proof to use to convince anyone who witnessed it of Moses' divine credentials:

The Lord said, 'What have you there in your hand?' 'A staff,' Moses answered. The Lord said, 'Throw it on the ground.' Moses threw it down and it turned into a snake. He ran away from it, but the Lord said, 'Put your hand out and seize it by the tail.' He did so and gripped it firmly, and it turned back into a staff in his hand. 'This is to convince the people that the Lord the God of their forefathers, the God of Abraham, the God of Isaacs, the God of Jacob, has appeared to you.'[8]

To hedge his bets, just in case the Pharaoh and his acolytes turned out to be too pig-headed to believe what they saw, and too obdurate in sticking to their illusions to accept the miraculous reincarnations of the staff and the snake as sufficient proof of the Hebrew God's omnipotence, Jahveh armed Moses with several other miracles to be staged at the Pharaoh's court for the Pharaoh's and his courtiers' consumption. Only when all the spectacular wonders on display failed to change the Pharaoh's mind did God abandon the attempt to enforce his will through staging spectacles of miracle-making, and resort to a series of gory plagues – to punish the sceptics for their sin of dismissing the evidence shown to them.

To be recognized as 'the true God', God needs to be seen doing miracles. Humans need to witness him at that work to recognize him as 'the true God': that is, the supreme force they desperately seek, a force they can trust to help them when they reach the end of their own ability to cope, and to protect them when they face a danger they find it impossible to repel. Humans need miracles to pave the way to the condition of 'voluntary servitude' – the name given by Étienne de la Boétie (as Michel Montaigne informs us) to the state he thought human beings were inclined to long for most strongly: a state of mind and mode of acting made so desirable by humans' chronically brittle and uncertain existential condition.

Entering that 'voluntary servitude' is a temptation difficult to resist. On the one hand, a power stronger than merciless reality, able to undo the evil done and make it possible to 'start from the beginning' as if the tragedy never happened, is precisely what humans need to salvage their hopes and their readiness to go on living, despite the apparently all-powerful adversity of fate. Humans need to believe there is such a power, such a court of appeal empowered to quash reality's verdicts – and they need miracles to support that belief. On the other hand, they need to believe that this awesome power is inclined or at least can be persuaded to stand on their side (German soldiers going into battle used to be reminded by the inscription engraved on their belt buckles, 'Gott mit uns!'), and that its grace is able to overpower even the most perverse scheming of the forces of evil. Humans need to be reassured (or at least allowed to hope) that the tremendous power in all its enormity and superiority might be – will be – used to their advantage, rather than making their fall irrevocable.

Carl Schmitt, arguably the most clear-headed, illusion-free anatomist of the modern state and its inbuilt totalitarian inclinations, averred that the genuine mark of all sovereign power, divine or human, is its capacity to make exceptions to a rule:

> *The exception is that which cannot be subsumed*; it defies general codification, but it simultaneously reveals a specifically juridical formal element: the decision in absolute purity…There is no rule that is applicable to chaos. Order must be established for juridical order to make sense. A regular situation must be created, and *sovereign is he who definitely decides if this situation is actually effective*…
>
> The exception does not only confirm the rule; the rule as such lives off the exception alone.[9]

In *An Enquiry Concerning Human Understanding* (1748) also quoted above, David Hume wrote that miracles 'are observed chiefly to abound among ignorant and barbarous nations; or if a civilized people has ever given admission to any of them, that people will be found to have received them from ignorant and barbarous ancestors, who transmitted them with that inviolable sanction and authority which always attend received opinions.' Yet even though knowledgeable and civilized nations like ours whole-heartedly accept Hume's view that miracles can hardly be proved to happen, the thirst for miracles shows few, if any, signs of subsiding; nor does the number of people wishing, with all their hearts, that miracles would happen – and so, as one would expect, there is also no fall in the number of those who declare, and try to convince whoever is craving to be convinced, that what they've accomplished or are able to accomplish is not far short of miraculous. And no wonder, given the volume of uncertainty permeating human lives, and the growing evidence that the inherited, learned, memorized and recommended routines prove – over and over again – to be inadequate, let alone foolproof, in tackling the contingencies and risks of daily life. The rising pile of dashed hopes and failed promises undermines the trust invested in the routine and indeed 'the normal' as such, in the extant institutions meant to guard the orderliness and predictability of the shared world: all too often their promises and assurances seem no less illusory and hazardous and so no more reliable and trustworthy than those coming from sources they would denounce as 'ignorant and barbarous'. All in all, after a couple of centuries of disenchanting nature, it is the turn of the disenchantment itself to be disenchanted...

A few minutes' stroll through cyberspace would be enough to find out that, to paraphrase Shakespeare, there are things of which philosophers did not and would not dream...Miracles do happen today as much as they did in ancient times, if we believe the holy scriptures. Here is just one example, picked at random at miracles. otsm.com:

Recently I flew from Glasgow to Calgary in Canada. I had to get a connection flight from Calgary to Lethbridge. I boarded the Zoom airplane at Glasgow feeling rather excited about flying out to Canada to visit friends. Shortly after boarding, the pilot announced that they could not get the plane started. We all sat in the plane which seemed like forever while technicians tried to get the plane started. Finally the plane was ready for take-off. We were now one hour behind schedule. The pilot said that he would try to make up for lost time. This never happened. As we got closer to Calgary I kept looking at my watch. There was no way I was going to catch my connecting flight! Well I am not a religious person. But I clasped my hands together and in my mind I pleaded with God; 'Please help me. Please God, you have got to help me. I need your help so much, please do not make this holiday a disaster...God I will have friends waiting on me at Lethbridge...please, please help me. Make a miracle happen so I will catch my connecting flight.' The plane finally touched down at Calgary at 2.30 p.m. My connecting flight was due to leave at 3.05 p.m.! How was I going to make it? I had to first get out of this plane. Then I had to get through customs. My luggage, I had to get my luggage. I had to then find the Air Canada desk and check in my luggage. How was I going to manage to do all this? Well I managed to get through customs very quickly! Then I managed to quickly get my luggage. When I finally got to the Air Canada desk I was puffing and panting. It felt like I was on the verge of a heart attack! I quickly explained everything to the young man behind the desk, saying in a panic, 'I don't know what I am going to do!' The young guy told me not to worry and that he would make sure my luggage went on board the charter flight. He told me to hurry and directed me to the correct gate. Well, making this long story short, I made my flight by the skin of my teeth! People would say that this was luck but it has nothing to do with luck! I'm telling you that God heard my prayers. A miracle happened! He made all those things happen quickly. The customs, the luggage, the check-in. God was making sure I would catch my connecting charter flight. I have being thanking Him almost every day since. I am so grateful. This has actually made my faith in God much stronger. The time I got to the check in desk it was 2.45 p.m., and the flight was leaving at 3.05 p.m. The guy that help me with my luggage, he was an 'angel' bless him. All I can say is this I know that all of this had nothing to do with luck. God made it all happen for me.

What does this prove? That miracles happen to people who believe in miracles. That if you want to witness a miracle, you must first pray for it to happen. And that you will believe that you did indeed witness it happening, if things go as you prayed they would...

25 February 2011

On Facebook, intimacy, and extimacy

'Facebook is the leading social networking site having overtaken main competitor MySpace in April 2008.' 'Facebook attracted 130 million unique visitors in May 2010, an increase of 8.6 million people.' 'The website's ranking among all websites increased from 60th to 7th in worldwide traffic, from September 2006 to September 2007, and is currently 2nd.'

These quotes, supplied by the apparently constantly updated Wikipedia website, are the latest information about Facebook's phenomenal success: its uncommonly fast and relentless ascent, leaving all other internet novelties and passing fashions far behind, and beating all records of growth in numbers of regular users, and so also in the website's commercial value. Indeed, according to yesterday's *Le Monde*, the current value of Facebook has now reached the unheard-of sum of 50 billion dollars. And as I write these words, the number of Facebook's 'active users' is passing the half-billion barrier. Some, of course, are more active than others – but at least half the active users are on Facebook on any given day. As the owners of Facebook inform us, an average user has 130 (Facebook) friends, while between them users spend over 700 billion minutes per month on Facebook. If that astronomical figure is too big to digest and assimilate, let me point out that if it is divided equally between Facebook's active users, it would give each one of them roughly forty-eight minutes per day. Alternatively, it could represent 16 million people spending twenty-four hours a day, seven days a week on Facebook.

By all standards, its success is truly astounding. The twenty-year-old Mark Zuckerberg must have stumbled on some kind of a goldmine when he invented (some people say stole[10]) the Facebook idea and launched it, for the exclusive use of Harvard students, on the internet in February 2004. That much is pretty obvious. But what was that gold-like ore that Lucky Mark discovered and goes on mining with fabulous, and steadily rising, profits?

On the official Facebook site you'll find the following description of the benefits credited with tempting, attracting and seducing those half-billion people to spend a good deal of their waking time on Facebook's virtual expanses:

> Users can create profiles with photos, lists of personal interests, contact information, and other personal information. Users can communicate with friends and other users through private or public messages and a chat feature. They can also create and join interest groups and 'like pages' (formerly called 'fan pages', until April 19, 2010), some of which are maintained by organizations as a means of advertising.

In other words, what the legions of 'active users' enthusiastically embraced when they joined the ranks of Facebook's 'active users' was the prospect of two things they must have been dreaming of without yet knowing where to seek and find them until Zuckerberg's offer to his fellow students at Harvard appeared on the internet. First, they must have felt too lonely for comfort, but for one reason or another found it too difficult to escape from their loneliness with the means at their disposal. Second, they must have felt painfully neglected, unnoticed, ignored, and otherwise shuttled on to a side-track, exiled and excluded, but once again found it difficult, nay impossible, to lift themselves out of their hateful anonymity with the means at their disposal. For both tasks, Zuckerberg offered the means they had so far sought in vain and terribly missed; and they jumped at the opportunity...They must have been ready to jump, feet on the starting blocks, muscles tense, ears pricked for the starter's shot.

I wonder: had Zuckerberg been born thirty or forty years earlier, had he been trained by his teachers to unctuously regurgitate Sartre's homilies or to repeat after Foucault as if quoting from Holy Scripture that the 'author is dead', had he learned from the apostles of 'New Criticism' that it is downright silly, and disqualifying for a student to connect artistic texts with any personal details of the author's life – would it have occurred to him that it is precisely the 'personal details' that make the author, and that therefore his young colleagues would be itching to match the glory of the celebrated authors by making public their own 'personal details'? And in the utterly unlikely case that it would have occurred to that earlier Zuckerberg, would the millions of active users have leapt to his invention and would the billions of dollars have followed them? It was only over the course of the last twenty years that, as Sebastian Faulks points out in *Faulks on Fiction*, 'far from being banned from comment, the author's life and its bearing on the work became the major field of discussion'. And, he adds, this watershed change 'opened the door to speculation and gossip. By assuming that all works of art are an expression of their authors' personality, the biographical critics reduced the act of creation to a sideshow.' I suspect (or rather I am sure) that it was only in the last twenty years that Zuckerberg could have had his revelation and brought his tidings to his fellow students, while finding his fellow students prepared to follow the Master along the road he showed them...

As Josh Rose, digital creative director of the ad agency Deutsch LA, has recently observed, 'The Internet doesn't steal our humanity, it reflects it. The Internet doesn't get inside us, it shows what's inside us.'[11] How right he is. Never blame the messenger for what you found to be bad in the message he delivered, but do not praise him either for what you found to be good...It depends, after all, on the recipients' own likings and animosities, dreams and nightmares, hopes and apprehensions whether they will rejoice or despair at the message. What applies to messages and messengers applies in a similar, even if not quite the same way to internet offers and their 'messengers', the people who display them on our screens and bring them to our attention. In this case, it is the uses that we, Facebook's 'active users', all half-billion of us, make of those offers that render them, and their impact on our lives, good or bad, beneficial or harmful. It all depends on what we are after; technical gadgets just make our longings more or less realistic and our search faster or slower, more or less effective...

Let us have a closer look now at those offers. The first one concerned the means of escaping loneliness. Let me quote once more from Josh Rose's musings:

> I recently asked the question to my Facebook friends: 'Twitter, Facebook, Foursquare... is all this making you feel closer to people or farther away?' It sparked a lot of responses and seemed to touch one of our generation's exposed nerves. What is the effect of the Internet and social media on our humanity? From the outside view, digital interactions appear to be cold and inhuman. There's no denying that. And without doubt, given the choice between hugging someone and 'poking' someone, I think we can all agree which one feels better. The theme of the responses to my Facebook question seemed to be summed up by my friend Jason, who wrote: 'Closer to people I'm far away from.' Then, a minute later, wrote, 'but maybe farther from the people I'm close enough to.' And then added, 'I just got confused.' It *is* confusing. We live in this paradox now, where two seemingly conflicting realities exist side-by-side. Social media simultaneously draws us nearer and distances us.

Admittedly, Rose is wary of passing unambiguous verdicts – as indeed one should be in the case of such a seminal yet hazardous transaction as exchanging sparse incidents of offline 'closeness' for the massive online variety. The 'closeness' traded away was perhaps more satisfying, yet time- and energy-consuming and beset with risks; the 'closeness' traded in is no doubt faster, calling for almost no effort and being almost risk-free, but many find it much less able to quash the thirst for fully fledged company. You gain something, you lose something else – and it is awfully difficult to decide whether your gains compensate for the losses; besides, a once-and-for-all decision is out of the question; you will find it as brittle and until-further-notice as the 'closeness' you've acquired.

What you've acquired is a network, not a 'community'. As you'll find out sooner or later (provided, of course, that you don't forget or fail to learn what 'community' was all about, busy as you are piecing networks together and pulling them apart), they are no more similar than chalk and cheese. Belonging to a community is a much more secure and reliable condition than having a network – though admittedly more constraining and with more obligations. Community watches you closely and leaves you little room for manoeuvre (it may ban and exile you, but it won't allow you to opt out of your own will), while network may care little or not at all about how obedient you are to the network's norms (that is, if the network has norms to obey, which all too often it doesn't) and so will give you much more rope, and above all will not penalize you for quitting. But you can count on community to be a 'friend in need, and so a friend indeed', while networks are there mostly to share in the fun, and their readiness to come to your rescue in the event of a trouble unrelated to the shared 'foci of interest' is hardly ever put to the test and would pass it even less frequently. All in all, the choice is between security and freedom: you need both, but you cannot have one without sacrificing a part at least of the other; and the more you have of one, the less you'll have of the other. On security, the old-style communities beat networks hands down. On freedom, it is the other way round (after all, it takes just one push of the 'delete' key or omitting to answer messages to get free of its interference).

Besides, there is all that enormous, indeed abysmal and unfathomable difference between 'hugging' and 'poking' someone, as Rose puts it...In other words, between the offline prototype and online variety of 'closeness', between depth and shallowness, profundity and superficiality, warmth and coolness, the heartfelt and the perfunctory...You choose, and in all probability you would go on choosing and you could hardly stop choosing, but it is better to choose knowing what you are choosing – and to be prepared to pay the price of your choice. This is at least what Rose seems to imply, and there is no quarrelling with his advice.

The content required to make the relationship 'meaningful' has changed considerably – and particularly drastically in the last thirty or forty years. It has changed so much that, as is suggested by Serge Tisseron, relationships considered 'meaningful' have moved from *intimité* to *extimité* – intimacy to 'extimacy' (see his *Virtuel, mon amour*, 2008).

Alain Ehrenberg, an insightful analyst of the convoluted trajectory of the modern individual's short yet dramatic history, attempted to pinpoint the birth date of the late modern cultural revolution (at least of its French branch) that ushered in the liquid modern world we continue to inhabit; a sort of equivalent for the Western cultural revolution of the salvo of the battleship *Aurora* that gave the signal for the assault on the Winter Palace and triggered seventy years of Bolshevik rule. Ehrenberg chose an autumnal Wednesday evening in the 1980s, when a certain Vivienne, an 'ordinary Frenchwoman', declared on a TV talk show, and so in front of several million spectators, that because her husband, Michel, was afflicted with premature ejaculation, she'd never experienced an orgasm throughout her marital life.

What was so revolutionary about Vivienne's pronouncement to justify Ehrenberg's choice? Its two closely connected aspects. First, acts quintessentially, even eponymically *private* were revealed and talked about *in public* – that is, in front of everyone who wished or just happened to listen. And second, the *public* arena – that is, a space open to uncontrolled entry – was used to vent and thrash out a matter of a thoroughly *private* significance, concern and emotion. Between them, the two genuinely revolutionary steps legitimized *public* use of a language developed for *private* conversations between a strictly limited number of selected persons: of a language whose prime function had hitherto been to set the realm of the 'private' apart from that of the 'public'. More precisely, these two interconnected breakthroughs initiated the deployment in public, for the consumption and use of a public audience, of a vocabulary designed to be used for narrating private, subjectively lived-through experiences (*Erlebnisse* as distinct from *Erfahrungen*). As the years went by, it became clear that the true significance of the event had been an effacing of the once sacrosanct division between the 'private' and the 'public' spheres of human bodily and spiritual life.

Looking back and with the benefit of hindsight, we can say that Vivienne's appearance in front of millions of French men and women glued to their TV screens also took the viewers, and through them all the rest of us, into a *confessional society*: a hitherto unheard-of and inconceivable kind of society in which microphones are fixed inside confessionals, those eponymical safe-boxes and depositories of the most secret of secrets, the sort of secrets to be divulged only to God or his earthly messengers and plenipotentiaries; and in which loudspeakers connected to those microphones are perched on public squares, places previously meant for brandishing and thrashing out issues of shared interest, concern and urgency.

The advent of the confessional society signalled the ultimate triumph of privacy, that foremost modern invention – though also the beginning of its vertiginous fall from the peak of its glory. The hour therefore of a Pyrrhic victory, to be sure: privacy invaded, conquered and colonized the public realm, but at the expense of losing its right to secrecy – its defining trait and the most cherished and most hotly defended privilege.

What is secret, like other categories of personal possessions, is by definition the part of knowledge not to be shared with others, or whose sharing is closely controlled. Secrecy draws and marks the boundary, as it were, of privacy – privacy being the realm that is meant to be one's own domain, the territory of one's undivided sovereignty, inside which one has the comprehensive and indivis-ible power to decide 'what and who I am' – and from which one may launch and relaunch campaigns to have and keep one's deci-sions recognized and respected. In a startling U-turn from the habits of our ancestors, however, we have lost the guts, the stamina, and above all the will to persist in the defence of such rights, those irreplaceable building blocks of individual autonomy. In our day, it is not so much the possibility of a betrayal or violation of privacy that frightens us, but the opposite: a shutting down of the exit from privacy. The area of privacy has turned into a site of incarceration, the owner of that private space being condemned and doomed to stew in his or her own juice; forced into a condition marked by an absence of avid listeners eager to wring out and tear our secrets from the ramparts of privacy, to put them on public display, to make them everybody's shared property and a property everybody wishes to share. *We seem to experience no joy in having secrets,* unless they are the kind of secrets likely to enhance our egos by attracting the attention of the researchers and editors of TV talk shows, tabloid front pages and the covers of glossy magazines.

'At the heart of social networking is an exchange of personal information.' Users are happy to 'reveal intimate details of their personal lives', 'to post accurate information' and 'to share photographs'. It is estimated that 61 per cent of UK teenagers aged thirteen to seventeen 'have a personal profile on a networking site' enabling 'socializing online'.[12]

In Britain, a country in which the popular use of cutting-edge electronic facilities lags cyber years behind the Far East, users may still trust 'social networking' to manifest their freedom of choice, and even believe it to be a means of youthful rebellion and self-assertion. But in South Korea, for instance, where most of social life is already routinely electronically mediated (or rather where *social* life has already turned into *electronic* life or *cyber* life, and where most 'social life' is conducted primarily in the company of a computer, iPod or mobile, and only secondarily with other fleshly beings), it is obvious to the young that they don't have even so much as a sniff of choice; where they live, living social life electronically is no longer a choice but a 'take it or leave it' necessity. 'Social death' awaits those few who have as yet failed to link up into Cyworld, the South Korea's cybermarket leader in the 'show-and-tell culture'.

It would be a grave mistake, however, to suppose that the urge to make a public display of the 'inner self' and the willingness to satisfy that urge are manifestations of a unique, purely generational and age-related urge and addiction of teenagers, keen as they naturally tend to be to get a foothold in the 'network' (a term rapidly replacing 'society' in both social-scientific discourse and popular speech) and to stay there, while not being quite sure how best to achieve that goal. The new penchant for public confession cannot be explained by 'age-specific' factors – at any rate not *only* by them. As Eugène Enriquez recently summed up the message of the fast-growing evidence gathered from all sectors of the liquid modern world of consumers,[13]

Only if it is remembered that what was previously invisible – everybody's part of the intimate, everybody's inner life – is now called on to be exposed on the public stage (principally on TV screens but also on the literary stage) will one comprehend that those who care for their invisibility are bound to be rejected, pushed aside, or suspected of a crime. Physical, social and psychical nudity is the order of the day.

The teenagers equipped with portable electronic confessionals are just apprentices training and trained in the art of living in a confessional society – a society notorious for effacing the boundary that once separated the private from the public, for making public exposure of the private into a public virtue and obligation, and for wiping out from public communication anything that resists being reduced to private confidences, together with those who refuse to confide them.

As early as in the late 1920s, when the transformation of the society of producers into a society of consumers was in an embryonic or at best incipient stage and so was overlooked by less attentive and far-sighted observers, Siegfried Kracauer, a thinker endowed with an uncanny capacity for gleaning the barely visible, still inchoate contours of trends prefiguring a future still lost in a formless mass of fleeting fads and foibles, noted:

> The rush to the numerous beauty salons springs partly from existential concerns, and the use of cosmetic products is not always a luxury. For fear of being withdrawn from use as obsolete, ladies and gentlemen dye their hair, while forty-year-olds take up sports to keep slim. 'How Can I Become Beautiful' runs the title of a booklet recently launched on to the market; the newspaper advertisements for it say that it shows ways 'to stay young and beautiful both now and for ever'.[14]

The emergent habits which Kracauer recorded in the 1920s as a noteworthy curiosity in Berlin have spread like a forest fire since then, turning into daily routine (or at least into a dream) all around the globe. Eighty years later Germaine Greer could observe that 'even in the furthest reaches of north-western China, women laid aside their pyjama suits for padded bras and flirty skirts, curled and coloured their straight hair and saved up to buy cosmetics. This was called liberalization.'[15]

Schoolgirls and schoolboys avidly and enthusiastically putting their qualities on display in the hope of attracting attention and possibly also gaining the recognition and approval needed to stay in the game of socializing, prospective clients needing to amplify their spending records and credit limits to earn a better service, would-be immigrants struggling to gather brownie points and supply them as evidence of demand for their services in order to have their applications accepted: all three categories of people, apparently so distinct, and myriads of other categories of people forced to sell themselves on the commodity market and wanting to sell themselves to the highest bidder, are enticed, nudged or forced to promote an attractive and desirable *commodity*, and so to try as hard as they can, using the best means at their disposal, to enhance the market value of the goods they are selling. And the commodity they are prompted to put on the market, promote and sell is *themselves.*

They are, simultaneously, *promoters of commodities* and the *commodities they promote.* They are, at the same time, the merchandise and their marketing agents, the goods and their travelling salespersons (and let me add that any academic who ever applied for a teaching job or research funds will easily recognize their own predicament in the experience). In whatever bracket they may be filed by the composers of statistical tables, they all inhabit the same social space known under the name of the *market.* Under whatever rubric their preoccupations would be classified by governmental archivists or investigative journalists, the activity in which all of them are engaged (whether by choice, necessity, or most commonly both) is *marketing.* The test they need to pass in order to be admitted to the coveted social prizes demands them *to recast themselves as commodities*: that is, as products capable of drawing attention, and attracting *demand* and *customers.*

'To consume' nowadays means not so much the delights of the palate, as investing in one's own social membership, which in the society of consumers translates as 'saleability': obtaining qualities for which there is already a market demand, or recycling the qualities already possessed into commodities for which demand can be created. Most consumer commodities on offer in the consumer market derive their attraction and their power to enlist keen customers from their genuine or imputed, explicitly advertised or obliquely implied *investment* value. A promise to increase the attractiveness, and consequently the market price, of their buyers is written – in large or small print, or at least between the lines – into the description of all products, including the products that are, ostensibly, to be purchased mostly or even exclusively for the sake of pure consumer pleasure; consumption is an investment in everything that matters for individual 'social value' and self-esteem.

The crucial, perhaps the decisive purpose of consumption (even if it is seldom spelled out in so many words and still less frequently publicly debated) in the society of consumers is not the satisfaction of needs, desires and wants, but the commoditization or recommoditization of the consumer: *raising the status of consumers to that of sellable commodities*. It is ultimately for that reason that passing the consumer test is a non-negotiable condition of admission to the society that has been reshaped in the likeness of the marketplace. Passing that test is a *non*-contractual precondition of all the *contractual* relations that weave and are woven into the web of relationships called the 'society of consumers'. It is that precondition, allowing no exception, tolerating no refusal, that welds the aggregate of seller/buyer transactions into an imagined totality; or, more exactly, allows that aggregate to be experienced as a totality called 'society' – an entity to which can be ascribed the capacity of 'making demands' and of coercing the actors to obey them – and so also the status of 'social fact' in the Durkheimian sense.

The members of the society of consumers are themselves consumer commodities, and it is the quality of being a consumer commodity that makes them bona fide members of that society. Becoming and remaining a sellable commodity is the most potent motive of consumer concerns, even if it is usually latent and seldom conscious, let alone explicitly declared. It is by their power to increase the consumer's market price that the attractiveness of consumer goods – the current or potential objects of desire triggering the consumer's actions – tends to be evaluated. 'Making oneself a sellable commodity' is a DIY job, and an individual duty. Let us note: '*making* oneself', not just *becoming*, is the challenge and the task.

Being a member of the society of consumers is a daunting task and a neverending uphill struggle. The fear of failing to conform is elbowed to the side by the fear of inadequacy, but it is no less haunting for that reason. Consumer markets are eager to capitalize on that fear, and companies turning out consumer goods vie for the status of the most reliable guides and helpers in their clients' unending effort to rise to the challenge. They supply 'the tools', the instruments required by the individually performed job of 'self-fabrication'. The goods they represent as 'tools' for individual use in decision-making are in fact decisions made in advance. They were ready-mades well before the individual was confronted with the duty (represented as an opportunity) to decide. It is absurd to think of those tools as enabling individual choice of purpose. These instruments are the crystallizations of irresistible 'necessity' – which, now as before, humans must learn to use, and obey, and learn to use to obey in order to be free...

Does not Facebook's mind-boggling success result from providing a marketplace where necessity can meet daily with freedom of choice?

26 February 2011

On building fortresses under siege

Pat Bertroche, running for the US Congress on behalf of Republicans in the state of Iowa, proposed on his blog (http://affordance.typepad.com) that illegal immigrants ought to have microprocessors grafted into their bodies: after all, he explains, I can graft a microprocessor into my dog's body if I wish to be able to find it. Why not do the same to the illegals? Indeed, why not?

In recent European reports from the scenes of massive clashes between pro-democratic protesters and the forces defending dictatorial regimes throughout the Arab world, two types of information took pride of place. One was the plight of the citizens of the reporting countries: their lives were in danger; they should be moved away as soon as possible to a safe distance from the outbreaks, from the southern to the northern coast of the Mediterranean; this was the government's most urgent task, any delay would be criminal. The other was the danger that the northern coast of the Mediterranean would be flooded by the refugees fleeing for their lives from the civil wars raging on the southern coast; this was the government's most urgent task, any delay would be criminal. One could hear similarly deep sighs of relief in two simultaneously transmitted and reported news items from blood-soaked Libya: one about the boat packed with British evacuees mooring at Valletta, the other about crowds of Libyans running for shelter – but towards the Egyptian and Tunisian borders. The first reaction of the Italian government to the news of the change of regime in Tunisia was to send additional navy units to guard access to the Italian island of Lampedusa from Tunisian asylum-seekers...And now François Fillon, the French prime minister, has announced that France will send two planes with medical help for liberated Benghazi. Nice gesture, you might say, testimony to our solidarity with the gallant fighters for democracy, and our willingness to join them in the battle. You might say that if you had not read Fillon's own explanation: this is one of the measures to stop the wave of immigrants threatening to flood the Mediterrean countries. The best way to stop it is to make sure that the situation in Libya will soon stabilize...

It would be easy, but wrong, to explain these as extraordinary events or emergency measures. For almost two decades the policy of the Schengen countries on the northern side of the Mediterranean has been to 'subsidiarize' the detection and confinement of would-be immigrants inside their native countries or in their immediate neighbours on the southern coast. In virtually every case, the 'bilateral agreements' were signed or entered into unofficially with tyrannical and corrupt regimes, profiting – alongside the gangs of unscrupulous smugglers – from the misery of the impoverished and persecuted exiles, thousands of whom never managed to cross the sea in gang-supplied, overcrowded, unseaworthy dinghies.[16]

And yet one cannot but note that the usual strictness of the European immigration and asylum laws is currently growing stricter, and the tough stance taken towards successful and prospective asylum-seekers is growing even tougher – all this unconnected with the unrest spreading from Tunisia to Bahrain. On the sudden hardening of Nicolas Sarkozy's posture towards the aliens who have recently turned into Frenchmen or Frenchwomen, Eric Fassin, a distinguished anthropologist and sociologist, comments in today's *Le Monde* that its purpose is to make all the other Frenchmen and Frenchwomen 'forget the defeat of the President's policies on all fronts – from (falling) purchasing power to (rising) insecurity', and most particularly to use the politics of national identity as a cover-up for replacing social protection with a market-operated free-for-all. Nothing new here, to be sure. The aliens inside (and particularly those who are domesticated) and the aliens at the gate (and particularly those who have good reason to be let through) have now been firmly fixed in the role of usual suspects. Whenever there is another public inquiry into another misdeed or misdemeanour, a failure or a flop in governing circles, these aliens are the first to be brought to the police station, avidly filmed and the footage shown on TV as frequently as that of the hijacked aircraft hitting the towers of the World Trade Center. Picking on the internal security problems generated by immigrants as the most urgent task of the French government was swiftly followed by the decision to put the biggest of bigwigs at the helms of the foreign affairs, interior affairs and defence departments. The meaning of the reshuffle was promptly spelled out by the President in a way that left nothing to the imagination: 'My duty as the President of the Republic is to explain what is at stake in the future, but above all to protect the present of the French', and this is why he decided to 'reorganize the ministries dealing with our diplomacy and security'. And so he appointed such persons as are 'prepared to confront future events whose course no one can predict'.

In the good old days of 2003 and 2004 when prices of stocks and real estate were climbing skywards by the day, GNP figures were going up while those of unemployment were standing still, and the wallets in the pockets of the middle classes and of those hoping to join them were still stuffed with credit cards, Nicolas Sarkozy's voice warmed up whenever he spoke of 'l'islam de France', of France's diversity, multiculturalism, even affirmative policy or positive discrimination, and their role in assuring peace and friendship in *les banlieues*. He had no patience with populists picking up Islam as a peculiarly suspect phenomenon demanding particularly watchful attention. In his *La République, les religions, l'espérance* (published in 2004), Sarkozy pointed out that Islam was one of the great religions, that the France of 2004 was no longer an exclusively Catholic country, that it had become a multicultural nation, and that instead of assimilation one should rather speak and worry about integration, a totally different kettle of fish: unlike the now abandoned postulate of 'assimilation', the policy of integration did not require the newcomers to renounce what they were. Even in 2008, when dark clouds were already covering the notoriously blue French skies, the President, as Eric Fassin reminds us, emphatically condemned the principle of 'consanguinity', demanding it be replaced with that of 'equality of chances', pointing out that 'the best medicine against

188 *February 2011*

communitarianism [*communautarisme*, in French discourse the concept of a population split into autonomous and partly self-enclosed and self-governing communities] is the Republic delivering on its promise'.

Well, it is an altogether different ball-game now, to borrow an American idiom. It all started in early 2010 with the hue and cry after the Roma settled in Grenoble (I recorded that episode earlier); Roma are, aren't they, the first among the first as usual suspects go? But the Roma incidents proved to be only humble *hors-d'oeuvres*; more to the point, appetizers. The presumption of symmetry between 'ceux qui arrivent' (the arrivals) and 'ceux qui accueillent' (their hosts), which until recently underlay the pronouncements transmitted from the government's buildings, has all but disappeared. No longer is an equal measure of respect required of both sides. Respect is now due solely to France, and paying respect is the duty of the *accueillis* (the 'received') – (well or badly received does not really matter). The French community (whatever that may mean), so the announcements announce, does not want to change its way of living, its lifestyle. But the unwritten condition for those 'received' if they want to remain 'received' is that they do change their mode of life, whether they want to or not. And, in line with the habit already noted as the trademark of modern hypocrisy by the great Frenchman Albert Camus (a Frenchman whose personal contribution to the glory of France is second to none), evil is once again done in the name of good, discrimination is promoted in the name of equality, and oppression in the name of freedom. For instance: 'We don't want to compromise on little girls' right to attend schools'...

This is a thorny issue, no doubt. That is why the slogans 'no tolerance of the enemies of tolerance' or 'no freedom for the enemies of freedom' sound so convincing. They assert as proven what had to be proved, pre-empting the question of whether those whose condemnation and suppression that slogan is meant to legitimize are indeed guilty of the transgressions of which they stand accused; and they omit the question of the right to prosecute as well as glossing over an illegal merger between the roles of prosecutor and judge. But does the prohibition against wearing headscarves in school indeed help to entrench the 'little girls' right to attend schools'?! André Grjebine of Sciences Po–Centre d'Études et de Recherches Internationales avers in the same issue of *Le*

Monde ('S'ouvrir à l'autre: oui. A son idéologie: non') that 'the alterity, perceived generally as the source of spiritual openness can also be a carrier of fundamentalism, obscurantism and closure'; would he not agree, however, that his order of reasoning, with all its appearances of impartiality and intention of *sine ira et studio*, is already a judgement in its own right (and moreover, as John Langshaw Austin would have said, a 'performative utterance', or 'perlocution'), only disguised? He did not mention, after all, that 'the spiritual closure, perceived by some as the carrier of identity and security, is just the same the source of fundamentalism and obscurantism – a connection at least as real as the one he preferred to put to the fore. Nor did he say that, much as the presence of spiritual openness in some may push some others to closure, it is the *absence* of spiritual openness that is the invariable and infallible mark of every and any fundamentalism. More often than not openness encourages, promotes, and nourishes openness – whereas closure encourages, promotes and feeds closedness...

Amin Maalouf, the Lebanese author writing in French and settled in France, considers the reaction of 'ethnic minorities', that is to say immigrants, to the conflicting cultural pressures they are subjected to in the country to which they have come. Maalouf's conclusion is that the more immigrants feel that the traditions of their original culture are respected in their adopted country, and the less they are disliked, hated, rejected, frightened, discriminated against and kept at arm's length on account of their different identity, the more appealing the cultural options of the new country appear to them, and the less tightly do they hold on to their separateness. Maalouf's observations are, he supposes, of key importance to the future of intercultural dialogue. They confirm our previous suspicions and conjectures: that there exists a strict correlation between a lack of threat perceived from one side, and the 'disarming' of the issue of cultural differences from the other – this as a result of overcoming impulses towards cultural separation, and a concomitant readiness to participate in the search for a common humanity.

All too often, it is the sense of being unwelcome and guilty without any crime being committed, and a feeling of threat and uncertainty (on both sides of the supposed frontline, among the immigrants and among the indigenous population alike) that are the principal and most potent stimulants of mutual suspiciousness, followed by separation and a break in communication, with the theory of multiculturalism degenerating into the reality of 'multicommunitarianism'.

Cultural differences, whether significant or trivial, glaring or barely perceptible, acquire in this way the status of building materials for the construction of ramparts and rocket launchers. 'Culture' becomes a synonym for a fortress under siege, and the inhabitants of fortresses under siege are expected to manifest their loyalty daily, and give up, or at least radically curtail, any contacts with the outside world. 'Defence of the community' is given priority over any other duty. Sharing a table with 'strangers', frequenting places known as the abode and domain of outsiders, to say nothing of romances and marriages with partners from beyond the boundaries of the community, become marks of betrayal and the foundations for ostracism and exile. Communities functioning on this basis become the means, first and foremost, of a greater reproduction of divisions and a deepening of separation, isolation and alienation.

A feeling of safety and the resulting self-confidence, on the other hand, are the enemies of ghetto-minded communities erecting protective barriers. A sense of security turns the terrifying might of the ocean separating 'us' from 'them' into an alluring and inviting swimming pool. The frightening precipice dividing a community from its neighbours gives way to a gentle plain inviting frequent walks and carefree strolls. No wonder the first signs of a dispersal of the fear afflicting a community so often cause consternation among the advocates of communal isolation; consciously or not, they have a vested interest in the enemy missiles staying where they are, aimed at the walls protecting the community. The greater the sense of threat and the more pronounced the feeling of uncertainty it causes, the more tightly the defenders close ranks and keep to their positions, at least for the foreseeable future.

A feeling of safety on both sides of the barricade is an essential condition of a dialogue between cultures. Without it, the chance that communities will open up towards one another and start an interchange which will enrich them by strengthening the human dimension of their bonds is, to say the least, slim. With it, on the other hand, the prospects for humanity are rosy.

What's at stake here is security in a much wider sense than the majority of spokesmen for 'multiculturalism' – who remain in a tacit (or maybe unintended, even involuntary) agreement with the advocates of the communal separation – are prepared to admit. The narrowing of the question of general uncertainty to the real or imagined perils of a two-sided cultural separateness is a dangerous mistake, drawing attention away from the roots of mutual distrust and disagreement.

First of all, people long for a sense of community today in the (mistaken) hope that it will give them shelter from the rising tide of global turmoil. That tide, however, which cannot be held at bay by even the highest community breakwater, is coming from very distant places, and no local powers are able to oversee, let alone control them. Secondly, in our intensively 'individualizing' and 'individualized' society, human uncertainty is rooted in a deep chasm between the condition of 'individuality de jure' and the pressure to achieve 'individuality de facto'.

Surrounding communities with walls will not help to bridge this gulf, and it will certainly render it harder for the many community members to cross to the other side: to the status of an individual de facto capable of self-determination, and not just on paper. Instead of concentrating on the roots and causes of the uncertainty afflicting people today, 'multiculturalism' draws attention and energy away from them. Neither side in the ongoing wars between 'them and us' can seriously expect its long-lost and much longed-for security to return following a victory; instead, the more jointly engrossed all of them are in the planning of future battles on the multicultural battlefield, the easier and more profitable a target they become for global powers – the only powers capable of profiting from the failure of the laborious task of building human community and of joint human control of its own condition and the circumstances shaping it.

All too often it is two miseries that confront each other on the battlefield of tribal skirmishes, that poor man's pitiable, high street replica of the haute couture wars of emancipation. One can understand those who are miserable, even while pitying their lot to be drawn into yet deeper misery by their confusion about causes and remedies. With a measure of good will, empathy and commiseration, that understanding can be recast into forgiveness. This hardly applies, however, to those who capitalize on the confusion of the miserable. As Richard Rorty put it, writing of the American case, somewhat but not totally different from the European variety:

> The aim will be to keep the minds of the proles elsewhere – to keep the bottom 75 percent of Americans and the bottom 95 percent of the world's population busy with ethnic and religious hostilities, and with debates about sexual mores. If the proles can be distracted from their own despair by media-created pseudo-events, including the occasional brief and bloody war, the super-rich will have little to fear.[17]

As recent experience shows, leaving little room for doubt, the super-rich would do anything, or almost anything, for the sake of having little to fear from the proles...

27 February 2011

On the American Dream: time for obituaries?

This is what Frank Rich writes in today's *New York Times*:

> The highest priority of America's current political radicals is not to balance government budgets but to wage ideological warfare in Washington and state capitals alike. The relatively few dollars that would be saved by the proposed slashing of federal spending on Planned Parenthood and Head Start don't dent the deficit; the cuts merely savage programs the right abhors. In Wisconsin, where state workers capitulated to Gov. Scott Walker's demands for financial concessions, the radical Republicans' only remaining task is to destroy labour's right to collective bargaining.
>
> That's not to say there is no fiscal mission in the right's agenda, both nationally and locally – only that the mission has nothing to do with deficit reduction. The real goal is to reward the G.O.P.'s wealthiest patrons by crippling what remains of organized labour, by wrecking the government agencies charged with regulating and policing corporations, and, as always, by rewarding the wealthiest with more tax breaks. The bankrupt moral equation codified in the Bush era – that tax cuts tilted to the highest bracket were a higher priority even than paying for two wars – is now a given. The once-

bedrock American values of shared sacrifice and equal economic opportunity have been overrun.

Were I to write a requiem for the American Dream (at least for the American Dream as dreamt by us, watching America from overseas with a mixture of hope and despair), I couldn't, by any stretch of the imagination, write it better. And I wonder who would. Though the fact that there are still people who feel and write like Frank Rich allows me to wonder whether the announcements of the American Dream's decease aren't, after all and despite everything, just a little bit premature?

It would be great if they were. Though for how long?!

March 2011

1 March 2011

On H. G. Wells's, and my, last dream and testament

In John Clute's exquisitely intelligent, erudite and perceptive introduction to a recent edition of H. G. Wells's 1933 book *The Shape
of Things to Come* (Penguin, 2005), once a bombshell but now
all but forgotten, we read that in his later years, well after the
traumatic experience of the Great War that left the nineteenth-
century world of optimism in ruins and sapped the foundations
of Whig view of history (both of the past and of the future), Wells
'became dislocated'. He and all his fellow sufferers of his generation were left scarred by the brutal and shameless cruelty, inanity
and absurdity of that war, and the scar would never truly heal.
But for Wells in particular, to be dislocated from the thrust of
history was to be dislocated from his central project, which he
wished to address to every able-minded person in the civilized
world. That project was to show what kind of a muddle the world
had got into, and to point the way forward.

Wells clutched stubbornly to his belief that there was and always
would be 'a way forward', no matter how numerous and varied
the hitches, obstacles, drawbacks and backlashes that might pile
up in front of humans who dared (were destined?) to follow it.
He never gave up his project, insists the author of the introduction

(that formidable exercise in simultaneously updating the book's ability to speak and the reader's ability to understand), but in the very last period of his life he addressed his audiences from a growing distance. Wells wouldn't budge from the position he had settled in from the start. Over long years filled to the brim with shocking disappointments, Wells stood more or less put; it was his intended audience that sailed off to the side and away...

To put it in a nutshell, Wells lost his once 'infallible sense of Zeitgeist', a sense that for two decades or more had been, by common agreement of enlightened opinion, his trademark: 'Wells was making the best possible argument for the triumph of European civilization'; though again, like so many of his contemporaries, he failed to anticipate the war... And Wells proved to be slower than many of his contemporaries in grasping the significance of that omission and count its casualties. Well into the war years, his writings show his unwavering trust that 'the Europe of 1910... after much dismantling and rebuilding, could be made to work.' His novels 'were fatally slow to register an evolving consensus about the First World War, not only within the intelligentsia but also in the hearts and minds of "ordinary" citizens'; 'To aftermath minds, that civilization was not a slate that could be wiped clean, not a correctible expression on the face of homo sapiens... but a mask disguising the true dreadful face of us all.' As to Wells, however, 'for good and for ill, he could not abandon the fight. He could not abandon the fight to make us see.' And this was despite his awkward sense of his failures of temperament: through the lips of Dr Philip Raven, a major actor in his *Shape of Things to Come*, Wells passes sentence on his own defects and incapacities: 'you cannot endure any conventional elaborations, any sideshows, needless complexities, indirect methods, diplomacies, legal fictions and tactful half-statements... How men of affairs must hate you – if and when they hear of you! Complications are their life. *You* try to get all these complications out of the way. You are a stripper, a damned impatient stripper.'

When I scan the records of my own life itinerary and set it against Wells's, I obviously find that my own few and by no means unquestionable merits fall well short of Wells's *strengths*: no match for the width and audacity of his vision, his literary talents, his sense of calling and his determination to see his mission through. But I am fully aware that I share his *weaknesses*, as listed one by one in Dr Raven's tirade. That brotherhood-in-flaws may allow me to surmise, even if tentatively and certainly with *très beaucoup – en fait toutes – proportions gardées*, some – wan as they may be – elective affinities between me, a humble craftsman, and he, the great artist...

But there is another justification for hypothesizing an elective affinity: this time not between characters or accomplishments, but between the historical contexts in which our respective labours gestated and into which they have been implanted; in particular, the effects of 'dislocation', so unerringly spotted by Clute in Wells – but, I believe, no less salient, if not yet stronger, in my own life story (Wells, unlike me, was, after all, spared the experience of a refugee or an exile – of both the 'foreign' and the 'internal' variety). The sense of 'being dislocated', when I think about it, has accompanied me for as long as I can remember: a sense of being out of place and out of time; and most certainly, that sense of distance separating me from 'men of affairs' – a physical as much as spiritual distance, of their choice as much as my own. I readily admit to having found the condition of 'being dislocated' pleasurable, nay deeply satisfying; and considering what my dislocation was from, also an honest, ethically praiseworthy choice... Before I read and absorbed Clute's intimations, I ascribed those diffuse yet ubiquitous and obstinate feelings, perhaps wrongly, to my inborn claustrophobia. Cerebrally as much as viscerally, I fear crowds, abhor hue-and-cries, and detest herd instincts and stampedes.

My dislocation was many-faceted. Childhood experience of being forcefully held at a distance from the world of my belonging and refused entry, doubled by wartime exile from the world I tried hard, though in vain, to join; after homecoming, a distance gradually yet unstoppably growing between my hopes and expectations, and the repulsiveness of realities exacerbated by the hypocrisy of 'men of affairs'; a brief sojourn in yet another country, this time with the experience of being 'in' but not 'of' the place; and finally, the other half of my life lived in a country so wondrously hospitable to foreigners, though on condition that they do not pretend to be natives...

Thus far, however, that has been a roster only of, so to speak, topographical dislocations. Perhaps (who can really say, hand on heart?), as a result of a predisposition formed through the series of 'topographical' dislocations, a more serious variety of dislocation, and surely one more closely related to that of Wells, did and does mark my professional profile: my own version of 'dislocation from the *Zeitgeist*'. Wells and I being almost two generations apart, the manifestations of a similar dislocation are bound to differ, however – indeed, be almost reversed. Wells's dislocation forced him to struggle to salvage the 'we can do it' self-confidence of the Enlightenment, Modernity and Enlightened Modernity, against the *Zeitgeist* of imminent catastrophe, a second fall and the ultimate Apocalypse ('It is possible to forget now, seventy years on, how profoundly *depressed* our world was in 1933, how great the odds seemed against the survival of civilization,' as Clute puts it). My variety of dislocation, on the other hand, expressed itself in resisting the happy-go-lucky *Zeitgeist* of the brave new world, the self-contented, stand-offish and insensitive world, a world believing in no alternative to itself, glad to live on borrowed time, and so prone to mistake the second fall for a second coming and to pretend that it 'can do it', while doing all it could to avoid doing what yearned and cried out to be done in order to save and redeem its targeted victims and collateral casualties.

In a nutshell, Wells struggled, against all odds, to save our self-confidence. What I was trying to do was to save our self-criticism; against all odds and pretensions to the contrary, to sap, or at least weaken our self-conceit. Wells searched for the silver linings under the darkening clouds; I tried to uncover the dark rocks and dark tides lurking behind the dazzling, yet improvised ad hoc and ephemeral lighthouses.

And yet...The spirit of the time might have done a veritable U-turn, protagonists and antagonists might have changed sides, but what all that turbulence failed to achieve was a cutting of one more link supporting the guess of elective affinity. Here it is, the farewell declaration jotted down by Wells on the final pages of *The Shape of Things to Come* in the name of 'the last government on Earth', its parting shot and apology for laying down arms, bound to be issued once it had come to the conclusion that there was 'nothing left for the government to do' (a declaration, let's remember, penned down by H. G. Wells in the depths of world-wide despair):

This is the day, this is the hour of sunrise for united manhood. The Martyrdom of Man is at an end. From pole to pole now there remains no single human being upon the planet without a fair prospect of self-fulfilment, of health, interest, and freedom. There are no slaves any longer; no poor; no doomed by birth to an inferior status; none sentenced to long unhelpful terms of imprisonment; none afflicted in mind or body who are not being helped with all the powers of science and the services of interested and able guardians. The world is all before us to do with as we will, within the measure of our powers and imaginations. The struggle for material existence is over. It has been won. The need for repressions and disciplines has passed. The struggle for truth and that indescribable necessity which is beauty begins now, unhampered by any of the imperatives of the lower struggle. No one now need live less nor be less than his utmost.

Writing for a change at the peak of the world's self-congratulatory celebration of its as-never-before opulence and comfort, I would have to try very hard indeed if I needed to add to or take away a single sentence from that description of the world worth living and struggling for...But I haven't felt such a need. And I still don't.

Notes

1 Other scholars have arrived at different limits, sometimes twice as large as Dunbar's. According to a recent entry on Wikipedia, 'anthropologist H. Russell Bernard and Peter Killworth and associates have done a variety of field studies in the United States that came up with an estimated mean number of ties – 290 – that is roughly double Dunbar's estimate. The Bernard-Killworth median of 231 is lower, due to upward straggle in the distribution: this is still appreciably larger than Dunbar's estimate. The Bernard-Killworth estimate of the maximum likelihood of the size of a person's social network is based on a number of field studies using different methods in various populations. It is not an average of study averages but a repeated finding. Nevertheless, the Bernard-Killworth number has not been popularized as widely as Dunbar's.' Unlike the researchers named above, who focus on groupings in various contemporary human populations, the prime objects of Dunbar's field and archive studies and the suppliers of the raw data from which Dunbar's number was calculated were primates and pleistocene populations; therefore, Dunbar's proposition that, given the structure of the neocortex shared by primates and their younger human relatives, the size of the primeval horde sets limits to the number of 'meaningful relationships' in humans needs to be taken as an assumption rather than a corroborated finding.

2 At www.controlacrisi.org/joomla/index.php?option=com_content &view=article&id=10464&catid=39&Itemid=68 (accessed June 2010).

3   Walter Benjamin, 'Theses on the philosophy of history', in Benjamin, *Illuminations: Essays and Reflections*, ed. Hannah Arendt (New York: Schocken, 1968), pp. 257–8.

4   See Günther Anders, *Le temps de la fin* (1960; Paris: L'Herne, 2007), pp. 52–3.

5   Michel Agier, *Le couloir des exiles. Être étranger dans un monde commun* (Bellecombe-en-Bauges: Éditions du Croquant, 2011).

6   T. R. Malthus, *An Essay on the Principle of Population* (1798; New York: Oxford University Press, 1999), Oxford, p. 61.

7   This and following quotations are from Leon Shestov, *Athens and Jerusalem*, trans. Bernard Martin (Athens, OH: Ohio University Press, 1966), pp. 424–6 and 68–9.

8   *Exodus* 4.

9   Carl Schmitt, *Politische Theologie*, pp. 19–21, emphasis added: see discussion in Giorgio Agamben, *Homo Sacer* (Stanford: Stanford University Press, 1998), pp. 15ff.

10 This particular claim of theft, like most of those made and contested during the Californian 'gold rush' of 1849 and thereafter, did not find unambiguous resolution in the courts; but then the internet at the start of the twenty-first century, like California in the middle of the nineteenth, was a uniquely lawless place, without private property, licensing fees or taxes, and – in the case of California – with guns taking the places of judges and policemen.

11 At http://mashable.com/2011/02/23/social-media-culture/.

12 See Paul Lewis, 'Teenage networking websites face anti-paedophile investigation', *Guardian*, 3 July 2006.

13 Eugène Enriquez, 'L'idéal type de l'individu hypermoderne. L'individu pervers?', in Nicole Aubert (ed.), *L'individu hypermoderne* (Toulouse: Érès, 2004), p. 49.

14 In *Die Angestellen*, essays first serialized in the *Frankfurter Allgemeine Zeitung* through 1929, and published in book form by Suhrkamp in 1930. Here quoted in Quintin Hoare's translation: Siegfried Kracauer, *The Salaried Masses: Duty and Distraction in Weimar Germany* (London: Verso, 1998), p. 39.

15 Germaine Greer, *The Future of Feminism*, Dr. J. Tans Lecture (Maastricht: Studium Generale Maastricht, 2004), p. 13.

16 Among the most recent summaries of the state of the game immediately preceding the explosion of unrest in the Arab countries, see Alain Morice and Claire Rodier in *Le Monde Diplomatique*, June 2010.

17 See Richard Rorty, *Achieving Our Country* (Cambridge, MA: Harvard University Press, 1997), p. 88.